Front-Line and Experimental Flying With the Fleet Air Arm

Front-Line and Experimental Flying With the Fleet Air Arm

"Purely by Chance"

Commander
G.R. (Geoff) Higgs AFC RN

Pen & Sword
AVIATION

First published in Great Britain in 2010 by
PEN & SWORD AVIATION
An imprint of
Pen & Sword Books Ltd
47 Church Street
Barnsley
South Yorkshire
S70 2AS

Copyright © Commander G.R. Higgs AFC RN 2010

ISBN 978 1 84884 262 5

A CIP catalogue record for this book is
available from the British Library

Typeset by Acredula

Printed and bound in England
By the MPG Books Group

Pen & Sword Books Ltd incorporates the Imprints of Pen & Sword Aviation,
Pen & Sword Family History, Pen & Sword Maritime, Pen & Sword Military,
Wharncliffe Local History, Pen & Sword Select, Pen & Sword Military Classics,
Leo Cooper, Remember When, Seaforth Publishing and Frontline Publishing

For a complete list of Pen & Sword titles please contact
PEN & SWORD BOOKS LIMITED
47 Church Street, Barnsley, South Yorkshire, S70 2AS, England
E-mail: enquiries@pen-and-sword.co.uk

Website: www.pen-and-sword.co.uk

Contents

Acknowledgements

Being absorbed in writing for over a year is not the most sociable of pastimes, and I fully acknowledge my wife Pat's tolerance in the many hours I spent in isolation. For her help and encouragement I am greatly indebted, as I am to my son, David, who provided invaluable computer and legal expertise and to Kate, my daughter, for her patience in periodically reading the text. The most profound comment from them was, 'Who are you writing this for?' I didn't know either, since I had moved the goalposts!

My thanks also to John Gaut, former FAA pilot and friend of long standing who read my story and helped with useful suggestions, to Ted Whitley with whom I had the good fortune to serve for a number of years and who allowed me to quote his 'Union Yarn', and to Sir John Treacher for permission to quote from his excellent book *Life at Full Throttle*.

I am grateful to my editor, David Morris, for the trouble and time he has taken wading through the manuscript proofs trying to make sense of my corrections and suggestions. And finally I am indebted to Peter Coles for having the courage to publish my memoirs in the full knowledge that many others could have written a similar and doubtless more interesting life history.

Preface

I began writing these memoirs in response to the not too infrequent urgings of my family to put something of my life on record, solely for private use. I never kept a diary and it was therefore something of a challenge.

However, I got down to it, temporarily ceased my primary pastime as an amateur water colourist and spent the next year or so recollecting events of a naval career that had been, 'purely by chance' like many others, the outcome of a world war. This was my original title for my memoirs, but I was persuaded that it did not have marketable value as a title, and my publisher wisely suggested the alternative. But as I picked up the threads it became more of a narrative than just a few reminiscences and in due course I was persuaded to offer it for publication.

In the course of my writing I have not referred to any outside source for information or corroboration, relying solely on personal recollections supported by my logbooks and personal photographs. I realise the shortcomings of this approach, but it arose from first intentions to produce a simple family record, and as time went on I felt disinclined – or perhaps too idle – to conduct the sort of research a more competent author would undertake. If, therefore, there occur any errors of fact the fault is entirely mine, and while I am not aware of, nor intend, any offence to the various characters who may appear from time to time, I unhesitatingly apologise if I have transgressed.

For the same reasons of initially producing a private family record, I avoided any tendency to become too technical in recording various happenings that I felt would bore the layman. Again, this may have been a mistake, since I realise it will be less than complete for the more discerning reader.

As I continued with events of the past I experienced many moments of sadness at the loss of so many good friends who, for one reason or another, did not stay the course. The hazards of flying they accepted willingly, as we all did, but those of us who rose to the challenge and survived can only reflect, 'There but for the Grace of God ...'

CHAPTER 1

In the Beginning

'And why do you want to join the Royal Navy to become a pilot? Why not the RAF?'

So the interview had progressed after the initial pleasantries in a building in Whiteladies Road, Bristol. It was early 1943 and I was seated, somewhat nervously, in front of three senior naval officers who were doing their best to put this 17-year-old at ease.

I had rehearsed this totally expected question numerous times with nice pat answers. But now my mind was a blank and I was tongue tied.

'Is it just the uniform?' one of them asked.

'Oh no,' said I, 'we went to Weymouth.'

'I see.' said another of them. 'So?'

And then it all flooded out and I told them about Alan Cobham's circus and an aeroplane known as the Spider at Whitchurch airport in the early 1930s. I had gone with my father and sat on the grass outside the fence – it was too expensive to go inside the airfield. It was a warm and wonderfully sunny day and at the end of the flying display I was hooked.

They had listened politely to my ramblings without impatience.

'But you earlier mentioned Weymouth', one commented.

'Yes, that was a few years later', I replied. 'We were on holiday and the bay was full of warships.'

The sea has always had a fascination for me, I suppose because it was synonymous with holidays. We had always mucked about in boats and trips round the bay, that sort of thing. I tried to explain this to the Interview Board, and I suppose it must have had some success; they were still listening politely, although they must have heard this sort of waffle many times before.

Then more questions – why had I left school early, what had I learnt in the Air Training Corps, did I have any of my family in the Royal Navy – yes, brother and sister – and so on.

Eventually, after they had discussed together out of my hearing, the President of the Board announced that I was too young for immediate consideration. My heart sank. But then, observing my disappointment, with a smile on his face he added that subject to a medical examination they would recommend entry under the 'Y' scheme for training as a pilot in the Fleet Air Arm nearer my 18th birthday. I cannot recall subsequent events. I left, floating on air, caught the wrong bus back to my office for work for which I had no inclination.

So it was that a short while later, after I had taken and passed a medical examination, a letter arrived confirming the Board's decision and enclosing a black badge embroidered with a 'Y' for wearing on my ATC uniform. I would be called up for training shortly after my birthday.

As far as I recall it was late November when the early morning post produced a travel warrant with instructions to join HMS *St Vincent* on 3 January 1944. The Allied invasion of Europe was still in the future, there was still plenty of war left, and in a macabre sort of way we all hoped to be part of it. Such was the misplaced enthusiasm of youth. But these were unusual and exciting times for late teenagers whose experience of life away from home had been restricted to the annual family holiday – and this more recently limited by the war.

And so on 3 January 1944 I followed my brother and sister into the Royal Navy. My mother took my departure in her usual stoical manner, no tears, anxious for me to do well and full of optimism. My father accompanied me on the local train to Bristol Temple Meads for the main line to Salisbury and on. These were the days of compartments, and we were joined by several American soldiers of whom at this time there many thousands deposited in or around Bristol in the build-up for the forthcoming invasion of Europe. We had already seen much evidence of this in the construction of temporary camps, including one on the local golf course, where the 14th and other fairways became Tin Pan Alley, Broadway or other such familiar names to them. The American soldiers had been well received by the locals, and in turn their generosity knew no bounds.

Those in our compartment were no exception. We got into animated conversation during the journey, asking about their home life and families, and they in turn seemed awestruck by the blitz on Bristol and what we had suffered. Large cartons of Lucky Strike cigarettes were produced which they insisted we accept. Much later I would wonder how many of these five American soldiers survived the invasion, which was to come five months later, and the subsequent fighting.

Such was the fortune of war that I was now to embark on the opportunity of a lifetime, an experience nothing in my earlier life could have anticipated. But I am ahead of my story.

Early Life

I was born on 25 September 1925, the third of four children, into a very happy if impecunious and occasionally tempestuous family. My father at that time had been working for the Great Western Railway since his youth and progressed to engine, or locomotive, driver status. Every small boy then aspired to be a train driver, and I suppose I was no exception until, later, after the Whitchurch display, I was dedicated to aeroplanes, with little hope then of achieving such lofty ambitions.

My mother kept a tight ship. We went to Sunday School and church as a matter of course. My maternal grandfather was a lay preacher, which he took extremely seriously. In the First World War he had courageously admitted to being against the war – any war – and any question of fighting. To kill was totally alien to his nature. Although a Conscientious Objector, he nevertheless volunteered to join the Medical Corps as a stretcher bearer, accepting fully that the casualty rate was at least as high as for front-line troops. The experience dwelt heavily upon him, and he took to composing poetry, at which he showed considerable flair. He was in every way a very kindly man whom I remember with much affection.

When I was 10 we moved home, and hence schools. I was within a year of taking the scholarship examination, not a good time to change schools. Fortunately I had been well schooled at Knowle Park, particularly by an excellent teacher, Miss Horler. Her brother was the well-acclaimed Sydney Horler, author of numerous thrillers. In her somewhat matronly way she imbued an enthusiasm for learning, no mean achievement with 9/10-year-olds.

And so my arrival at the new junior school, Sea Mills, was quite painless. The school had a positive attitude towards sport, and boasted a number of well-above-average players, particularly footballers. At least two of these went on to achieve professional status at the highest level.

The previous excellent teaching showed up well against my fellow pupils, and at the end of the first and only complete year there I was awarded a prize for coming top of the form. More important, I passed the scholarship examination for entry to a number of grammar schools in Bristol.

Thus it was that at the age of 11 I arrived at Cotham School, a relatively small school of some 350 boys or so. Cotham had been born out of the nineteenth-century 'City School' founded by the Merchant Venturers in Bristol for their own children. Cotham adopted many of the former school's traditions. It had an excellent reputation for scholastic achievement, which I doubt I did much to enhance. Professor Paul Dirac, the renowned physicist and Nobel Prize winner, was an old boy, and there were many other distinguished 'Old Cothamians'.

Academically my achievements were modest in the extreme, and perhaps it was that undue emphasis on sport, notably cricket and football, contributed to this. An enthusiastic wicket keeper, encouraged by the cricket master to 'stand up' to even the quickest bowlers – and one such was a very tall boy with the famous cricketing name of Hobbs – ensured selection for the first eleven at the young age of 14. My batting wasn't up to much – perhaps a very average No. 6 or No. 7. In retrospect I fancy I may have been too keen to protect my wicket rather than score runs, of which there were generally all too few. In defence I was not tall for my age, I was with much older boys and it was common for the opposition to field 17- and 18-year-olds around six feet tall, bowling very fast. However, I survived in the team by virtue of my wicket keeping, at which I like to think I was a shade more than competent.

Unfortunately my school days were about to come to a premature end. At the age of 15 I became very ill with severe pneumonia, meningitis and other complications. My eventual recovery was in no small measure due to the total dedication of the family doctor, Dr Munday, who for much of two consecutive nights scarcely left my bedside. He was to be in constant attendance for many weeks. This was before the days of automatic hospitalisation and – fortunately perhaps – today's NHS, since his clinical care could not have been bettered. Shortly after this, although beyond the age for call-up, he volunteered for Army duty and left his practice.

Thus many weeks away from school at a critical juncture left me well behind my contemporaries. This and the disruptive affect of the war – the blitz on Bristol was in full flow, with sleepless nights in the Anderson air raid shelter after yet another air raid siren – combined to take the interest off further schooling, and much against the wishes of my mother in particular I left without formal qualifications.

So I learnt about life in the outside world. The small firm I joined was a fortunate choice. It was scarcely more than a one-man band, but what a man! Mr Pauli was the owner of a strontium surface-mining company, and also senior partner of a firm of sugar brokers. From him I was to learn much about the commercial world. Responsibility was expected and accepted. It was a very enjoyable period in my life, and when I left to go to war it was with some sadness, only mitigated by the anticipation of what lay ahead.

My brother Graham and I were very close. We had much in common and enjoyed most things equally. On occasions he could be very stubborn and intractable, but it never affected the affection we held for each other, which lasted until he died. We enjoyed cycling and frequently embarked on short cycling trips complete with two-man tent and the inevitable – in those days – primus stove.

We were both members of a local boys' club, superbly run by a Mr House, a seaman by calling. The club premises, which had snooker and table tennis tables, were funded by I know not whom or how, but we paid only a nominal amount when selected for the club's cricket or football teams, which could not have covered the hire costs of the pitches. There must have been a Good Samaritan somewhere, but I never discovered where, although the generosity of Mr House knew no bounds

Shortly before my brother left home, having volunteered for the Royal Navy, we cycled from Bristol to London and back, a distance of some 220 miles, to visit an aunt. We had previously traded in our bicycles for a tandem on which we were able to achieve the respectable average of around 20 mph. It was a challenging adventure for a 15- and 17-year-old, but despite the most appalling thunderstorm on the return journey we were pleased to have done it. In due course my brother left for initial training, and subsequently spent the rest of the war years at sea, punctuated only by short courses ashore.

The demands of the war had accelerated the pre-service training organisations, and in 1942 I joined No. 1837 Squadron Air Training Corps based at my old school. In due course it would find more suitable premises close by, with an adequate HQ building and small parade ground.

The squadron was commanded by a former WW1 pilot with a pronounced limp. He and his supporting instructors generated enthusiasm by competition from which we all benefited. The tedium of drill and square bashing was offset by interesting lectures and squadron sports against similar organisations in the Bristol area. I would be given a corporal's stripes for needling the local authority into providing football and cricket pitches without charge!

Shortly after the move to the new premises came an opportunity to apply for training as a motorcycle dispatch rider. I volunteered and was fortunate enough to be selected. The group of eight were subjected to the most rigorous training, involving steep gradients over soft ground, sand dunes and time trials. There were one or two failures in the group, but for the rest, who could fail to be six feet tall at being given ownership – albeit temporary – of a 250 cc Ariel or Norton? Heady days for a not yet 17-year-old, particularly when on completion of the course night-time duty entailed journeys of up to forty miles to deliver messages, dispatches or small parcels to Army units in the Gloucestershire area.

Blackout restrictions of course were in full force at this time, and all road transport was subject to an angled, slotted shield over the headlights. This restricted a rather poor beam to only a few yards ahead on the road, and demanded total concentration in the very dark environment. There were no street lights or other form of illumination. Such conditions resulted in an amusing incident on one night duty. During training I had become friendly with a cadet, Ashton Reed, from another ATC squadron. We were to become lifelong friends. After completing the course we teamed up together for night duty, and occasionally, when carrying sensitive material, we were required to ride together for security. Returning from an Army HQ in the Cheltenham area well into the night, I was leading, with Ashton a cricket-pitch length or so behind me, and was keeping a general watch on him through the rear-view mirror. At some stage, after rounding a sharp left-hand bend, I looked behind and there was nothing! No dipped headlight and no Ashton.

So I backtracked some several hundred yards to the corner to hear a plaintive call from my left – Ashton! He had failed to see and negotiate the sharp bend, and proceeded straight on through a churchyard gate, wrapping himself round a former person's gravestone. Fortunately the gravel path in the churchyard had alerted him to impending danger, and the impact with the long-gone person's headstone was of minor proportions. All was well apart from a dented pride. Ashton later trained as a pilot with the RAF, and we saw a lot of each other after the end of the war.

By this time I had been promoted to flight sergeant. My left sleeve was a motley collection of badges, with my rank badge surmounted by the Y scheme and then the squadron badges. Mounted on a motorcycle, which we were allowed to collect before parade, and on which we would take our WJAC girlfriends home, it all seemed terribly important. One of the four WJAC was the sister of a former school friend. I had only met Betty once or twice before, usually at Lloyds Bank, where she was a cashier, and which I visited often in the course of my work. But our friendship now blossomed.

The more mundane routine of the ATC was punctuated by occasional flight experience from a local RAF airfield. Any pilot then, of course, was a hero, but I remember being more than impressed by a languid individual, a sergeant pilot, who piloted the Airspeed Oxford I flew in from RAF Locking, Weston-super-Mare. Gosh, I thought, how can he be so nonchalant and matter of fact, as we flew out over the Bristol Channel and down the Welsh coast, all at low level? No flying overalls in those days, he wore his normal uniform resplendent with RAF pilot's wings and the inevitable white silk scarf casually draped round his neck. Sadly he didn't say a word to any of us during the whole flight, and after landing he stalked across the grass as if we didn't exist. Hero worship went down a peg or two, but he wasn't typical. ATC cadets were generally well received at RAF stations.

Then came the moment of truth: January 1944 had arrived. I was given a rousing send-off by my squadron friends and many others, and went to war.

CHAPTER 2

To War

The train from Bristol terminated at Salisbury. Southern Railway took over from the old Great Western, and if one was lucky a connection would arrive within a half-hour or so. Later experience would show how shallow such hopes were, and travel, during the night especially, could result in hours on a dimly lit platform devoid of any creature comforts, with waiting-rooms locked for the night.

On this journey, however, all was well, and I arrived at Portsmouth Harbour station directly alongside the ferry which would take me across the Solent to Gosport. From there a short walk of perhaps a mile would land me outside the gates of HMS *St Vincent*, the training establishment for aspiring naval aviators which would be my home for the next three months.

It was a bleak and forbidding-looking place. Built sometime in the early nineteenth century, it had been condemned at least twice, but reprieved on each occasion by the necessities of this or that war or crisis as a general naval barracks. Now it had become the home of that select bunch of aircrew recruits who were privileged to wear a white cap-band. At least that is how we saw ourselves.

We soon discovered that HMS *St Vincent* was the sole preserve of a Chief Petty Officer gunnery instructor by name of Wilmott. Nominally in overall charge of parades and general discipline of trainees, his influence was everywhere. Wilmott and *St Vincent* went together like fish and chips for all the many cadets who passed through his hands. He was either liked or disliked according to your point of view, but no one would dispute his success at turning boys into men during the short period they were there.

Legendary stories of CPO Wilmott abound. I heard after I had left *St Vincent* of one such that occurred during the pilots' course following mine. Wilmott delighted in his role of parade commander, which, in fact, he performed very well. Cap pulled down to the front over his eyes, head thrown back, swagger stick tucked firmly under his left arm, ramrod straight, he was very much the Guards sergeant-major – only better, as one would expect of a chief gunnery instructor Royal Navy.

Apparently, I was told, on one particular day, taking the course for drill, he had them formed up on three sides of a square facing him prior to marching the whole lot past him in close order, line abreast and wheeling in formation at each corner of the parade-ground: a difficult drill exercise.

Wilmott was rather a short man, and in order to oversee events to his satisfaction, he had mounted a small platform on top of a trailer pump house, a contraption placed there in case of fire. Now it was his habit while taking parade to give emphasis to his shouted orders by throwing his head back, clutching his swagger stick with the palm of his left hand and taking a step or two back. All good parade-ground showmanship. Only this time, obsessed with the standard of wheeling in front of him, he performed his usual routine forgetting entirely that he was not on terra firma but two feet up on the TPH platform. He disappeared!

Shortly he emerged from behind the platform, cap askew, clutching his false teeth, looking a trifle shaken – but certainly not stirred. He carried on with his orders almost without a pause, and it says much for the force of his personality that no one laughed. I only wish I had been there to witness it.

Lectures in navigation, seamanship, theory of flight, meteorology and signals, including Morse and semaphore, would occupy much of our time when we were not square bashing under the watchful eye of Chief Wilmott. Much of this was plain sailing to me since I had had a good grounding in the ATC. Armament training, mostly with .303 rifles, necessitated a march of several miles to Brown Down range, where one could guarantee a brisk on-shore wind to add to the difficulties of cold hands trying to hit a distant target. I never quite mastered it, and only much later would I discover I was partially closing the wrong eye looking through the sight!

On arrival we had been placed in 'Divisions' – in my case Collingwood – which determined the dormitory you would share and the numbered mess. The dormitories and attendant wash facilities were basic. Thirty to forty trainees housed in each dormitory in double bunks would share totally inadequate washing facilities and lavatories. Showers were rugby style, with hot water at a premium. For most of us it was a shock to the system, but you learnt quickly.

Occasional long-weekend leave after duty on Friday until Sunday evening was a welcome break from the very strict discipline, and I suppose we were all chuffed to return home and show off our new uniforms. It was on one such weekend leave to Bristol that I first met up with John Gaut, who I discovered lived quite close to my home. I had not come across him before, but many years later we would meet again and become lifelong friends.

He would relate the amusing story of the 'automatic spud peeler'. It was the custom for each mess deck to provide a duty rating whose job it was to assist in the galley for a short period in the forenoon, as well as be responsible for collecting the food for the mess at meal-times. The usual duty in the galley was 'spud peeling', and he told me of the occasion when he and another rating were on such duty, and instead of manual peeling they had been allowed an automatic peeler, but the difficulty was that it was on the slow side.

'I know how to make this go faster', said the knowledgeable one, and proceeded to tinker with the mechanism. He succeeded, but like the Sorcerer's Apprentice he couldn't stop it. Spuds were spewed out everywhere at a high rate, all over the galley floor. The galley staff were not amused, but the upside was that at the end of Wilmott's week's punishment both John and his erstwhile chum were expert spud peelers.

Towards the end of our time at *Vincent* we would take examinations to determine whether we would go on to flying training or not. I had had the misfortune a week or so before to badly sprain my right ankle during a vigorous game – laughingly called rugby – on the sports field. I recall it combined the subtleties of football with the rougher elements of the oval ball game, depending on the particular player's background. No matter, it resulted in marked incapacitation, alleviated by the kind support of one Maurice Graham, who, being a very sturdy lad, piggy-backed me much of the time.

His kindness was ill rewarded, however, by CPO Wilmott, who, seeing him carrying me across the parade-ground at a steady walking pace, became apoplectic. This was a heinous crime to him; his parade-ground was hallowed ground, and you always doubled or walked round it.

'Double, that man', he bellowed.

'But sir,' said Maurice, breaking into a sort of stumble, 'he's heavy.' Answering back was more that the exalted CPO could take. He turned puce and his response reverberated across the parade-ground.

'In my office!' he shouted back, and we knew what that meant. Fortunately he had a human side to his rough exterior, and in his office shortly afterwards, after a short lecture, he did the unthinkable – almost apologised!

A little later on during the seamanship exam, my 'ankle' helped me in another way.

'Come and tell me what this knot is and then tie one yourself', said the CPO – much retired but recalled for war service. As I got uneasily to my feet, he saw my difficulty and said, 'Oh sit down, lad, and I'll tie this sheepshank for you.' The rest of the examination went much the same way. He was a very nice fatherly figure who had told us many amusing yarns of his time in the Royal Navy before the war.

There were a number of failures on the course, I suspect as much due to attitude as anything else, since potential officer material was much in the forefront of the selection process for continued training. The original course of some 300-plus was made up of overseas trainees from New Zealand, South Africa and elsewhere in addition to the Y-scheme entries who made up the bulk. There were also a number of transferred RN ratings, leading seamen, chiefs and petty officers who aspired and had volunteered for retraining as aircrew. The latter were an interesting bunch. One I recall to this day seemed bent only on increasing his list of conquests of the fairer sex, and would relate, *ad nauseam*, the finer details of his exploits on return from his night ashore in Portsmouth. Unfortunately his bunk was directly adjacent to mine, and he pounded my inexperienced ears unmercifully.

About the same time as the examination results were announced we were asked to state our preference for flying training. This meant Canada or the United States. Rumour had it that the Americans were pernickety about trivial things and operated a system of demerits. These were given for a variety of non-flying instances of so-called misbehaviour. Not making your bed exactly in accordance with the US bed-making manual, for instance, earned you ten demerits. Twenty demerits by the end of a week resulted in a formal interview and a warning of termination of training. Thus there were two means of being 'washed out', as it was known, with general demeanour and flying considered of equal importance.

I had no problem with this, but I didn't want to put it to the test. The American training was also longer. So I opted for Canada, and to Canada I would go. We had now been promoted to leading airmen. On arrival at *St Vincent* we had become acquainted with 'Blue Line' cigarettes and were given a free ration of 200 cigarettes a month. This we would now lose, so the increase in pay on advancement to leading airman was very welcome.

In retrospect perhaps the loss of the Blue Line privilege did us a favour. Although smoking in those days was commonplace, the Blue Line was hardly to be compared with the Players or Wills cigarettes of the day, and over a period they might have caused untold damage. The more extreme description would say they were the sweepings off the Woodbine cigarettes floor, and you couldn't get any lower than that. Woodbines were the cheapest on the market, generally sold in packets of five in a little paper packet to those who couldn't afford anything better.

We left *St Vincent* with anything but sadness, richer for the experience perhaps but otherwise keen to get on to the proper stuff, flying. I would not see many of my course members again. We would be divided into much smaller groups for our various destinations for pilot training or, in the case of potential observers, to Trinidad. A week's embarkation leave at home, fond farewells to old friends, then to Greenock on the Clyde to join the Cunard liner *Queen Elizabeth*, bound for New York. Recently completed, she had yet to earn her keep as a fare-paying passenger ship, but had already done sterling service in transporting thousands of American servicemen to the UK. In contrast, the east–west sailings were relatively light in numbers, and cabin accommodation was spacious even for lowly leading airmen.

As with similar fast passenger ships, we sailed alone without convoy, and once we had cleared the Irish Sea area, without escort for the transit to New York, where we arrived without apparent incident, although I learnt later that the ship had changed course on one occasion to avoid a possible U-boat threat. I had my first glimpse of the Statue of Liberty before we tied up at Pier 90, the traditional berth of Cunard.

Any thoughts of seeing the city were soon dispelled. With indecent haste we were whisked off to a waiting train for the onward journey to Canada, or, to be more precise, No. 31 PDS, at Monkton, New Brunswick. No. 31 Personnel Dispatch Station out east in the sticks seemed a strange place to locate a reception centre for trainees destined for central or western Canada, and we thought, 'What the hell are we doing going the wrong way from New York?' After all, a train direct to Ontario, where we would be trained, would have taken considerably less time without taking account of the eventual train journey back west from Monkton. But the world moves in mysterious ways, and Monkton was probably selected because of its proximity to

Halifax and St John, where many of the ships berthed, ignoring the logic of an alternative reception centre for New York arrivals.

But there it was, we duly settled in for an indeterminate time to wait our turn to travel to St Eugene, which we now knew would be our first destination for flying training.

For us Monkton was dead time: no objective, no work, nothing to do except report once a day to show we were still there. But it wasn't all bad. We enjoyed the luxury of food long since forgotten. There was an excellent choice for every meal: steak for breakfast if you wished, orange and other juice by the gallon, and the quantities of everything unlimited. For the next eight months we would suffer the same hardship!

There was to be no formal leave because of the uncertainty of departure, but for some time it had been standard practice to wriggle under the perimeter fence to see what the outside world had to offer. There wasn't much, but one milk-bar-cum-café was renowned for its high standard of waitresses, and was duly given the business. I doubt if they were much above average, but to us, starved of female company, they were wonderful. Through one of the girls we were introduced to a farm of sorts where they hired out Indian ponies but no saddle! So I had my first experience of riding. I managed to stay aboard, as did my two friends, and we returned the next day for more punishment

Monkton was easily forgettable. We were there far too long with nothing to do, waiting impatiently for departure to flying training. When it did come I nearly lost it – there was a hitch. I was in the sick bay, having contracted tonsillitis, and was plainly going to miss my course if I stayed there. So I bribed a medical orderly to bring my clothes, and escaped without authority. There was hell to pay. The pompous and very angry senior medical officer threatened all sorts of retribution for violation of hospital orders. 'This is an offence for which I should put you on a charge,' said he, 'particularly as you have involved a member of my staff.'

Things looked black, and I became distinctly worried that my initiative had rebounded on me. Things were smoothed over, however, and I recovered sufficiently to be allowed to proceed with my course on condition that I reported to the medics on arrival at the next staging place, Victoriaville.

There had been rumours of stopping-off after leaving Monkton at a place called Victoriaville for a short period *en route* to EFTS at St Eugene.

13

Reasons were vague, but the general impression we gathered was a touch of showing the flag by parading through the town for the benefit of the locals. Why Victoriaville – a small- to medium-size town some miles north-east of Montreal – we never discovered. It boasted a military barracks but not much else.

However, we duly arrived, were billeted in the barracks and were put through mini boots and gaiters training in preparation for a march through the centre of the town. It was all rather quaint really, thirty or so Britishers, rifles at the slope, resplendent in highly polished boots and gaiters striding down the Main Street to the music of some patriotic tune or other, to the acclaim of a fair number of locals, who no doubt wondered what on earth it was all about. So did we!

It was to be a short interlude, however. Barely a week later we would be on the train to St Eugene, a final journey of some 600 miles since leaving Monkton, through mainly open country with little signs of habitation. It was hardly memorable except for the plaintive whistle of the train throughout the night as we proceeded quite literally down the High Street of small towns.

CHAPTER 3

Flying Training

No. 13 EFTS, St Eugene, Ontario

So we arrived at last at St Eugene, the home of No. 13 Elementary Flying Training School, a few miles from the station, wondering what the next few months would bring. We were not to be left with our thoughts for long. Stories abounded as we sighted the empty beds of those who had failed at one stage or another. Not the sort of thing to inspire confidence in nervous, newly arrived would-be pilots. But it seemed a pleasant enough place and our first glimpse of our aircraft mount, the DH Cornell, thrilled us with anticipation.

The Cornell was a low-wing monoplane, built in Canada to replace the earlier Tiger Moth. It was not unlike the much later DH Chipmunk built in the UK. It benefited from an enclosed cockpit to contend with the harsh Canadian winter conditions, and in every way was a delightful little aeroplane to experience the first thrills of flying.

In due course we were allocated to this or that flying instructor, a Royal Canadian Air Force officer with whom we would stay for the duration of the course. Mine was a minor disaster named Mason. A rather seedy-looking chap, Flg Off Mason in the first few weeks was more often sick than available. This presented quite a problem.

After my first flight with Mason on Tuesday 4 July, I then didn't see him for a further two weeks, and this at a stage when continuity was essential. The first week resulted in only two instructional flights, and the next, only one. Three flights in two weeks with three instructors. This didn't bode well. Instructors brought in at the last moment had not the same commitment to another instructor's pupils, and by the beginning of the third week I had visions of the empty bed routine, Meanwhile many of the other students had by this time gone solo. I was to wait until 26 July for that formidable experience, and when it came it was a bit of an anti-climax.

15

I had waited impatiently for some days for this moment, and now Flg Off Mason had swallowed his nervous disposition and sent me solo. There was no feeling of apprehension – only that of relief. I started up, taxied out ready for the take-off. I was enjoying myself. Now down the runway, take off, then straight ahead to 400 ft before turning left cross wind and then climbing to the circuit height. Downwind, pre-landing checks completed, only I would not land on the first approach; this was to be an overshoot as instructed. Round again; downwind checks then cross wind for the approach and then landing, quite a decent one, I thought.

Now, less than two hours later I was confronted with the periodical twelve-hour flying check. The chequered instruction had done me no favours, and I knew that having been sent solo later than usual I was viewed with suspicion. The twelve-hour check passed without difficulty, but unsurprisingly, because of my history, a further progress check loomed, and I was given two hours to improve. But to improve on what? I didn't think I had any particular problems, but the delay before going solo rang the alarm bells, and I was mentally and ignominiously on my way home – and disgrace! That was how failure was viewed.

Then the Good Lord came to my rescue in the form of the squadron commander, a somewhat older and aged pilot of many years in contrast to the majority of instructors, who had only recently qualified for their own 'wings'. Thus after the permitted two hours, I would be given a progress check – known by all as a 'wash-out check' since that invariably followed. I think I was, at that time, justifiably resentful at the turn of events and the haphazard progress. However, as it happened, I need not have worried.

On the Sunday morning Flt Lt McPherson took me aside in his office.

'Now then, young Higgs,' said he, 'what seems to be the problem?'

'I don't know', I replied, not knowing what else to say, since I was not troubled by anything so far with my flying.

"Right,' he said after a pause, 'I'll see you at the aircraft in a few minutes. Please make sure my parachute is there.' Then he added, 'I shall climb in the back, and when I've done so, start the engine, taxi out, take off when permitted by the runway controller, carry out a circuit and overshoot, and then land without any further word from me.'

'Yes sir', I said, with a slight sense of relief at his warm and friendly attitude, a most welcome change from the distant and uncommunicative Mason.

16

I made sure his parachute was properly stowed in the back seat, strapped myself in the front cockpit and waited, but not for long. He was as good as his word, arrived very quickly and climbed in. 'All right,' he shouted, 'I'm strapped in, forget I'm here.'

So I did. Started up, taxied out and in due course took off and did his bidding. After landing, across the intercom came, 'Right, now taxi back down the runway and we'll do a little general flying.'

I took off again and settled into a pleasant half-hour's flying, responding to the occasional instruction. All went well and in a short while, 'Let's go home' came from the rear, which I promptly did, carrying out a second highly respectable landing.

The subsequent debriefing was short, complimentary and to the point. 'Nothing wrong with your flying. Well up to scratch. I'll have a word with your instructor.'

I think he may have had more than 'a word', because later that day I was sent off for a second solo flight. More than relieved at events, I had now been given a bit of an accolade by the man who mattered most.

For the rest of the course I never looked back. The routine was much the same: ground school, link trainer to polish instrument procedures and of course flying. Frequently three flights a day now and occasionally four, we had alternate weekends free but otherwise flew seven days a week. And so we approached the end of August and the end of the course, with only final examinations to contend with. I had now completed sixty-five hours' flying. In contrast to the miserable start in July, nearly fifty hours were achieved in the three weeks of August.

I had the dubious pleasure of the chief flying instructor, who was also the base commander, for my final navigation flying check. Sqn Ldr Michaud, a French Canadian, whom I remember to this day, had the reputation of not much caring for the Brits, and I suppose I was more than a touch apprehensive, but I need not have worried. He was quiet and very polite, and I passed without difficulty. Earlier in the course he had crossed swords with two RN lieutenants who, together with three Canadian lieutenants, had joined the course at Victoriaville. We never discovered the cause of their confrontation, but it centred on their conduct in the RCAF officers' mess, and was serious enough to have both these career officers sent back to the UK, where, no doubt, apart from the detrimental effect on their careers, they would be asked to explain themselves. The three Canadians stayed with us throughout flying training, and later on to Yeovilton, where, sadly, one was to die in an aircraft accident.

The other two qualifying final tests, general flying and instrument, followed a day or two later. I passed both, and the ground school examination and so the threat of early return to the UK had passed – for the moment. There was now the challenge of the formidable Harvard.

During the relatively short time at St Eugene I and a few friends were able to visit Ottawa. There was nothing of any interest around the base. St Eugene was hardly Las Vegas – a small, unpretentious town between the Ottawa and St Lawrence rivers, whose claim to fame, for us, was solely due to being on the main line between Montreal and Ottawa. Ottawa, though, was something else. It was the first opportunity to see anything of Canada, and various notices on the official notice-board encouraged you to stay with Canadian families who had kindly expressed their willingness to entertain you for the weekend. In our case Mrs Earl and her daughter would be our hosts.

The short train journey from St Eugene took a little under the hour. I recall the compartment even now because it was quite different from the standard train at home. It was open plan, with half devoted to large swivel-armchairs, the other half with seating similar to that of the London Underground. Very novel to us and extremely comfortable.

The Earls' home was on the outskirts of the city, a modest house, but the welcome was very warm and friendly. Our host had thoughtfully rustled up some female company for the Saturday, and we were able to relax at the nearby beach, which I recall was somewhat unimaginatively called 'Sandy Beach'. It wasn't, it was mostly pebbles, but it mattered not. Our hosts were staunch Presbyterians and deemed it proper that we should not neglect that aspect of the weekend. So off to church we would go on the Sunday morning with more than a sense of righteousness before returning to St Eugene in the late afternoon. A most enjoyable break; we didn't see much of the city, but the unstinting hospitality of the Earl family had been more than enough.

No. 14 SFTS, Kingston, Ontario

And so towards the end of August I would leave St Eugene with a sense of relief and much more confident about the future than I had been some weeks before. We were bound for Kingston and the next stage of our flying training. Kingston, lying on the shores of Lake Ontario, was of modest size but noted for its military academy. The most striking thing on arrival was the atmosphere and attitude of the instructional staff, who, unlike at St Eugene, were RAF officers or sergeant pilots, a number with operational experience. No longer treated like expendable fodder, we were now regarded very much as potential pilot material, and their job was to make it so. They were to do their best.

From the start I enjoyed every minute of it, and although there were to be failures among us, I never once felt threatened. We were now just over half the number with which we had started. Severe pruning had taken its toll, but in many ways those who remained felt all the safer for it. Instructors were allocated, in my case Flg Off Hodson, with whom I struck up an immediate rapport. A very likeable chap, it would transpire that he was to be my instructor for only a short time. He had previously applied for front-line operational service and was delighted when this was granted in September. Sad as I was at his departure, this was to be the icing on the cake. Flg Off Hayter, his replacement, was a splendid fellow and we hit it off straight away. The relationship was more than instructor/pupil, we became good friends, and as a consequence the rest of the course would be plain sailing and thoroughly enjoyable.

About half-way through the course a most extraordinary accident happened. A student, flying solo, landed on top of another aircraft which had taxied onto the runaway in preparation for take-off. Fortunately this aircraft was also flown by a student, who, as was customary, was in the front cockpit. The consequences otherwise would have been disastrous, since the rear section of the aircraft behind the front seat and where an instructor would have been was completely destroyed. Miracle of miracles, both student pilots were unhurt, but the outcome was a progress check and failure for one of them.

The Harvard was a big step up from the more basic Cornell. Designed to prepare students for operational aircraft, it possessed many of their characteristics: a more powerful engine with a constant-speed propeller to maximise all conditions of flight, it could bite you hard if you were careless. It was ideally suited for armament training, and one of the pleasures of the course later on would be a detachment to a relief airfield at Gananoque, twenty or so miles from Kingston, specifically to conduct concentrated armament practices. The beauty of this was that the detachment took place towards the end of the course after all final flying tests had been satisfied, and so was completely without pressure.

Despite the intensity of the course – four hours of ground school instruction on the same day as three or four and, on occasions, five flights of about an hour each – there were periods of relaxation during occasional free weekends when it was possible to visit Toronto or Montreal. The more adventurous would cross the border and hitchhike to Syracuse or take the train to Buffalo. The latter was a fair journey, though, just about twice the distance of Toronto, which we favoured. The appeal of Syracuse lay solely in its reputation for very attractive girls at the large college there, and many a long-lasting liaison resulted. Some to my knowledge went the distance.

I can't say Toronto held much attraction for me, nor, for that matter, did Montreal. We usually put up at one of the Forces Hostels, which cost pretty well nothing, burnt the candle at both ends and arrived back at Kingston having achieved the minimum of sleep in the process. But we were young, barely turned 19 years of age, and guaranteed to be bright eyed and bushy tailed the next morning – or so we thought.

I recall only one visit to both Toronto and Montreal. It was enough, and, in fact, the weather in Montreal was so cold on the occasion of our only visit – minus something or another – that we retreated to the warmth of a cinema for a film we had no intention of seeing. It made such an impression on me that I have now forgotten the name of the film, even though we sat through it twice!

At the sharp end of business, as the course progressed the flying became vastly more interesting. Much attention was given to formation flying and basic flight or battle drill. Low-flying exercises featured prominently. The local area, particularly to the north of Kingston, with its barren wasteland and many lakes, was conducive to the lowest of low flying. My instructor was inclined to let me have my head on these occasions – to his cost. With excessive confidence on one occasion late in the course, I persuaded myself that a very narrow gap between a line of trees was negotiable for me to fly through without climbing over the top. But it wasn't. In the process of trying to correct my mistake by a shallow turn to port to miss the tree on the right, I made a fool of myself by clipping a small branch on the tree to my left with my wingtip – Horror of Horrors!

From the rear cockpit came a strangled but very restrained comment: 'Clot!' said Flg Off Hayter, which in the circumstances sounded more like a vote of confidence! Back at base, of course, he had to take responsibility, which I felt was unjust, but that's the way the 'cookie crumbles' for instructors, as I was to learn much later on.

Fortunately the damage was slight, involving only the replacement of a small section of the wingtip. The damage to my pride was another matter.

But Hayter harboured no ill will; in fact I believe he took some satisfaction in encouraging me to fly so low as a prelude to forthcoming operational demands.

By the end of November we had virtually finished the course, taken all final flying examinations to qualify for the much-coveted 'wings', and would prepare to go to a relief airfield some twenty miles to the east of Kingston for final intensive armament training. There we would carry out air-to-air gun firing against a towed target, and a dive-bombing exercise using 2? lb bombs. These, apart from the inaccuracies caused by the pilot, seemed to have their own idiosyncrasies, and their flight path would vary widely. Throw in the wind variation, which was always totally unpredictable from some two thousand feet, and you knew that the chances of hitting the target were much the same as a golfer's 'hole in one'.

Gananoque was rightly known as the 'Gateway to the Thousand Islands', an incredibly beautiful cluster of islands at the eastern extremity of Lake Ontario. They were of varying sizes – some very small, with scarcely room for one dwelling, others quite large, where the numerous homes of the wealthy could be seen. It was a pleasant place to spend a week, very relaxing, with no pressures to distract us. Snow covered the ground to some depth. Well compacted, it did not restrict the flying, and of course we benefited from the experience of coping with the vicissitudes of these conditions. At the end of the week we returned to Kingston having become well adapted to slithering down the runway after landing and having learnt to anticipate poor braking on the ground.

The final ground school examination was all that remained, and this I negotiated without difficulty, but I had put in a lot of work prior to this and would have been disappointed had it been otherwise. Unlike the 'stop-go' at EFTS, the course had gone smoothly without interruption. The instructional staff were excellent and greatly contributed to an enjoyable and rewarding experience.

On arrival back at Kingston from Gananoque, and after the ground subject examination, we had rounded off events with the 'Link Trainer' test, an exercise of little consequence, and I was pleased later on that day to get back up in the air for my last flight at Kingston. This was Monday 11 December 1944, and for me it was a sad occasion.

Four days later on Friday the 15th was 'Wings Day', when all our endeavours would be rewarded by the formal presentation of the long-looked-forward-to naval pilot's wings badge. On the day, eager enough with anticipation for this important occasion, imagine my utter delight when I discovered I had been selected top student, having come top of the flying course and second in the ground school examination! I was accordingly presented with the 'Admiralty Prize' and, perhaps understandably, felt ten feet tall. My thoughts went back to six months earlier when – by the Grace of God!

Coincidentally with the award of the flying badge we were promoted petty officers, temporary acting, but nevertheless petty officers with a considerable uplift in pay. There was slight irony here because RAF students in Canada on being awarded their wings would, if selected, be commissioned there and then. We would have to await our return to the UK. This perhaps was of little consequence other than that they would travel home in officers' quarters, whereas we would still be 'cattle class'.

The great benefit of training in Canada had been the broad spectrum of weather conditions. We had flown in all sorts of weather, experienced a lot of cloud flying with its attendant instrument training, and operated in the snow conditions of Gananoque as well as Kingston over several weeks. By comparison our fellow students in America had experienced only the totally hospitable weather of Pensacola in the south – one hundred per cent sunshine and no correspondingly bad weather.

Agreeable as this must have seemed to them at the time, it would be a climatic shock for those who returned to the harsher flying conditions in the UK. It was perhaps as well that a fair percentage of them would form up in new squadrons in the USA after completion of operational flying training at Jacksonville in Florida, and then proceed direct to the Pacific, where with any luck they would experience largely fine weather – south-west monsoons permitting.

And so in mid-December the survivors of the original flying course entrained for Halifax and the return home. The loss rate over the previous months had been high, about fifty per cent, but accepted as about average for all courses. One of two had been back-coursed for one reason or another. At any rate those lucky ones – and there must have been an element of luck in it – who had survived would now embark in the good ship SS *Louis Pasteur*, a former transatlantic liner of French origin. Not quite *Queen Elizabeth* standard, she was showing her age and the effect of numerous wartime crossings as a troopship. How she came to be in British hands I never discovered, since with the collapse of France all French ships had been ordered by the Pétain government to sail for ports in Vichy France or North Africa.

Accommodation on board was cramped and uncomfortable, with poor ventilation. By chance I had been given 'the buzz' that there was a slot available in the after 4-inch gun deck crew. This meant a decent bunk in the gun deck quarters, with plenty of fresh air for sleeping, and was highly recommended! So I joined the starboard watch of X gun for the voyage home and very nearly qualified for the Atlantic Star. If the voyage had lasted two more days I would have! It was not to be.

We completed the crossing in six uneventful days, practising gun drill but never firing the gun in anger. The U-boat threat had greatly diminished and the weather was unusually kind to us for the time of the year. And so we arrived in Liverpool in time for Christmas leave.

Christmas 1944 must have been one of the most enjoyable occasions for me. Two weeks overseas and disembarkation leave, meeting old friends and, I suspect, not a little showing-off of new pilot's wings and crossed anchors on the left sleeve. And for once I had a little spare money to enjoy. Life could not have been better.

Unfortunately, my brother was not there to share the experience. He was now in HMS *Royalist*, a cruiser, which for some time had been engaged in convoy protection duty round the North Cape to Russia. By any standards it was one of the more arduous and exhausting duties at sea at that time. A high state of alert twenty-four hours a day as soon as they left UK waters, with a constant U-boat threat as well as the risk of enemy aircraft attack; and for those merchant ships that did manage to make Murmansk, a welcome about as warm as a slab of wet cod. However, *Royalist* and my brother survived and would be 'rewarded' with a warmer spell of duty in the Mediterranean. But welcome as this change was, there was still plenty of action there.

Leave over, I was to report to HMS *Macaw* near Bootle, Cumberland, where Their Lordships would reveal who would be commissioned and who would be the unfortunate ones who would remain petty officers. It was a godforsaken place of very temporary huts, devoid of any form of entertainment and miles from anywhere – unless you counted Bootle – which we didn't. It was some miles away, anyway, and we were without any form of transport. In its defence its sole purpose was to receive such as myself from overseas, awaiting a further appointment after the selection process.

Mr Gieves' (naval tailors), representative was a permanent fixture there, waiting to measure you up and add you to his list of customers.

'But', I said when he asked to measure me, 'I don't know yet whether I've been selected.'

'Oh, don't worry sir,' he said, 'you will be all right. By the way, do you dress right or left?' I hadn't a clue what he was talking about!

It soon became obvious that Gieves was the best source of information in the Royal Navy, and here they had clearly been given advance notice of those to be commissioned.

Much later on they would ask if they could measure me for tropical uniform, and I knew that they knew where I was destined long before I was told officially. Anyway, they were right. I was duly given the King's Commission as Midshipman (A) RNVR. They don't come much lower than that. But I didn't care, I was very proud when I put on my uniform for the first time. A few of the older ones, who were over the age of 19?, the minimum age for one-stripers, had been made sub-lieutenants, but it mattered not, since we would all serve the same qualifying time to lieutenant.

Very wisely Their Lordships had injected a short refresher flying course before operational training, and in due course No. 9 (P) Advanced Flying Unit at RAF Errol near Dundee beckoned for those selected for fighter training. Others destined for TBR training would go to a similar unit at RAF Tealing. I had been nominated for fighters, which pleased me greatly and really rounded things off. I had no wish to trundle around dropping torpedoes from Barracudas or such like.

It was now the end of February, and I had not flown since early December. But it all came back to me, rather like riding a bicycle, and my instructor was kind enough to say that there was nothing more he could teach me as far as the Harvard was concerned. And so the five weeks there was a bit of a jolly, mostly formation flying, usually solo, and towards the end a period of night-flying.

There was one more hurdle before Fighter School. A short instrument course at the so-called Naval Advanced Instrument Flying School, HMS *Godwit*, based at Hinstock, a sleepy establishment in Shropshire. This turned out to be quite painless, bordering on the farcical. A small handful of hours of instrument flying in the Airspeed Oxford, a twin-engine aircraft, which seemed rather odd for pilots destined for single-seat fighters, followed by an even more ludicrous forty-five-minute flight in a Tiger Moth for an instrument spin recovery.

This turned out to be a climb lasting some thirty minutes to height, putting the aircraft into a spin, recovery, and then landing. It was well known that spin recovery in the Tiger Moth was best left to the aircraft. Under no circumstances were you to attempt to assist by the use of stick or rudder. It would come out of the spin by itself. Any attempted assistance by the pilot was liable to upset it! It was all rather a waste of time, but I suppose it justified their existence, and for me it was another tick in the logbook. So it was that two weeks later I would achieve my goal, arrival at No. 1 Naval Air Fighter School, to fly the mighty Vought Corsair.

No. 1 Fighter School, RNAS Yeovilton

RNAS Yeovilton was the home of the fighter school, and had been for many years. It was well known to us as a tough, demanding course, and of course, apart from the short period at Hinstock, we were back in a naval environment for the first time since leaving *St Vincent.* It seemed a friendly enough place, a collection of temporary buildings for our accommodation with quite large double cabins. A similar collection of buildings constituted the wardroom mess. Adequate and comfortable, it would remain unchanged for many years afterwards until, in the 1990s, permanent accommodation was built.

I had now lost many of my friends from the original flying course; some hadn't quite made it, others had been selected for TBR training, and one or two were to go to RNAS Henstridge, a satellite of Yeovilton, for conversion to Seafires. I can't recall at the time whether I envied them the opportunity to fly the glamour aeroplane, or not. The Corsair was in any event the 'hot ship', and anyway, I would join a Seafire squadron later on, whereas the reverse opportunity would not occur for them to fly the Corsair.

Yeovilton was very much geared to creating a front-line environment. The instructors were seasoned operational pilots, and for the first time a sense of urgency prevailed. The Corsair was a huge step up the aircraft ladder – the latest and most potent fighter aircraft in both the United States Navy and our own. It had terrific performance for its day, and was rugged and ideally suited for carrier operations, although in its early days it had been rejected by the USN for difficulty in landing aboard carriers. Fortunately the US Marines adopted it, and so did we. Eventually the USN sheepishly followed, but in fairness the aircraft had by then been redesigned in the cockpit area to improve the view. Even so, when the aircraft was 'sat up' in the landing configuration, the view ahead was considerably restricted, demanding a curved approach onto the deck.

Gradually over the next few months we would tame the beast and learn all the tricks of the trade to use it in its operational role for fighter combat and ground attack. Early in the course we would become acquainted with the technique for carrier landing. These were known as aerodrome dummy deck landings, ADDLS for short, and we were to practise these for most landings with the aid of a 'batsman' on the end of the runway.

Then, towards the end of the second month, the course at Yeovilton would be interrupted by a short detachment to the Naval School of Air Warfare at St Merryn in Cornwall. Here we would carry out air-to-air live firing against a drogue towed by a Lysander, similar to that we had previously practised in the Harvard, but at twice the speed. The practice known as quarter attacks would commence by flying an opposite and parallel course to the towing aircraft, offset by a suitable distance, turning in towards the target at some juncture to initiate a 'curved pursuit' in order to commence firing from astern at an angle of forty-five degrees. We were, emphatically, not to continue firing after reaching the fifteen-degree position, since it was considered unhealthy for the safety of the drogue-towing pilot. Numerous examples of over-enthusiasm by attacking pilots would be quoted, some with fatal consequences, and the union of drogue-towing pilots wanted none of this! We were thus given very strict instructions on the matter, and the towing pilots were all too keen to report even minor violations. I didn't blame them.

Not long before our detachment to St Merryn, the end of the war in Europe had been officially declared on 8 May 1945. It was a memorable occasion, a Tuesday, and we happened to be carrying out dinghy training in Yeovil. It was also Market Day. On hearing the news of the German surrender, dinghy drill was abandoned and forgotten, and there occurred a general exodus to the nearest convenient hostelry for refreshment. It was, I recall, just after midday, and none of us saw the light of day until early evening, and only then because the naval bus driver wanted homewards and threatened to leave without us. Happy days!

Our watering hole on arrival was already full of farmers having their own little celebration, and in short time we would be toasting each other to greet the great news. Another round and, 'Up the Navy', they would shout in friendly fashion. 'Up the Pigs and Cows', we would retort until, later, a little the worse for wear, it all became a trifle silly. Fortunately the bus driver came to our rescue. But it was rather a special day, not to be forgotten. Somehow there was an air of sadness on the way home. It began to dawn on us that the end of the European war meant less opportunity to get to the 'sharp end' and a slice of the action. There were always the Japanese, of course, but the war at sea in the Pacific had been largely an American affair, and not in the forefront of our minds. This would now change.

On return from St Merryn we would concentrate on more ADDLS in preparation for carrier qualification. It was during one of these practice sessions that we suffered the loss of one of the Canadian lieutenants, who stalled his aircraft on the final approach and was killed. This was extremely sad. He was away from home, which made it that much worse, and we were within a week or so of the end of the course. To compound the matter, most of the course were at the end of the runway, watching the landings, as we were enjoined to do, and witnessed the tragedy. Not to be recommended.

We had lost a good friend who had been with us throughout the whole of our flying training. We felt a particular sadness for the other two Canadians, who would return to Canada with the unenviable task of visiting their friend's relatives. The visit to the local church for the service and burial would be our second in a matter of weeks. Shortly before this, one of the instructors, Lt Norcott, was killed during a quite normal sortie. The cause was never established. Curiously, I would become quite friendly with his younger sister, Sadie, some years later when I myself was instructing.

By the first week of July we were considered operationally ready, subject only to carrier qualification. I had, I thought, coped with the course pretty well and hoped my instructors would be of a similar mind. Unfortunately, in one sense, as it turned out, I was given an above-average assessment for night-flying, which made me a strong candidate for a night-fighter squadron.

But first we were to repair north to Ayr, and to 769 Squadron for carrier qualification. The ship was HMS *Premier*, an escort carrier of small – very small, I thought – dimensions, scarcely big enough for the Corsair. There, after a short session of ADDLS with the ship's deck landing control officer, I found myself airborne from Ayr bound for the Firth of Clyde and HMS *Premier*. I climbed to 2,000 ft, switched on the YE beacon to home to the ship, which I duly located. Good grief, I thought, on seeing it from 2,000 ft, they are surely joking. But they weren't, and my thoughts were interrupted by a call from the ship.

27

'Corsair orbiting Mother [parent carriers were always known as 'Mother'], this is XYZ [her call sign], interrogative your call sign?' I had forgotten to call the ship on approaching her. 'XYZ, this is Green 2', I replied, somewhat sheepishly, which immediately brought the invitation to join the circuit in preparation for landing. So I did, with much trepidation.

As I descended into the circuit, *Premier* began to look a little more acceptable, still far too small, of course, but there she was ploughing along at her maximum speed of around 16 knots, belching black smoke and kicking up an untidy-looking wake. Now, downwind, flying parallel but opposite to the ship's course, with undercarriage, flaps and – remembering to put my hook down – I prepared to turn in towards the deck when opposite the stern, as I had been briefed. No, I thought, this can't be right, I shall land ahead of the ship. Nevertheless, ignoring my misgivings, I initiated a hard turn to port to counteract the ship's speed and the current tailwind, and settled into a nice, steady, curved approach to track the ship's wake a little astern of the round-down.

By this time the batsman was in sight and beginning to wave his arms around in familiar fashion. He is giving me a 'Roger', which is fine, so I'll put my life in his hands. Keep the nose of the aircraft up and speed steady, just follow his instructions, which I did. And then 'Crunch', I'd landed and was aboard. Almost simultaneously, the hook snatched a wire and the aircraft came to a stop, throwing me hard forward against the harness.

The relief, not to say surprise, was enormous. I was right, the ship was small. I could see very little flight deck ahead, and not a lot to each side. Now the flight deck crew were waving me back to disengage from the wire, and signalling to raise the hook before pushing me back to the stern. Over the R/T came, 'Green 2, we're pushing you back for take-off. That was OK, well done.' The batsman appeared at the side of the aircraft, gave me a grin and a 'thumbs up'. I was relaxed, I now knew what to expect.

Without delay he held up the board with the take-off checks, I gave him a 'thumbs up', he rotated his flag to signal full throttle, lowered it and, brakes off, off I went down the flight deck for take-off, circuit and the next landing. So it went on until I had completed the requisite eight landings, and landed for the last time feeling a shade pleased with myself. Now, following the flight deck crew's signals, I taxied ahead of the barrier and parked before switching off the engine.

When I reported to the bridge, they seemed satisfied with my performance, the more so because earlier another pilot had distinguished himself by entering the barrier on his second attempted landing, damaging the aircraft beyond repair by the ship's aircraft engineers. Thus, I was informed, said pilot would now take my aircraft to complete his landings, and I would return to Ayr in the back of a Swordfish! Not entirely to my liking, but who was I to protest?

Shortly, a Swordfish landed on, and I, together with another passenger, climbed in the back. Twenty minutes later we landed at Ayr. It was now the 9 July, and I had completed all my training. It had been a long eighteen months, but by the grace of God and the inevitable good fortune the many vicissitudes had been overcome. All that now remained was to wait and see what the future held; but first a short period of leave.

CHAPTER 4

Fully Fledged
- 891 Squadron

The 'future', we had previously been told, meant a front-line squadron for some, but not all. Others would be appointed to a second-line or training squadron. The remainder would report to a 'pool' for an indefinite time, where they would await a vacancy in one squadron or another. I was fortunate to be given an appointment to a front-line squadron, but my above-average night assessment had come home to roost. It was to be a night-fighter squadron, No. 891, currently based at RNAS Eglinton near Londonderry, Northern Ireland. My eldest sister was already serving there as a Wren, and I knew I would have to mind my Ps and Qs! We were on close terms, but she wouldn't care to have the misdemeanours of her younger brother visited upon her in the closely knit environment of a naval air station.

In mid-July, after a short leave, I travelled north to Stranraer via the dreaded Carlisle, a junction I would come to know all too well over the years. It was always an interminable wait, usually of unknown length, but at least I was now travelling first class. The night ferry to Larne arrived in the early hours of the morning and we entrained to Londonderry. On the ferry I had met several others destined for Eglinton. One, Ben Turner, I discovered was also joining the same squadron.

After what had been a very long, more than thirty-six hours of continuous travel, I announced myself at the wardroom and was given my cabin number and directions to get there. Leave your gear, they said. We'll get transport to bring it up later! It was just as well. Apart from the main wardroom buildings, accommodation was scattered around an area of a mile or so, and mine, of course, was about as far away as you could get. Accommodation was a Nissen hut divided into four cabins, with basic facilities and not a lot else. No hot water, which would be brought to you every morning by a steward with a kettle of tea. By the time he had walked the distance, it was cold.

I had by this time discovered that the squadron was equipped with the Grumman Hellcat II (NF), the NF denoting that it was equipped with radar for night-fighting; only at that time it wasn't. It would be a number of weeks before the first radar fitment took place.

The morning after arrival I reported to the Squadron CO, a New Zealander, as were, as I was to discover, the majority of the other pilots in the squadron, which had been formed a month earlier. The welcome from the CO was tepid and I warmed to him not at all. His first words were, 'So you've come from Yeovilton flying Corsairs. I suppose you think the Hellcat is a bit of a come-down?' He went on, 'Well, it isn't.'

We, Ben Turner and I, hadn't said a word at this stage, and were not unnaturally bemused at this uncalled-for and unfriendly attack. His aggressive attitude was to persist for the next three months. He seemed to have a perpetual chip on his shoulder and was rude to everyone, but particularly towards the non-New Zealander. I would come across him on a number of occasions in the future to discover he was still of the same raw arrogance towards others.

It was a relief, therefore, to meet the rest of the squadron and friendly faces. The senior pilot, Peter Picot, also a New Zealander, was charm itself. Out of a completely different mould from the CO, he came of good stock from Wellington, where his family owned a chain of very large department stores. He was to act as the foil between the CO and the rest of the squadron, but in truth it was never a happy squadron, as events would show.

Nevertheless there was no lack of enthusiasm. I was assigned to 'Black Flight' as deputy flight commander, with Ben as my number four. Jock Melville – thank Heavens, a Scot – was the flight commander. We got on well.

Only a week or so after my arrival a squadron party/dance had been organised in Londonderry. These occasions were a normal opportunity to get together off duty with the chiefs and petty officers and the ratings, not forgetting the squadron Wrens who were employed to do cine-assessing and other support functions, including ensuring the 'coffee boat' was always available for the pilots after a sortie. To match numbers, as was customary, an invitation had also been sent to the Chief Wren for 'X' number of other Wrens who wished to join us. There was never any shortage of volunteers!

I had by this time been pleased to see my sister on a number of occasions, usually taking a walk together off the camp. Both our lives were busy. She seemed to have a lot of friends and was to keep me well informed of station events outside my narrower world of the squadron. As far as I can recall, the squadron dance/party was a success, a lot of 'Liffey water' was consumed and much merriment was made.

During the course of the evening it would seem that a petty officer Wren attached herself to me without, as far as I can recall, which is perhaps not a lot, much encouragement. The upshot was that on the naval bus returning to Eglinton we sat together. For reasons unknown to me then, but revealed later, this seemed to excite the interests and amusement of the other Wrens on the bus. Arriving back at the station I think there was a suggestion that we might meet again.

However, the upshot of this was a telephone call the next day from my sister: could we meet later after duty? We did, and of course, she had heard through the grapevine of said PO Wren's latest conquest!

'Not on your life,' said elder sister, or words to that effect, 'she's not for you', and went on to explain that said PO Wren had the dubious reputation of being the station bicycle – although these perhaps were not her exact words.

Meanwhile, back at the farm, flying was going ahead apace. Two and three flights a day, six days a week including either a Saturday or a Sunday, mostly patrol formations to get the whole squadron together, or other battle drill. We kept the squadron Wrens busy with our air-to-air cine-camera work, and there was some night-flying and the inevitable ADDLS in preparation for what we understood would be embarkation in HMS Ocean in September, and deployment to the Pacific for the war against Japan.

On 12 August we left Eglinton for RNAS Nutts Corner, near Belfast, as part of the plan for embarkation. We carried on much as before but suffered several setbacks. During one night sortie, having taxied out in turn behind the flight commander, I stopped behind him at the end of the runway prior to take-off. Then all hell broke loose: the 'stick', or control column, began to whip in frenzied fashion all over the place in the cockpit. Petty Officer Rogers, following me, had failed to stop. His propeller, which had already demolished most of the tail unit, was steadily eating its way towards my cockpit. Not amused, and with a few choice words, I managed to taxi back to dispersal. Unfortunately, some time later Rogers would fail to return from a night cross-country exercise, and would be found high up in the Mourne Mountains.

He was our first and only loss, although not long before, one of the New Zealand pilots had stalled late on the approach during an ADDLS session and crashed inverted alongside the batsman and, once more, the assembled company of squadron pilots. It was a very nasty accident. He was severely injured but lived to be sent back to New Zealand after some months' recovery.

Around this time I became friends with the Corsair again! The 'pool' aircraft required a test flight following some minor rectification or other, and by some good fortune it fell to me to carry out said duty. Twenty minutes into the flight, checking flaps and undercarriage operation in accordance with the test schedule, a spray of liquid filled the cockpit. I had suffered a hydraulic failure. Somewhere near Coleraine at the time, I was fortunately also not far from RAF Ballyhalbert, where I was able to carry out an emergency landing without flaps. A Stinson Reliant returned me to Nutts Corner later that day.

Events elsewhere were gathering pace. The atomic bombing of Japan had taken place in August, and so, on 2 September, the war against Japan ended. We celebrated in fine style wondering what the future would now bring for the squadron. But meanwhile, thoughts were on the beer and Liffey water, which flowed faster than its namesake. In the early hours I was offered a lift back to my cabin by the squadron AEO (air engineer officer) in his motorcycle and sidecar. Leavings the precincts of the wardroom, he took the first corner – against the sidecar – too fast, promptly throwing me into a ditch! Hoots of laughter from one or two others leaving at the same time, who had wisely refused the charitable offer of a lift.

Every indication from the Admiralty was that we, with all others, were to continue as planned for the time being, which meant embarkation in *Ocean* at the end of the month. But here came the crunch point, and the lack of empathy from the CO now revealed itself. The New Zealanders, to a man, with the exception of the CO, decided that they would not put their lives at risk in deck landing to no purpose, as far as they could see, and flatly refused to continue. More than shades of mutiny. The atmosphere in the wardroom mess was bolshie. Despite assurances from various quarters, the position was irrecoverable: the New Zealanders were adamant and wanted nothing more than to return home. The Admiralty was so informed. Wisely, no doubt, after consultation with the New Zealand authorities in London, they accepted the situation and disbanded the squadron, and in so doing avoided any unpleasant publicity.

In the event our sister squadron, 892, took our place embarking in *Ocean* in November. Its life was short, however. After a short deployment to the Mediterranean it returned home to disband in February. Meanwhile, we flew our aircraft to RNAS Stretton on 25 September, my birthday. It was a very disappointing birthday present. In accordance with the US Lend Lease Agreement, all American aircraft supplied to the UK would either be paid for, returned to the USA, or dumped in open water. UK policy was the latter, thus avoiding 'a spend' we did not have. Our new Hellcats were to suffer this fate with indecent haste. At the time it seemed criminal.

The end of hostilities, particularly coming unexpectedly, was bound to cause all sorts of manning and other operational difficulties, and it was no surprise to me or the many others to be sent on leave indefinitely while Their Lordships sorted themselves out. So home on leave I would go. The war was over. I hadn't fired a gun in anger, and wondered whether it had all been a waste of time, not to say money.

CHAPTER 5

After the War

The extended period of leave was a mixed blessing. Uncertainty about the future dominated the next months. What should I do? Find a job in anticipation of demobilisation. There had been no indication of what lay ahead, and like all wartime volunteers my commission was 'hostilities only'. I contemplated contacting my old employer, and through him, Mr Barratt, chairman of Albright & Wilson, to see what might be offered. I felt that with two years' broad naval training and travel experience I was marketable. In the end it seemed best to wait for a move from the Admiralty.

Like many others at this time, they seemed to have forgotten about me. In the confused state that then existed I had not been receiving my monthly pay, largely, I suppose, because I was not borne on any ship's books. It was only through the generosity of my mother, who could ill afford it, that a reasonable social life was sustained

Ashton Reed, my old friend who had qualified as a pilot in the RAF, was also at a loose end on leave, and it became all too easy to forget about the serious business of earning a living. We had much in common; both firm jazz enthusiasts, we were known to imbibe a little at an agreeable pub called the Cambridge Arms. Our common interests extended to an attractive girl he had recently befriended, whom he unwisely brought to the Cambridge one evening. He was now to discover she had a shared interest! But he bore no grudge. We remained close friends until early in 1946 he was called back to the RAF for demobilisation. Later, he was to go to Kenya, where he would join his uncle, a planter, but I cannot recall of what.

Then two things happened. The Admiralty, after a gentle reminder, re-established my pay and back-pay, enabling me to reimburse my creditors, and almost simultaneously invited me to take a four-year extended commission. I should have, but I didn't, think twice about accepting, living only for the moment and ignoring the fact that in four years most of the sought-after jobs would have been taken by the wise ones who would get into the job market on demobilisation. Nor could I expect that my old employer would look upon a delayed return to civilian life with much favour.

I was also aware that the offer of university places on demobilisation for officers and some senior rates would be forfeited. In my case it would have meant a foundation course prior to entry, and I had spent the last two years and more 'in school' and was not particularly attracted to the idea.

So I gratefully accepted the offer of extended service in the Royal Navy, changed my wavy RNVR stripes for straight ones and looked forward to the future. It wasn't long in coming. I would be appointed to HMS *Colossus* for 1846 Squadron, flying Corsairs again, and felt the wait had been worth while. My appointment went on to say that I was to join HMS *Devonshire* at Portland for passage to Ceylon, where I presumed I would find *Colossus*.

And so at Portland with four others who, like me, were to join 1846, I was ferried out to *Devonshire*, lying at anchor off shore. My fellow pilots had been trained in the United States, in Florida, half-formed a squadron there and were then disbanded.

Devonshire was a relic of the pre-war Navy, a three-stack County-class cruiser currently engaged in transporting navy personnel between home and foreign stations. It was clearly her captain's intention to maintain standards in every respect. At 10,000 tons she was a comfortable ship, retaining all the characteristics of her pre-war design in commodious accommodation and a quarterdeck large enough to play football. It was scrubbed daily and the brass work highly burnished.

Our reception in the ship was cordial, but hardly with open arms. Understandably, the ship's officers were less than enthusiastic at *Devonshire* being used as a 'trooper'. For some of them it meant doubling-up in cabins where before they had enjoyed a single, and in the wardroom mess facilities were similarly stretched. Apart from the four of us there were a number of other officers taking passage, which almost doubled the normal complement, with a knock-on effect in wardroom catering and seating.

We sailed for the Mediterranean and beyond, calling at Gibraltar, Malta and Port Said before entering the Suez Canal. The ship usually spent a few days in most places, which allowed a little shore leave for local familiarisation. For those of us seeing naval ports we had only read about before, this first experience was deeply moving and would remain so for a long time, never diminished by later frequent visits.

At Port Said we were inundated by scores of craft of one sort or another before we had anchored, their occupants all bent on flogging their wares, some attempting to climb the ship's side, only to be rudely ejected without ceremony.

Here I would make the acquaintance of Simon Artz, a large store-cum-bazaar where it was possible to buy almost anything. Simon Artz was then, and perhaps still is, an institution in Port Said. A meeting-place for all and sundry, one never purchased anything without first taking tea with the proprietor or one of his staff. All very civilised – and persuasive! I learnt very quickly the art of bargaining and the numerous methods of fending off the persistent street urchins who badgered you to buy whatever they had to sell, from watches and cameras to leather work, or even their sister.

The temperature had now risen considerably, and during our subsequent passage through the Suez Canal it became almost unbearable. In the ship there was no relief during the long, slow transit, the many fans merely redistributing the hot air; one could only look forward to the relative improvement we hoped to find in the Great Bitter Lakes.

Little boys running along the banks of the Canal kept pace easily with the ship, smiling and waving their arms, occasionally making rude gestures, but all in friendly fashion. In those days the British enjoyed an enviable relationship with the Egyptians. Eventually we reached Aden. Aden is either a godforsaken place or a magical experience, depending on your point of view. I rather tended towards the former, but could see the other side. A British protectorate for centuries, it possesses an excellent anchorage, and was then still regarded as of considerable strategic importance. It would remain so for a good many years to come until largely external pressures dictated otherwise. Eventually it would become the capital of Yemen.

We were now, after more than two weeks, on the last leg of our journey. Their Lordships had provided us with an all-expenses-paid cruise which others would envy. Boring it had not been. During actual passages various activities had been engineered to pass the time, including some very competitive tugs-of-war. The pilots, in particular, had made a number of friends in the ship, and the initial standoffishness resulting from the domestic upheaval had long since disappeared.

One particular engineering midshipman in the ship remained a good friend for a very long time. Several years later he arrived at RAF Syerston as a student pilot. I was then an instructor there, but he was not one of my students. 'Red' Webb, or more usually known as Webby, I never knew his Christian name, but the 'Red' stemmed from the colour of his hair, I would come across frequently in the future, and we always kept in touch.

Some years later he telephoned to invite me and my wife to London for the Ceremony of the Keys at the Tower. He turned out to be quite an authority on the more historical London pubs, and so we were enjoined to pound the streets of East Central, visiting one or two of Webby's favourite hostelries before returning to the Tower. Here he had a connection with one of the Tower Wardens, a retired Sergeant Major, and we were thus able to enjoy the privilege and hospitality of their mess before and after the ceremony.

But back a quarter of a century to 1946 and arriving at Colombo, I had other things on my mind. My immediate destination was HMS *Ukussa*, the naval air station at Katukurunda, some miles east of Colombo. The ship arrived in Colombo harbour shortly after sunrise. It was already very warm, and bidding farewell to our friends in *Devonshire*, grateful for their tolerant hospitality, I stepped ashore on the jetty for my first experience of Ceylon. Instantly I fell in love with the place. The atmosphere, everything about it, was magical, making a huge impression on me. The Sinhalese people seemed warm and friendly, all with smiling faces. I was captivated. Ceylon, the jewel in the sea, its tear-drop shape suggesting that India had been crying to lose it.

I was to return again within a year, only for my feelings to be reinforced and unchanged. In later life I would hanker to return many times, only to be afraid that youthful memories had not told the truth and I would experience a great sense of disappointment. Some things are best left as first impressions, uncluttered and unimpeded by later, more mature experiences. It's all part of life's rich pageant, and must remain in ordained fashion.

Opposite the jetty the Grand Oriental Hotel stands proud, a relic of the former grandeur of colonial days. The 'Raffles' of Colombo, perhaps without the same opulence, it must have greeted many a traveller in the past – as it now did us. Here I enjoyed a long, cold drink while waiting for the naval bus, fascinated by the busy traffic of bicycles and rickshaws and men chewing betel nut, which they unceremoniously spat out in the street. Within a short time the bus arrived for the short journey through palm trees and paddy fields, bouncing along indifferent roads to our new but temporary home. I now knew that *Colossus* was not in Ceylon at all, but thousands of miles away off Simonstown, where the squadron had been disembarked to the South African airbase at Wingfield.

The ship, with the squadron, was due to arrive in Ceylon towards the end of the month so we had a week or so to kick our heels with not a lot to occupy us, or so we thought. Katukurunda was formerly a RAF station until 1942, when it was transferred to the Royal Navy primarily for use as a repair yard and reserve aircraft storage. Literally cut out of the jungle, the accommodation, built largely of bamboo, was basic and open to the elements. It was also open to the monkeys. Officers' cabins, or 'Bandas', consisted of a room with a small verandah, and these were regularly visited by our little friends, particularly in the early evening when the occupants were away at dinner. Woe betide anyone who left any possessions in the open unguarded. Newcomers learnt fast!

I was now to discover the delights of oriental food, particularly the Ceylon version of Indian curry. The wardroom at Katukurunda may not have been up to much, but it rated the best Sunday lunch you could wish for. The curry was historic, as one well-known food buff is wont to say. Unimaginable dishes of every description to please the eye; perfectly cooked and backed up with fruit, the likes of which I hadn't seen for years – if at all. It helped to make the time for the return of the squadron pass without too much pain.

Within a few days I was in the back of a twin-engined Expeditor to Cochin on the south-east coast of India to collect a Corsair as a spare for the squadron on its return. A day later I repeated the exercise. Pretty straightforward except that local rules prohibited prolonged flight over the open sea by single-engined aircraft, and so I was compelled to skirt the coast from Cochin to give the shortest sea transit to return to Ceylon. It took over two hours, as long as the much slower Expeditor flight time over the more direct route. For a carrier-borne naval aircraft there was a touch of irony about such precautions.

CHAPTER 6

14th Carrier Air Group, 1846 Squadron, HMS *Colossus*

I joined the squadron on its return to Katukurunda, and was distinctly chuffed to discover the senior pilot was none other than Peter Green, who had been one of my instructors at the fighter school. Quietly spoken and modest, despite his considerable wartime record, he greeted the newcomers as equals; consequently he held the respect of us all. I was also to meet for the first time Hank Adlam, an extrovert with a larger-than-life approach to everything. I would discover later in Colossus that his evening entertainment after a 'gimlet' or two before dinner was liar dice. He would cajole the younger members to take part, but, significantly, seldom seemed to pay the forfeit of a 'round' at the bar.

We new boys slotted in very well. We weßre welcomed into the squadron football team, where we provided much-needed new talent, later only losing to the 'Royals' in the ships' knockout cup. Katukurunda also boasted an excellent hockey pitch. I had never played before, but learnt a great deal from playing with the local Sinhalese chaps and using the much better curved Indian-style stick. It stirred my interest, and henceforth hockey would become my preferred winter activity

The time at Katukurunda passed very pleasantly. With the forbearance of the squadron's native driver and squadron truck, I learnt to drive, mainly around the airfield perimeter track, occasionally on the base roads, until I became competent to his and my satisfaction. Former experience riding motorcycles was a great help, and of course all squadron pilots were required to ride the allocated 'duty boy' motorcycle in the course of their duties.

For light relief from flying, the squadron jeep was available for recreational purposes. I recall on one occasion, with three or four others in the back of an open jeep, being driven by a more senior squadron officer, to Galle, south of Colombo, where there was a fine beach. It took us along dirty, dusty tracks through native settlements where no quarter was given by our intrepid driver to animals, poultry or even people, who scattered at our oncoming. In retrospect it was disgraceful: a disgusting example of the attitude which still persisted in a few, but thankfully not many, of my associates.

In mid-May we left Kat to embark in *Colossus*. On 17 May I carried out my first deck landing since qualifying in *Premier* nearly a year before. By this time the ship had sailed round the other side of Ceylon to the vicinity of Trincomalee, or Trinco, as it's commonly known, so we had a flight of nearly two hours before embarking. All aboard safely except for one: Sub Lt Beechinor fails to catch a wire and enters the barrier.

For the next month we consolidated our embarked flying, exercising with two other light fleet carriers, *Vengeance* and *Venerable*, as well as HMS *Jamaica* and *Norfolk* exercising their gun crews with mock attacks. Dive-bombing with practice bombs and live strafing attacks were a regular feature in mass attacks against towed targets or designated areas. We practised group flying with the Barracudas of 827, our sister squadron, and discovered how difficult it was to get in a firing position behind these slow-moving monstrosities when well handled by their pilots.

These aircraft had had a very chequered career, and been responsible for a great many casualties, usually when recovering from torpedo dives. On retracting the dive brakes at the bottom of the dive at low altitude, the aircraft would veer sharply to the right, out of control. This fault was not recognised for some time, and many of the accidents were ascribed to 'pilot error' until the remedial action of winding on pre-trim was circulated to aircrew.

The period was also to give most of us the first experience of being catapulted, or boosted, as it was known. Exciting to find 90 knots on the clock in a second or two! And the old hydraulic catapults were not the gentlest of rides. Unfortunately we suffered another barrier on landing – Eric Beechinor does it again! Only on this occasion he had been allowed to fly Commander Air's personal Corsair to make up squadron numbers. Tubby Lane's (Commander Air) 'There goes my bloody aeroplane' over the flight deck broadcast was worth listening to.

In late June we departed Trincomalee – and Ceylon – in fine style. We were boosted off with the ship at anchor – even more than normal boost, which loosened a joint or two – so that the ship and aircraft could pass the flagship and provide the customary salute at the same time. It raised a well-earned Bravo Zulu (well done!')from the C-in-C, and was a nice way of leaving the Far East station. I was sorry to leave the area so soon. We had enjoyed the friendly rivalry with *Vengeance* and *Venerable*, both in the air and ashore in Trinco at the Clappenburg Club. Little did I then know that my absence from Ceylon would not be for long.

The Arabian Sea gave us its usual mixture of weather conditions, very rough at times, then Aden again, the Red Sea and the Canal. Curiously, I felt like an old hand at Aden; it was only a month or so since we had called there in *Devonshire*, and now I would change my opinion of Aden. It was hot, very hot and arid, but in the intervening period from my last visit, I began to look beyond the obvious things and soak in the atmosphere. No doubt about it, it was a place of some fascination. Surrounded by high, inhospitable mountains to the north and east, it was perhaps more than the refuelling and trading stop for which it was renowned; but exactly what was hard to say.

Market-places were everywhere, but the main centre of trading and bartering activity was the 'Crater', a small townlike place within the city, but approached from the coastal area through a narrow pass in the mountains. It was a noted hostile place, and generally out of bounds to ships' companies. I think it might have been on this occasion, but with the patronage of a young officer from the Port naval staff, I sallied forth with a few friends one afternoon – to test the temperature, as it were. It turned out to be a crater in every sense of the word, giving an immediate impression of isolation, of being cut off from the safe world we had left behind. There was only one way in and one way out. Innocent or normal looks or glances from the Arabs there would suddenly seem belligerent and threatening. There was that atmosphere about it. However, for the moment it was all imagination, we engaged in some bartering of one or two things to take home and came to no harm. But it wasn't always like that. Robberies were commonplace, particularly with single visitors; it had not earned its hostile reputation for nothing.

Many years later, I would arrive in Aden in rather different circumstances. I was at that time seeking a suitable location to conduct tropical trials for the Buccaneer Mk 2 aircraft, and had flown a Canberra aircraft there from Masirah Island, which like Aden was on my list of possibilities. In the event this was the time of withdrawal from overseas bases, and at Aden the Army was having a difficult time of it. The Crater in particular had come in for a certain amount of notoriety and much publicity arising from the actions of a Colonel Mitchell, who against orders had gone into the area with the Scots Guards to take overt action against these very Arabs who were disrupting events and threatening an orderly withdrawal. But back to 1946 and *Colossus*.

Colossus, as many ships were at that time, was being used as a temporary troopship to return serving personnel overseas to the UK at the end of the war. The war had been concluded some many months by now, but the staged return of those serving overseas would take some time. Thus we had been asked to provide passage home for a number of Wrens who had been serving on the naval staff in Aden. So before leaving, we embarked these young ladies, conducting them to specially prepared quarters on board, away from the leering eyes of the sailors. Almost without exception they were sad to leave. No doubt they had been in great demand for social occasions and had loved it there. Now they would return home to greater competition.

Our main concern now was to meet our scheduled passage time, and no flying was possible until we reached the Med in early July, nearly three weeks after the last flight. Diversionary airfields were mandatory now in peacetime, which was perhaps just as well. On my second flight I suffered another hydraulic failure, only this time it squirted straight in my eyes, temporarily blinding me as I flew downwind prior to landing aboard. I had just lowered the undercarriage at 700 ft, and for a few moments had little idea whether the aircraft was straight and level, climbing or descending – a few sticky moments.

I immediately called the ship. 'Alpha Zulu [ship's call sign], this is Red 2, I have a hydraulic leak in the cockpit and in my eyes. At the moment I am unable to see outside or the instruments. Am I looking good from you?'

Back from the ship, 'Red 2, you are OK. Keep going as you are for the moment.' I acknowledged, and shortly things improved. I could now see sufficiently to know where I was, so I called the ship again.

'Alpha Zulu, Red 2, I cannot lower flap, propose flapless landing. Any instructions please?'

'No, in your own time, we are ready to receive you, just add another 10 knots on the approach but cut slightly earlier when the batsman signals', which I did. I caught number two wire. Apart from a noticeable harder entry into the wire all went well.

Another first, I thought. Flapless landings anywhere, ashore or afloat, were never practised, and I thought I had done pretty well as a relatively inexperienced carrier pilot; but no one else seemed impressed. There were no Bravo Zulus handed out.

With no further flying possible and the ship flying her paying-off pennant, the atmosphere aboard was relaxed and easy. *Colossus*, although not myself, had been away from the UK for eighteen months, and most of the ship's company – but not all of the aircrew – had served in the ship for the full deployment. In early 1945, when *Colossus* sailed from the UK to join the British Pacific Fleet, the war in the Far East was still in full flow, although that in Europe was drawing to a close. However, hostilities against the Japanese would cease on 15 August, and so the ship and its air group would not arrive in time to see any action. Everyone now was keen to get home.

Meanwhile, there were celebrations to be had before then. Bawdy songs and slightly (?) raucous behaviour had long been a feature of evening gatherings in the wardroom of carriers by the aircrew, generally much enjoyed by the other ship's officers as well. It was not at all uncommon for the executive commander and other senior officers to join in these riotous proceedings. Most of the words to the songs originated from talented squadron officers, many to the tune of well-known ballads or folk music.

In *Colossus*, however, there was one unique to that ship, simply because it had been written by and about two of 827 Squadron aviators – Peter Cane and Paul Bartlett, the latter the observer to the former. They were a very close pair, as is usually the case of a pilot and his observer, and would be expected to sing for their supper with their party piece on sing-song evenings, which on the way home was almost every evening. Their ditty would go:

We're the Twins, Ting a Ling Ling
We're —— (repeated three times)
We're the Brothers St John and we know all about
When we're out, there's no doubt
We're so much alike in our figure and height.
Then:
We're the Twins …
(second verse, more risqué, but not a patch on other songs that would be sung that night.)

But it was the Noel Coward presentation and mannerisms that had everyone rolling in the aisle.

Fleet Air Arm songs are legendary. Some originated well before the Second World War from early carrier days. Others found their source in derivations of rugby songs or during time at university. They greatly added to the *esprit de corps* of naval aviators.

We left the Med and Gibraltar, and the ship arrived in Portsmouth on 23 July. Meanwhile the squadron had flown off to Gosport, a well-established naval air station of pre-war standing. The squadron was now disbanded, and the aircraft, which we had grown very fond of, were destined for the same fate as 891's Hellcats. With 827 Squadron, we had formed the 14th Carrier Group. Rumour had it that it would now re-form with Seafires and Fireflies.

As far as *Colossus* was concerned, she had finished her days under the White Ensign, and with indecent haste she was sold to the French Navy to become *Arromanches*. As part of the general reduction of the fleet after the end of the war, a similar fate befell HMS *Venerable* and HMS *Vengeance*, our two sister ships in Ceylon. In due course they became HrMs *Karel Doorman* of the Royal Netherlands Navy and *Minas Gerais* of the Brazilian Navy, the latter after a short loan period to the Australian Navy.

Ironically, in 1968 the Dutch sold *Karel Doorman* to the Argentinians, a transfer that would cause considerable concern a decade or so later when *De Mayo*, as she was now named, could not be found in the early stages of the Falklands war. Much fruitless time was spent in searching for her, since the threat to the task force from her A4 aircraft with Exocet missiles could not be ignored. In the event, although she was eventually located in harbour, her unknown whereabouts had caused the Carrier Group to shift position to remain outside her potential missile threat.

Now, back in Portsmouth from Gosport, another squadron appointment had been hinted at before I left the ship. Meanwhile a few weeks' 'foreign service' leave. Paul Bartlett, I had discovered, was a Bristolian. His father was to meet him on arrival, and he had very kindly offered me a lift home in his father's car. We returned to the ship from Gosport, packed our things, made our farewells and retired to the Queen's Hotel in Southsea where Paul had arranged to meet his father.

I arrived home and looked forward to my leave. My relatively long-standing girlfriend, Betty, had now been demobilised from the WRNS and had returned to work for Lloyds Bank in Bristol. We were now to resume our friendship. They were halcyon days of youth, no apparent cares, a regular salary and the prospect of steady employment for the foreseeable future. Tennis, the theatre and concerts occupied much of our time. The odd pint at the local at lunch-time with my father on his days off were all very agreeable.

A week or so after arriving home, I met up with Paul and one or two others for a small reunion. Horts in Broad Street was then a fashionable hostelry, and to Horts we would go in a car borrowed by one of the team, whose name I've forgotten. Now, parked outside our selected establishment, we disembarked for Horts Bar, studiously ignoring the 'No Waiting' sign in this narrow street. It was about twelve thirty, I recall. Hours later we surfaced outside, showing all the signs of a most excellent liquid lunch.

'Good afternoon, sir, is this your car?' It was the local constabulary asking the obvious.

'Uh, yes,' said our driver, 'is there something wrong?' The constable, an affable lad, it seemed, commented on the fact that there was a 'No Waiting' sign directly above the car.

'Moreover,' he added, 'to my knowledge you have been parked here for over three hours.'

'Good Heavens,' said our redoubtable driver, not to be put off, 'has it really been that long? You see,' he added, 'we have been having a sort of reunion.'

And he proceeded to explain the circumstances; how we were all intrepid naval officers, aviators in fact, just back from the Far East; the rest of us sat back and said nothing; he was doing a great job and we were full of admiration. At this the face of the law lost its officious look and creased into a smile, and he began to describe how his father had served in the 'Andrew' for twenty-odd years. He himself was not a Navy man, said he, but 'done a stint in the RAF'.

After a little more of this and that over the next fifteen minutes, with a lot of the nodding of heads, he enquired of our intentions. Well, we said, we were hoping to turn round and go back up to Baldwin Street. 'Right,' said our new-found friend, 'get in and I'll give you a hand with the traffic.' Which he did, marching into the middle of the road and stopping traffic to allow us a clumsy six-point turn, and then waving us on our way. It was our lucky day.

The time passed very quickly, and my expected appointment to a Seafire squadron was not long in coming. But first a conversion course: where? Back to Eglinton! So to Northern Ireland again, only this time we would take the ferry from Heysham to Belfast. A number of ex-1846 pilots were to join me in the new squadron, but there would be a few new faces, one or two of these already Seafire qualified. We were fortunate to have, as one of the new faces, one Peter Tod, a two-ringed straight striper, but a relatively inexperienced pilot, whose organising ability we would come to appreciate. We all assembled at Heysham, and Peter took over from then on, organising cabins, food and other matters with a proficiency we could only admire. He exuded confidence.

The conversion course flying Seafire Mk IIIs with that 'sewing-machine'-sounding Merlin engine, commenced at the end of August 1946, and lasted four weeks. The thrill of flying a 'navalised' Spitfire didn't quite hit the heights that might have been the case straight out of training and before experiencing Hellcats and Corsairs. A superb aeroplane in the air, delightful to fly, but unlike the Corsair or Hellcat, its shortcomings as a deck landing carrier aircraft were already well known to us.

The Seafire III was derived from the Spitfire Vc with slight modifications, and was the first of a number of Marks of Seafire provided for the fleet, but their general characteristics remained unaltered. With some sixteen hours of flying under our belts, mainly armament familiarisation, we left Eglinton for RNAS Maydown, its satellite airfield ten miles to the west, to join 804 Squadron.

CHAPTER 7

14th Carrier Air Group –
804 Squadron

Maydown had none of the permanency of Eglinton. It had been closed for some time at the end of the war, but now reopened to accommodate the 14th CAG consisting of ourselves and 812 Sqn operating Firefly Mk 1s. The Seafire we were to operate was the Mk XV, powered by the more powerful but much noisier Griffon engine. As a result it lost to a large extent that familiar Spitfire sound. Again it was derived from later Marks of Spitfire. The Mark XV also introduced the 'sting' hook, fitted on some, but not all. Its advantage was considerable compared with the belly hook. Unfortunately, I was allocated one of the latter, with all the shortcomings that I would later demonstrate!

We settled into our makeshift accommodation well enough. The base commanding officer was a Lt Cdr Bill Sykes, a somewhat eccentric fellow and aged aviator. His forte was to ride a horse for his duties instead of using his official car, and so he would appear for Sunday Divisions riding down the ranks and causing apprehension to all and sundry. We saw little of him, however: mainly in the wardroom from time to time. His duties could hardly be described as arduous, and he seemed to have a wide circle of like-minded local friends to occupy his spare time.

From the squadron point of view we had now been saddled with an air group commander, a totally unnecessary tier above the squadron commanders in their relationship with the ship's air officers. No. 804's new CO was Lt Cdr Bryant, and it was apparent from the beginning that he and Callingham, the AGC, did not get on together. The 812 Sqn CO, Wynn Roberts, had no such problem, and it was an inauspicious way for what should have been a close-knit team to look to the future. This apart, we worked up for the next three months, occupied with much of the mixture as before: formation flying, carrier drill and a fair measure of low-level bombing with 10 lb bombs, for which the Seafire was singularly inappropriate.

For me and some others there was a new activity – Army Co-operation, for which we had a carrier-borne Army liaison officer attached to the group. In fact, we had two, a captain and a major, very different characters – the major from a distinguished regiment, the captain from a run-of-the-mill one. But they and we got on extremely well for the whole of the commission. During exercises from Maydown, the pair of them would disappear into the bundu, giving us grid references of likely targets over the R/T, and then watch from a distance while we carried out our attacks. The attacks, using the camera gunsight, would be assessed later by the 'pongos'. All very entertaining: lots of low flying and much ribaldry in the bar at the end of the day.

In the early part of the work-up, closing to take up station in line-astern formation of Sub Lt Miles, I distinguished myself! Perhaps a shade over-confident in quite bumpy conditions, I managed to nick the fuselage of his aircraft with my propeller. It caused me to lose a couple of inches off my prop and Myles a little surprise. Nothing very serious, although it might have been, we both landed safely. It cost me a rap over the knuckles for over-confidence in the prevailing conditions, and a pint of Liffey water for Buster Myles.

The majority of the aircraft were due for minor modifications of one sort or another, for which we would fly them to RNAS Donibristle, near Dunfermline. I made three such flights from Maydown until finally, at the beginning of February 1947, all squadron aircraft were flown in to Abbotsinch on the Clyde for loading on board HMS *Theseus*. For the life of me I never then, nor later, understood why we didn't fly them on board in the conventional way. It was the first of the many imponderables I experienced during the commission, and it may have had some history in the ever-deteriorating relationship between Bryant, our CO, and the AGC.

Showing the Flag, HMS *Theseus*

Be what it may, the arrangements were to result in no flying for us for a month while the ship sailed to the Med and beyond to Ceylon. By now it all seemed very familiar: Gibraltar, Malta, Port Said, Aden; I had done it all before. Nothing had changed – not even the 'girls' in the 'Gut' at Malta.

Eventually, after three weeks, Ceylon again, but this time to Trincomalee, Katukurunda and other naval air stations having closed, leaving the original

China Bay airfield at Trincomalee and HMS *Bambara* as the only remaining facility for disembarked naval squadrons. It was in fact the oldest of the numerous naval air stations in Ceylon, comprising originally three separate airfields. These had been dispersed after the Japanese attacks in 1942, but reunited two years later.

We flew from the ship to our new home on 15 March, and carried out several weeks of concentrated – and very necessary – flying until in early April we embarked in *Theseus* for a period of work-up, for both the air group and the ship. I thus made my first deck landing in the Seafire nearly six months and some three thousand miles away after the squadron had first formed. Not the best of planning, I thought; but then, nor was much of the rest of the Far East deployment.

The weather at this time of the year was tropically hot, and the temperatures were soaring by mid-morning to well above 100°F. The metal on the aircraft would be untouchable after an hour or so, and the cockpits unbearable. So we would rise early, carry out briefing by 5 a.m., and be airborne well before six o'clock. After landing on, breakfast, then another flight before 8 a.m., after which we would shut down for the day. It seemed a short flying day, but there were many other things to do.

Over the next several weeks we operated as an embarked air group while the ship remained in the vicinity of Ceylon. It was all pretty much routine exercises until tragedy struck in the form of our first fatality. Peter Tod stalled his aircraft in the latter stages of the approach just short of the round-down. The aircraft rapidly rolled and entered the water inverted. He was only at about 100 ft when he stalled, and the end was inevitable. Regrettably, despite very quick reaction by the attendant destroyer, HMS *Constance*, neither the aircraft nor Peter was seen again. In itself this was distressing enough. Peter had been popular in the squadron, and his contribution in so many ways would be keenly missed. Worse was the fact that his brother, a sub-lieutenant RNVR doing his National Service, was not only on board but witnessed the whole thing from the 'Goofers', a popular place on the flag deck for off-duty officers to watch flight deck activity, particularly deck landings.

It was all very sad; and here, I thought, the planned flying programme since leaving Maydown was shown up for all its shortcomings. Peter was not an experienced pilot and could ill afford a month off flying. Not only with hindsight did I feel that this reinforced my view that we should have flown on board in home waters, and carried out continuation flying at Gibraltar, Malta and elsewhere during the eastward passage.

Whether this was the final nail in the coffin for our CO, Bryant, in the disagreeable relationship with the AGC I know not, but he departed almost immediately, to return to the UK. I had no great liking for him – he was an aloof figure – but I had even less regard for Callingham. He gloried in the unnecessary role of group commander. Squadron officers were beneath his dignity, and it is doubtful whether he knew more than a handful of their Christian names. Before embarking, he had had a Seafire stripped of its duck-egg blue and grey camouflage to a shiny silver metal finish, much to the aversion of the squadron ratings who were charged with keeping it polished. In keeping with his station, he sported a white flying suit; we wore the grey/green issue.

However, there it was, we were now without a commanding officer, and would remain so for many weeks. Jake Wright, the senior pilot, assumed temporary command. I liked Jake, Dartmouth trained and a thoroughly good egg. He was an extraordinary mixture of naval officer and philosopher who had also developed a deep conviction towards Buddhism. I recall many animated, and sometimes argumentative, discussions with Jake in the Clappenburg Club in Trinco on subjects so diverse that there seemed no end to his interests. Unfortunately, after this commission he would become the Navy's loss. The Royal Navy no longer provided him with the stimulus or challenge for his intellectual talents, and he retired on our return to the UK. Meanwhile he grasped the nettle of temporary command with confidence.

We remained in the vicinity of Ceylon for only a short while after Peter's accident, and it seemed to mark the beginning of a jinx period for me. Landing back on board after a successful group formation flypast over Colombo, my starboard oleo collapsed as I caught the wire. Nothing very serious, it was an all-too-common feature of the Seafire's undercarriage in deck landings, but it was my first deck landing incident. Although it was not 'pilot error', I was not pleased. This was the last flying for the ship before departing the area.

For a few days we enjoyed a rest period in Trinco harbour, gave an air group party for ship's officers and those from the air station at the Clappenburg Club, played team games in whatever version took your fancy, and then left Ceylon for the Andaman Sea. I was not to know that this would be my last acquaintance with my paradise island. I had grown more than fond of Ceylon, the people were among the most agreeable I had come across and there was no suggestion then of the conflict between Sinhalese and Tamil that would later develop with such bitter consequences. I had experienced both factions on the two sides of the island, and the later fighting seemed alien to the people I had known.

We arrived off Malaya in the second week of May and flew off to Butterworth Field, a Royal Air Force station a little north of Penang Island. Before that, however, we had paid a courtesy visit to the Andaman and Nicobar Islands, occupied by the Japanese during the war and now reinstated as a constitutional part of India by courtesy of the Queen Victoria's Own Light Infantry, who took the Japanese surrender three months after the official end of the war.

We called at both islands, seemingly to the bewilderment of the local population; they paddled out in their primitive boats, mostly naked, just looking at us. The *pièce de resistance* was Port Blair, capital of the Nicobars. The local chief was entitled to be called 'Queen', and was accordingly invited on board after the captain had made the customary courtesy call to her ashore, presenting the usual ship's crest as a gift. Her arrival in the captain's 'barge' that had been sent ashore was memorable!

I was on the quarterdeck at the time. A huge lady, she arrived with her entourage at the bottom of the gangway amid the honking and snorting sound of several piglets – her return gift to the captain! With great but delicate effort by a couple of stalwart seamen, she was steered up the gangway to the captain's quarters for refreshment, followed by her helpers carrying the wretched animals, still snorting! Later, upon her return, she was manoeuvred back down the gangway minus piglets. What happened to the piglets I know not, but it was all a priceless sight.

Now at Butterworth for two weeks, it was a quiet period for flying but a great deal of maintenance. Our hosts were in fact the Royal Australian Air Force, to whom the base had been leased. In our Seafires we tussled with their P51 Mustangs in the air before reliving it all in the bar afterwards. They could talk us down, but we always outfought them where it mattered. They were kind enough to provide us with transport to visit Penang, which then enjoyed, and probably still maintains, the status of 'duty free', as befits the first British Straits Settlement in the nineteenth century.

We were now to fly to Singapore, where *Theseus* had proceeded with 812, our sister squadron, after flying us off to Butterworth. Our destination, HMS

Simbang, Sembewang naval air station in the north of the island, a distance of over 400 miles, was stretching the range of the Seafire, and so we were fitted with overload, or drop, tanks. Unfortunately the system had not been satisfactorily tested at the time of leaving, which caused a rethink and change of plan. We now planned to refuel at Kuala Lumpur on the way south, and so we did.

It was an easy flight of about two hours, in loose formation seldom above two thousand feet, admiring the countryside. Shortly after leaving KL, relaxed and minding my own business, the second jinx arrived in the form of a call from my No. 2:

'Um – leader, you have just lost something.'

Me: 'What have I lost?'

No. 2: 'Your drop tank has just arrived in a paddy field and made a big splash.'

Oh hell, I thought, that'll cause some pollution with the rice. Then on second thoughts, no, it was empty, and the splash was obviously the tank hitting the wet paddy field. The exchange between my No. 2 and myself was of course heard by the rest of the squadron pilots, including Jake.

'Any problems?' said he.

'None', I said, and so we proceeded south without further incident, reporting it on our arrival at Sembewang amid the usual ribald comments from the chaps about unauthorised bombing and so on. Fortunately the jettisoning system was found to be intact and not activated. The second jinx was, as I knew, not 'pilot error', but it was disconcerting and I wondered what the third would be; they always come in threes. I would not have to wait long!

At Singapore *Theseus* was joined by HMS *Glory* and her escort, and so the Flag Officer, Rear Adm Creasy, who had embarked with his staff before leaving UK, would now earn his keep. The Far East cruise we were undertaking had been planned as the first 'goodwill' exercise by the Royal Navy after the conclusion of the Japanese war, visiting Malaya, Singapore, Hong Kong, Australasia and a number of the Pacific islands, some of which had only recently been fully liberated.

HMS *Glory* had been in or around the Far East for some time, and had vacated Trincomalee for Singapore only a month before our arrival. Like *Theseus* she had been commissioned too late to take part in the war. Her air group consisted of 806 Squadron equipped with Seafire Mk XVs and 837

Squadron equipped with Firefly Mk 1s to replace the obsolescent Barracuda. From hereon we would operate as a fleet, the two carriers with their destroyer escorts accompanied by RFAs for replenishment and occasionally a cruiser for exercises.

To the 'new boy' to the true Far East, Singapore was a culture shock. Despite the experience of the Middle and Near East, Malaya, but especially Singapore, was different. Singapore: gateway to the Orient, full of frantic activity by the majority Chinese population. A complete contrast to the more leisurely atmosphere that prevailed in Ceylon. Already, only a year or so after the war, the old colonial atmosphere had returned. I knew not of it, of course, but sensed it. There was an urgency about the place which was not apparent in Ceylon. It came as no surprise to me later, after the handover of Hong Kong, to find it the centre of the financial world in the region, and its future prosperity seems limitless.

Sembewang in the north part of the island was remote from most of the hustle and bustle of Singapore city itself, and I saw little of it. The air group had been allocated accommodation in the naval dockyard while the ship underwent minor maintenance. It was a little inconvenient but there was no spare capacity at the air station. We had now gone on to tropical routine, which meant early starts for flying and, more important to us, early ends to the working day. Swimming in the pool at the Officers' Club at HMS *Terror*, tennis and organised sport occupied much of our time, all of which passed very pleasantly.

Then we suffered another very unfortunate happening. My friend Buster Myles, whose tail I had clipped long ago at Maydown, was not merely an expert swimmer, he was more than that, he was the essence of the human fish. The *Terror* pool had very high diving-boards, and Buster occupied some time in demonstrating his considerable talents in one form or another off the top board.

One day after I had left the pool to return to my cabin he apparently had got into some difficulty during one of his complicated sequences off the top board, and landed awkwardly in the water. I learnt later that during the dive he had severely twisted his back and had been rushed to the naval hospital. As a result he was left behind after the squadron left Singapore, and the sad sequel was that on our passage south we were to learn with disbelief that he had died from internal injuries.

So by now at Singapore, with the 'flag-showing' cruise hardly started, we had lost two of our pilots. This was only slightly mitigated by the arrival there of the replacement CO. Jake had filled the gap very well indeed, but we needed the rank and experience of a replacement for Bryant to fend off the occasional interference of the AGC in squadron matters. Therefore we welcomed Fraser Shotton with open arms. Fraser, the ever laughing Fraser, was a revelation. An experienced pilot who had commanded a Hellcat squadron during the war and seen action in the Pacific, he was relaxed and always pleasant, and the pilots warmed to him. Later we would find he had another attribute: his deck landings were never two the same, but somehow he usually managed.

We spent a month at Sembewang. We carried out exercises with the Royal Air Force based there, celebrated the King's birthday with a combined flypast of the two air groups and RAF over Singapore city and generally prepared ourselves for re-embarkation. But in truth not nearly enough flying was planned. In the first three weeks I personally flew only eight sorties before flying out to the ship on 21 June.

Regrettably the importance of sound planning to involve solid continuation flying was still not recognised in the Royal Navy. There was a lack of appreciation at the higher levels, which failed to recognise the unique needs of the aviator. 'They' seemed to think it was all a little like ship's gunnery practice; it could be left for a while and would still come back as before. But in the air it doesn't. Left for a while it comes back without the fine tuning, and flying is an unforgiving pastime. It would be some time before the Royal Navy got rid of this pre-war attitude and those officers of high rank who couldn't broaden their minds beyond annual regattas and the nuisance of the aircraft carrier.

On the flight before I flew out to the ship, sure enough the third jinx beset me. In typical wartime fashion the runway at Sembewang had been laid with Sommerfelt tracking, metal strips as one sees nowadays at country fair shows and fairgrounds. Perfectly satisfactory, it permits operation on grass fields in very wet conditions which might otherwise be precluded. However, it can be more than a little rough for take-off and landing.

In the event on the final session of ADDLS before embarking, I had just touched down and was rolling merrily along the runway when I came to a grinding stop, heeled over and the undercarriage partially collapsed. For reasons unknown, my hook had dropped from its housing, engaged part of the metal tracking and brought me to a premature stop! Well, there we were, I thought, why does it have to happen to me? There was the natural engineer's reaction. Nothing wrong with the system, you must have inadvertently pulled the deck release mechanism. But of course he knew as well as I did that it was a silly comment to make.

The hook in the Seafire was manually operated up and down. It had to be rehoused by hand, and to lower it the pilot had to lean down to reach to the back end of the starboard side of the cockpit floor to locate a toggle with string on the end. It then required a firm jerk to drop the hook. It was quite a business, and inadvertent operation was simply not possible. Sub-lieutenant I may have been, and short as I was of a rank or two with the AEO, he suffered a piece of my mind for his hasty, ill-thought comment.

For three days we stayed in or around Singapore waters, operating with the *Glory* air group and occasionally providing 'trade' for the Royal Air Force aircraft from Tengah. I had now achieved my fiftieth deck landing, seventeen in the Seafire, and began to feel more at home taking off and landing aboard than on a runway. The beauty of it was, everything was close at hand, there was little taxiing to be done, the crew room and ops room were just below the flight deck, and when all was done for the day, one merely had to negotiate a couple of decks to the wardroom and cabin.

At the conclusion of this all-too-short flying period, we sailed south, through the Sunda Strait and into the Java Sea for passage to Tasmania, our next port of call. Meanwhile there had been frenzied activity in some quarters in anticipation of 'crossing the line' – the traditional Royal Navy ceremony to initiate novices into the brotherhood of the seas and as subjects of His Oceanic Majesty King Neptune as they cross the equator. It has always been recognised as a day for jollification. The ship is placed out of routine for the day, and officers and men share impartiality in the proceedings.

A canvas pool had been rigged on the flight deck, filled with water, and a dunking-chair placed on a platform alongside. Come the day and the time, at the Navigating Officer's signal, the Master-at-Arms, as the senior rating on board, declared proceedings open. As befits rank, the Admiral was the first to be initiated. It seemed unlikely that he had not crossed the equator before, but he took his punishment without protest. The 'Master', with a shaving brush the size of a ship's broom, duly prepared the Admiral with extensive soap and water lather for the wicked-looking razor wielded by the Chief Gunner's Mate. Honour satisfied, the Admiral was let off without the traditional full dunking. Others followed amid much ribaldry, skylarking and good humour. We had paid our respects to King Neptune and now proceeded south.

Now off the southern coast of Australia, *Glory* and her escort left us to pay a scheduled visit to Adelaide before meeting up with us again later on. With a diversionary airfield available, we joined them for a day's flying as they departed, and then ourselves continued our passage to Hobart. The day before entering harbour the air group announced the ship's impending arrival by disturbing the early morning with the roar of twenty-four unleashed Rolls Royce Griffon engines, flying quite low over the centre of Hobart. Looking down over the island, I had been surprised to discover how rugged and mountainous Tasmania was. I hadn't done my homework!

So we had arrived on what was really the second stage of our cruise.

Having landed back on board, we entered harbour with flags flying, flight deck manned in ceremonial fashion, and the Royal Marines band thumping out jolly music as only they can. It is always an impressive and emotional occasion for us, and no doubt for the crowds lining the jetty. It was doubtful that Hobart witnessed the arrival of many warships: not a popular port of call when Sydney and Melbourne beckon. It was really quite cold when we tied up alongside. Snow covered the distant mountains, but it was a welcome relief after the high temperatures and humidity of Singapore, and we looked forward to a pleasant two-day visit.

In time-honoured fashion we held the standard 'cockers' that evening in the hangar decorated with flags and bunting. All the 'right' people were there – or the wrong people, depending on one's view – but whoever they were they always enjoyed the experience of being invited on board a warship. It is never difficult making friends on these occasions.

Two aviator chums, Frank Steel and John Morton, and I were doing our duty entertaining a few guests in time-honoured fashion, bent only on ensuring that they were well supplied with refreshment and enjoying the experience. Guests on board invariably arrived with the expectation of providing return hospitality, and it was not long before we three were invited to join the doctor and his family the following day. Frank was not of our squadron, he was an observer in 812 Squadron, but I had known him for some time, and John was one of the original *Devonshire/Colossus* fraternity, and a fellow squadron pilot.

Unfortunately we had one day only after our arrival to appreciate Hobart and Tasmania, but I doubt we could have occupied our time better. We were collected from the ship as arranged and taken to their home in the northern outskirts of Hobart. It looked a cosmopolitan sort of place as we drove through it, nothing of particular note. It was, after all, a city of modest size, with a population then only a third that of Bristol. Our host introduced his daughter, who, together with her rather delicious friend, both much the same age as ourselves, suggested spending the day up Mount Wellington, a little north of Hobart, where the family owned a chalet. So we did, shoehorning the five of us into the doctor's adequate but not large car. Not a long drive, but the cold, although we had been warned beforehand and had taken suitable precautions, nevertheless surprised us.

The temperature was well below zero when we reached our destination, still well short of the summit. In those far-off days it was customary to go ashore in uniform; 'plain' or civilian clothes for officers on shore leave was yet to come. And ratings would not be permitted this privilege for three decades and more. Consequently our heavy reefer jackets and trousers, complemented by the substantial long naval greatcoat, proved more than suitable for the occasion. The greatcoats were much admired by the girls, to whom, of course, we gave way.

The chalet proved to be a touch more than the name conjures up in the mind. It was surprisingly spacious, well equipped and with views to die for. We were told the family spent much of the summer months there, enjoying barbecues outside on warm summer evenings. It seemed a far cry from the present. It was wonderfully relaxing, and we were in no hurry to return to the ship. But return of course we would, regretting that our stay was so short with these very hospitable people. We bade them farewell.

We sailed early next morning to join up with HMS *Glory* and her escort for Melbourne, where the two carriers tied up, one astern of the other. Meanwhile the *Theseus* air group had flown off in open waters to provide a flypast over the city to coincide with the ships entering harbour. By all accounts an impressive sight, witnessed by an unbelievably large crowd, who seemed to remain with us for the next ten days. Every day queues of visitors would assemble on the quayside, waiting to go on board one of the four ships, all 'open to visitors' throughout the stay.

The flypast always raised a cheer. We had perfected a large T formation of sixteen aircraft, the Fireflies providing the crossbar, with the Seafires down the vertical, plus two on either tip of the crossbar. It was my misfortune to provide the left 'tit' as it was known, line astern of the Firefly on the extreme left of the crossbar. Poor fellow, flying line abreast of four others, never easy, he had his hands full, and that meant I had to cope with all the sometimes extravagant manoeuvring while he tried to maintain station. We all worked up quite a sweat. With honour more or less satisfied, we broke up to make our way to the nearby Royal Australian Air Force base at Point Cook. It would be well over a week before we flew again – with one exception.

Ever since our disembarkation to Butterworth Field, the P51 Mustang had intrigued me. In the Seafire we had generally got the better of it in simulated air combat, but we were not oblivious to its fine wartime reputation, and I was keen to discover what it was made of. Tongue in cheek, chatting to one of the Australian pilots in the officers' mess bar a few days after our arrival, and discussing the various merits of our two fighter aircraft in amicable but progressively more assertive tones, oiled by a beer or two, I threw out my bait.

'Of course,' said I, 'I would never know whether the Mustang is as good as you say unless I flew it.'

It was a long shot, and I thought no more about it until much later after dinner. A voice behind me said, 'CO says you have permission to fly it tomorrow if you get your CO's agreement.'

It was my newly found friend leaning over the back of my chair. I thought it was Christmas, and immediately sought out Fraser. 'OK,' he said, 'but please don't break the b——y thing.'

So I got myself a highly rewarding flight in the aircraft that had been responsible for turning American Air Force daylight bombing missions during the war into something less than sheer suicide by providing long-range fighter escort. Curiously I had lost the Merlin engine when the Seafire XV was produced with a Griffon, only to rediscover its delights in the Mustang.

Anyway, all by the by, I appeared promptly at their dispersal next day, got myself suitably briefed by my flight lieutenant mentor in the crew room and together we walked out to the aircraft. I climbed in, familiarised myself with the cockpit and strapped up. Compared with the cramped space in the Seafire, it was spacious, reminding me of the reverse sensation I experienced with the Seafire after the Corsair. Everything seemed logically laid out, as I remembered with the Corsair and Hellcat, instruments and switches, no problem there, so I gave the thumbs-up to the ground crew, signifying ready to start. The response was a raised hand 'clear to start', which I did.

Immediately there was an air of familiarity about the proceedings, the unforgettably sweet sewing-machine sound of the Merlin. I knew I was at home. After the usual checks I taxied out and was pleasantly surprised at the improved forward view and the advantage of the wide undercarriage in ground stability compared with the Seafire. Here were the basics of a good carrier aircraft. The flight was pleasant but unremarkable. It handled well, perhaps not quite the agility of the Seafire but a good stable platform for tracking during air-to-air firing. I spent forty-five minutes or so enjoying myself, a few aerobatics – distinctly heavier on the stick and less inclined to wander – generally explored the performance parameters – until I thought about going home.

I returned to Point Cook and requested permission to land. Everything nice and straightforward, no problems, the aircraft sat down nicely on the runway when I cut the engine, none of the float and bounce tendencies of the Seafire. I hadn't broken it!

'How was it?' said my flight lieutenant friend after I had taxied in and stopped the engine.

'Fine,' I said, 'a very nice ride.'

On the way in to the crew room I waxed lyrical about his aeroplane, as befits the honour and confidence he had shown me, because, after all, although his CO had authorised the flight, it was his judgement that was on the line. His CO was waiting in the crew room.

'Thank you very much indeed,' I said, 'that was very much appreciated, especially when you didn't even know me a few days ago. I might have broken it!'

'Oh I don't think so,' he replied, 'I too have flown Spitfires, and anyone who can fly Spits would have no problem with the P51.'

Very generous, I thought. We had invited our Point Cook hosts on board for drinks and supper on the following day, and I made sure they were included.

It was difficult then – and the more so now – to understand the grave error of no planned flying during our stay in Melbourne until flying back on board nine days after our arrival. True, we were there primarily to 'fly the flag', and the aircrew to take their part acting as hosts, entertaining on board for much of the time, and of course being entertained, private guests, a cricket match at the Melbourne Cricket Ground against an Australian XI containing two Test players, which we lost. All that we understood and naturally enjoyed it all, partying well into the night. The Aussies rank with the Americans in unforgettable hospitality. But flying – no, that would have to come later – must get the priority right! Consequently the aircrew would spend most of the period on board the ship rather than Point Cook

By the time we departed Melbourne I doubt if many of us had averaged more than a few hours' sleep each night. The social life had been hectic and non-stop, either on board or ashore. Invitations to officers on the wardroom notice-board were mandatory. Either you volunteered or you were press-ganged. The Admiral had emphasised that we in the flagship in particular, but the others as well, of course, were expected to make it a memorable occasion. They were yet to learn how memorable. For some of the ship's ratings, Melbourne – and the local girls – offered more than life on board, and we had the expected absentees on sailing. At least two of them would be picked up by the patrols and returned to us later in Sydney, subsequently to take their punishment. For a ship under sailing orders, desertion invariably meant a custodial sentence and dismissal from the service.

Departing Melbourne to the usual fanfare of ceremonial and the inevitable large crowds of well-wishers, the four ships sailed for the local area to conduct various activities and evolutions, largely for the VIPs we had embarked for the occasion. And, of course, the Press, national as well as local, which had shown great interest and given a lot of coverage during our stay.

Back at Point Cook the air group took off at the appointed time to exercise with elements of the RAAF prior to landing back on board. Exercises completed, we joined 'mother' for land on. Remarkably without incident! Later the same day the whole air group took off again for group formation flying and other exercises for the benefit of our guests, not forgetting the Press.

Then the truth came home to hit us. I had already taken off and was orbiting with the rest of the squadron, waiting for the Fireflies to do the same, join up in flights of four, so that we could fall in astern of them. It was standard operating procedure for the lead aircraft after take-off to fly ahead of the ship for some distance before reversing course down the port side of the ship to allow subsequent aircraft time to get airborne, turn to port and join up in flight-of-four formation. The second flight would do the same, the first meanwhile manoeuvring to be in a position for the second to fall in line astern somewhere down the port side of the ship. Nothing very complicated, take-off intervals were generally predictable for a worked-up ship, and the manoeuvre only demanded timing and keen look-out.

The first four Fireflies had taken off, formed up and were at about one thousand feet on the port beam awaiting the arrival of the second flight. This flight had barely reached the height of the first when disaster struck. The Senior Pilot leading this four somehow managed to fly up and under the last aircraft of the first flight in the lead; the two aircraft collided, and now, out of control, both aircraft fell into the sea. It was a terrible tragedy. Four aircrew lost, including the squadron Senior Observer, seemingly without any reasonable explanation from straightforward bread-and-butter carrier drill.

Perhaps more of a tragedy was that the Senior Pilot, Lt Cdr Nat Hearle, had survived being shot down during the war and had suffered a number of years as a prisoner of war; he had not long since resumed his pre-war and wartime flying. This was a bad start, but more was to come.

After the ship had sorted things out and the destroyer escort, after searching with little hope for survivors, had resumed station, the remaining six Fireflies and nine Seafires continued with a curtailed flying exercise. There was little enthusiasm for continuing after the collision, and I doubt whether our performance during the rest of the exercise in front of our visitors did us justice. However, we fired our guns at towed targets, carried out low-level formation flypasts and generally entertained in the shortened time our fuel state allowed. The ship now prepared to receive us.

Having turned into wind, our VIPs no doubt wondering what was next on the menu, the remaining Fireflies, their pilots having been given a few words of encouragement by their CO over the R/T, landed on first – followed by the Seafires. The first two on safely, the pilot of the third aircraft somehow contrived to drift well over to port during the late stages of the approach, landed just short of the first wire but outside the raised section. Now on the extreme edge of the flight deck his port wing struck the batsman's wind breaker on his platform, and the aircraft continued up the deck into the port stanchion of the barrier, narrowly avoiding going over the side of the ship.

In the process the batsman, having done his best to avoid inevitable disaster, had abandoned his position and dived into the safety net provided alongside his platform to save himself from being hit by the aircraft wing. It was not to be for one of the batsman's 'tellers', the two ratings who provide ongoing information for him on the state of the aircraft and the flight deck. During the landings, one of the ratings faces aft, checking hook, undercarriage and flaps down, and this rating, sensing impending disaster and having seen the batsman disappear into the net, promptly followed him.

Unfortunately, the other rating, facing forwards to ensure the deck was clear, wires up, barriers up and 'Green' from FlyCo (who controls operations), was naturally oblivious to his perilous state and was struck by the aircraft wing. He was killed instantly.

This was a bad start to our resumed flying. In a professional sense the Press was having a field day, without, I am sure, enjoying the human side of it. The ship had now had enough. The rest of us were diverted back to Point Cook.

Glory too was having her own problems. Several barrier entries by her aircraft had contributed to an unacceptably high accident rate in the carrier group as a whole, and the loss of aircraft of this order could not be sustained if we were to continue the cruise. Not to be able to do so would have far-reaching and embarrassing consequences, and was unthinkable. Heads would roll!

So we in the remaining Seafires headed back to Point Cook. Our unexpected return had nothing of the spontaneous pleasure of our initial arrival nine days earlier. We were not exactly tails between our legs when we taxied in, but certainly a little shamefaced. Our professional pride had been dented in front of another Air Force, and while we – those of us now at Point Cook – had not been directly involved, on these occasions the 'can' is shared equally in the squadron. However, we were warmly greeted amid much sympathy, and a few Green Label beers later put things in perspective. The retard ground crew, meanwhile, had refuelled and put the aircraft to bed for the night, and we all anticipated a more successful tomorrow.

Next day, after flying back on board, preparations were under way for the funeral of Lt Cdr Hearle. He had been recovered from the sea by HMS *Constance*, our attendant destroyer, and transferred during the morning. This delayed our departure from Point Cook until midday, when we rejoined the ship, landing back on board without incident. The carrier group then headed for the open sea and Sydney, our next scheduled visit.

Despite the dreadful performance of the air groups, Melbourne had been a success as a 'flag-showing' visit. Many tens of thousands of visitors had continually taken advantage of the ships' 'Open Days' over the seven days in harbour. With the Governor of Victoria accompanied by other VIPs taking the salute, a full ceremonial march-past through the streets of Melbourne had taken place on 18 July. Led by the band of the Royal Marines, with twelve hundred officers and men, the route was packed with enthusiastic and cheering crowds, waving flags, with streamers and confetti thrown from high-rise buildings *en route*. It was perhaps the highlight of the visit.

The Royal Marine band, in full-dress uniform, always conscious of the occasion, excelled themselves playing 'Waltzing Matilda' and other Aussie music. The sailors were obviously irresistible; invitation lists multiplied and had no trouble being filled. Apart from what they could glean from Press and radio, the vicissitudes at sea were remote from most of the Melbourne population. Anyway, it was not their problem. Welcoming the first major deployment of RN ships to Australia since the end of the war was their business, and in this, as with Hobart and Sydney to come, Melbourne excelled itself. This was still Australia of old, part of the Empire, and then Commonwealth, no hint or thought then of Republicanism.

So to Sydney. Ready now for a fresh start, bowed but not broken, with two days' flying ahead of us before entering Sydney, we joined forces with the cruiser HMAS *Australia* and her several escorts for exercises, and hoped our luck had changed. Which it did – at least for the first day. We located and 'sank' *Australia* after she had broken off to act as the 'enemy', and successfully saw off attacks by Australian strike aircraft on the carrier group. The land-on was significant only for a 'There but for the Grace of God ...' landing by Bill Plews, who at one stage appeared to be landing his Seafire across the flight deck and not down it. Somehow he managed to snatch a wire just as he was about to go over the side, but ended up in the embarrassing position of looking over the starboard gun sponson.

The following day was the mixture as before, more close air patrols and top cover. After well over an hour's flying we returned for the land-on, Fireflies on first in time-honoured fashion, and then us. Echelon starboard down the starboard side of the ship, I broke off in turn to fly downwind, content with life and looking forward to lunch before the scheduled afternoon flight. Hook, flaps and undercarriage down, I was nicely placed on the approach, with the batsman seemingly satisfied with what he saw. Over the round-down now, I got the expected 'cut' from the batsman and waited for the tug of the wire. There was no tug and no wire! I had somehow contrived to miss them all, and now the barrier loomed large – which I duly entered.

Reviewing events later, I convinced myself that had my aircraft had a 'sting' hook instead of the 'belly' one it was fitted with I would not have had a problem. The belly hook hangs only about a foot below the undercarriage line, whereas the sting is a good two feet. But there it was. Yesterday I completed my sixtieth deck landing. Today was my twenty-third in the Seafire. Now I had broken my duck and was far from happy. I thought I had flown a pretty good approach and landing, but clearly something needed polishing – was I tweaking the stick after the cut?

Inevitably questions arise in one's own mind, and doubts about the next landing. But there had been no criticism or pointers from 'up high'. I had never felt unhappy about landing aboard – in fact quite liked it – so had no real qualms about the afternoon sortie. Still ...! The barrier entry had not been unduly harsh – a grinding of metal propeller on the barrier cables – and after shock-load testing of the engine, new prop and other damage dealt with, the aircraft should be serviceable in a day or two. For me there was the standard medical check and a word or two of encouragement from Fraser before lunch and my second flight for the day.

Early in the afternoon all aircraft took off for the concluding exercise with the Australian group. It was all uneventful, we seemed to have turned the corner, there were no flying horrors and, in a personal sense, although a little apprehensive, I had not worried overmuch about the land-on. I caught a decent wire and left the morning's events behind me. Longstanding practice says that the best recipe after an accident is to get airborne again as soon as possible; and so it appeared to prove. Unfortunately, time, particularly overnight, allows the mind to dwell!

On 24 July we were to enter Sydney for an extended twelve-day visit. Although not the last of the Australian cities to be visited, it was regarded as the climax, the most important one, and we intended making it memorable. By now, following the pattern we had set, the two air groups joined together for a ceremonial flypast over Sydney, sixteen from *Theseus* and ten from *Glory* – all they could muster after their share of accidents and general unserviceability. We took off in good order, formed up first in flights, then squadrons, followed by groups, and finally *Glory* Group fell in behind us: an impressive sight, twenty-six aircraft in close formation, marred only by the shortfall from *Glory*.

We flew low over the Heads leading into the harbour, above Sydney Harbour Bridge and over the city, circled once, which took some time manoeuvring this relatively large number of aircraft, and repeated the performance. Vast numbers of sightseers had already packed all the vantage points approaching the harbour, and from the occasional glimpse when we were able to divert attention from the demands of formation flying, they could be seen waving flags and obviously cheering.

It was a longish flight and required great concentration to maintain close-order formation. We could be seen wherever we were in the vicinity of the harbour, and there could be no let-up in relaxing station. Eventually we broke up to return to our parent ships and commenced the land-on. Downwind once more, I turned hard to port for the approach and settled into the groove. Everything nice and tidy, I took the 'cut' and waited for the wire. It was a long time coming and I began to despair. I was getting closer to the dreaded barrier again, and wondered why. Then a sharp tug and I had snatched the last wire! But I was not out of the wood by a long way. The aircraft rolled on, retarded by the wire but not sufficiently to prevent nudging the barrier. Oh hell, I thought, two in two days, what on earth am I doing?

Whatever it was, it was out of my hands now. One barrier is commonplace, particularly with Seafires, but two? Something amiss with the technique somewhere: but what? I saw the CO, who had been watching my arrival. He had nothing to offer. I had apparently floated just over the wires, but I hadn't looked fast on landing, touched down late and that was it. 'Wings' had asked to see me, he said. So up to FlyCo I went, expecting something of a rebuke. Instead, he was if anything sympathetic. Apparently he could see nothing wrong with my approach and landings, but obviously something needed to be sorted out. Full of apologies, I could only agree.

Our next disembarked period for the air group was planned to be during the ship's visit to Auckland some weeks ahead, and he had suggested to Fraser that he rest me from flying until then. So it was, I had now lost a little confidence but, at the same time, had no doubts that the problem, whatever it was, could be overcome.

Theseus, with *Glory* and escorts tucked in astern, entered the entrance to Sydney Harbour to unbelievable scenes of welcome. Small craft were everywhere and came perilously close in their efforts to take photographs or just to wave flags. Sirens sounded from near and far, and water cannon from various Harbourmaster craft created an impressive spectacle. Everywhere the shore was packed with well-wishers. It was a memorable and very moving experience.

Sydney, with its backcloth of the Sydney Harbour Bridge, is a wonderfully attractive harbour on entering round the Heads. The bridge connects the north, largely residential shore to the more industrial and shipping south side, and this is where we now headed to tie up to No. 2 wharf, Woolamaloo Bay, *Glory* and the two escorts astern of us. Our reception on entering harbour was to be the beginning of a non-stop round of receptions, invitations and parties of one sort or another from every imaginable source. All the ships' officers and ratings would need to draw on all their resources to stay the course. Hobart and Melbourne had been the starters, but Sydney was to prove the main course – with all the trimmings.

Fortunately, in one sense, the air group officers had been granted special leave for four days, presumably to wind down after the traumas of the last few weeks. This news had been transmitted to various reception organisations ashore, with the predictable result of producing numerous invitations to stay here, there, almost everywhere with anyone. Scanning through the formidable list on the wardroom notice-board, I was attracted by an invitation for four junior officers to visit Canberra, staying with the British High Commissioner and his wife. So, with three friends of similar mind, we hastened to place our names prominently at the top of the list, hoping that if there was a draw for places, our group entry would prove decisive. Before then – our leave would not begin for three days – we would play our part in hosting the many dignitaries and guests

As the ship was being secured alongside, there appeared on the quayside a number of ratings, deserters from Melbourne, handcuffed to naval military police. It was an unedifying sight which regrettably occurred all too often in the many ports we visited, and tarnished the reputation of the service which the majority had preserved.

The first few days were Melbourne all over again. The ships were made 'open to visitors' on selected days, but then, because of the large numbers, additional days were made available to accommodate them. The standard opening reception party by the Admiral, Captain and officers had now achieved military-type precision in every department. Food and refreshment, decorations and other innovations, standard of service by the excellent wardroom staff and, of course, music by the RM band chosen with care for the occasion and played from a temporary stage in the hangar created an atmosphere of relaxed sophistication. It was difficult not to be seduced by it all, and the reaction of our guests confirmed their appreciation of the efforts put in by the ship's company.

During the early part of the evening I was introduced to the High Commissioner and his wife by the Commander. I took to them at once. 'Mrs

High Commissioner' – regrettably I have no note and have forgotten their names – was especially easygoing, and obviously anticipated entertaining her young guests for a few days with a good deal of pleasure. Did we have any special needs or requests? The answer was no, just to get away from the ship for a break was more than enough. It was now Friday 25 July. They would arrange for us to be picked up on the Sunday for the 150-mile drive to Canberra, which, they were keen to emphasise, as the State Capital was a far cry from the fleshpots and other delights of Sydney.

State licensing laws then, in 1947, were odd by any standards, and totally counter-productive in achieving the hoped-for effect of reducing drinking. On the first occasion ashore, I looked with amazement at the number of drunks on the streets at around five o'clock in the evening. No liquor was allowed to be sold after six o'clock, with the predictable consequence that the dockyard mateys and others would fill their bellies with copious quantities of Cascade Green between knock-off time and six p.m.

Canberra was all we hoped it would be. Created entirely to house government buildings, foreign ambassadors' residences and other institutions of national importance, it had been planned with great care and was beautifully laid out. Almost all the buildings were of white stone, giving an almost clinical but pleasing appearance. Especially impressive were the Government Offices building and that of the Australian War Memorial, a vast edifice commemorating the fallen in two world wars.

The High Commissioner's residence was of a standard expected for the King's representative, quietly opulent but pleasing, with a homely look. Our hosts made us very welcome. They had arranged enough, but not too many, engagements of one sort or another, lunch-time drinks, evening cocktail parties and so forth, leaving sufficient free time for sightseeing and anything else we wished to do. We met a lot of very interesting people, diplomats from other countries, Australian government officials and, of course, their daughters, who had been dragged in for our benefit. It was all much as we had anticipated and wished.

We left for Sydney feeling refreshed and in good spirits, eager in due course to depart on the next and final stage of the Australian visit – Brisbane. It was evident when we arrived back on board that Sydney had excelled itself in inflicting on our ships' companies every conceivable form of welcome imaginable. In uniform ashore, everything was free, public transport, many free bars and restaurants, cinemas and theatres and even taxis would take you to your destination without charge. 'Good on y' mate' was a byword. In return the sailors by and large behaved themselves, leaving a good impression of the Royal Navy behind them, which, after all, was what it was all about.

Always of paramount importance when planning visits by HM ships is the need to ensure that the interests of the ship's company, especially the ratings, are near the top of the lists. Port or other places of call should, above all, be affordable as well as interesting, which means appropriate places of entertainment, bars, cinemas and so on, within easy reach of the sailors' pockets. There is little point in descending upon the likes of Bermuda, for example, where the costs of everything are more tuned to the wealthy from America and rich ex-pats than the more basic aspirations of Jolly Jack. In this respect Australia had been a resounding success – if anything, improving as we went along.

Sydney had been outstanding. It had always been accustomed to a regular influx of warships, particularly Allied warships during the recent war, whether for logistical reasons or simply R&R, leave and relaxation. Moreover, they had not forgotten the debt of gratitude they owed to those who had provided a buffer from the Japanese, who with the occupation of New Guinea had come perilously near their northern shores.

We slipped our berth at Woolloomooloo in late afternoon on Monday 4 August, twelve days after our arrival. It was time to get back to work. The following day, while still in the Sydney area, the ship went to flying stations. A short exercise had been planned, seemingly oblivious to the detrimental effects of the prolonged and hectic entertainment the aircrew had suffered, quite apart from nearly two weeks off flying, and apparently also forgetting the grim experience at Melbourne.

Eight Fireflies were ranged on deck for the flying programme. For some reason which I cannot recall, no Seafires were involved in the exercise, which, as it turned out, was providential. Immediately after start-up two Fireflies were declared unserviceable and pushed to one side. Then, having sent off the remaining six, the leader of the second section experienced undercarriage retraction problems and made an immediate return. This left scarcely more than half the planned number to complete the exercise.

Within the hour the five Fireflies returned for the land-on. The performance which followed was, even by recent experience at Melbourne, unbelievable and incomprehensible.

On this day, however, it took 812 Squadron by the scruff of the neck. All five aircraft duly came into the 'slot', flying down the starboard side of the ship, breaking in normal fashion with no hint of the events to follow. Wynne-Roberts, the CO, landed first and taxied ahead of the barriers to the forward deck park, already occupied by the two which had been unserviceable at take-off. The barriers were raised prior to receiving the second aircraft. This and the third aircraft landed without incident, but then it all went wrong.

The fourth aircraft, flown by Lt James, approached, touched down a little fast and late, bounced heavily and cleared both barriers, finishing up on top of Wynne-Roberts's aircraft, taking both aircraft over the port side of the ship; and, tragically, one of the squadron ratings, who was sitting on the CO's aircraft wing in preparation for after-flight checks.

The attendant destroyer stationed on the port quarter closed the scene rapidly and was able to recover both aircrew before the aircraft disappeared. James suffered a broken leg, but of the rating there was no sign, despite an exhaustive search. It could have been much worse – and worse was to come!

After the wreckage in the deck park forward had been sorted out and the search for the unfortunate rating regretfully abandoned, the last aircraft was called in. Lt Butterworth, having witnessed things from afar, now started his approach, perhaps with some misgivings. Over the round-down now, he touched down well up the deck quite heavily and bounced, missing all the wires. He too now cleared both barriers, narrowly missing the island with his wingtip in the process, and proceeded to land on top of a Firefly on the starboard side. Both aircraft disappeared over the starboard bow, taking with them a fork-lift truck which had been minding its own business.

The escort, HMS *Cockade*, was now working overtime. Having scarcely had time to resume its station on the port quarter of the carrier, it now turned smartly to starboard to carry out its second act of mercy. By the Grace of God both Butterworth and his petty officer observer were picked out of the water, unharmed, none the worse for their adventure other than getting a good soaking. Both were later returned to their parent ship, together with Lt James and his observer from the previous almost identical happening. Lt James was to have his broken leg properly attended to in the sick bay.

We had now lost nearly half 812 Squadron's aircraft in less than a month, together with four officer aircrew and a squadron rating. In addition, another pilot would be unfit to fly for some months. Lt Butterworth would fly no more. He had previously been involved in another quite serious accident, and for him this latest episode was the last straw. Later on in Singapore he would be flown home, subsequently to leave the service.

Even now, more than half a century afterwards, I find these two occurrences quite bizarre. Unlike the Seafire, the Firefly was a purpose-built carrier aircraft with all the features required for its task. Strong, wide undercarriage, excellent forward view and good controls, it had no vices and was ideally suited to carrier operations. Later on in my career, when I had carried out numerous deck landings in this aircraft myself, I would come to regard it as probably one of the easiest of the many aircraft I had operated from an aircraft carrier.

Why then should this extraordinary sequence of events have occurred, involving two relatively experienced pilots? The only possible conclusion is that it was the direct result of too much high life, lack of sufficient current flying practice and prolonged gaps between all-too-short periods at sea devoted to the ship's primary purpose. This state of affairs could not continue.

The adverse publicity generated by Australian Press and radio reports was not well received back home, and questions were being asked. Locally it was dominating all the good, very hard work which all the ships had put in during our port visits. The situation was causing embarrassment to all concerned, not least to ourselves at the sharp end. Those with the responsibility for planning and organising the deployment would now reflect on the effects of thoroughly flawed planning. Spasmodic flying during a tour involving long periods spent in port hosting parties and other forms of entertainment is not an acceptable peacetime risk.

What signals passed between the Flag Officer, Rear Adm Creasey, and the Admiralty I can only imagine. But it was clear to the most optimistic of us that it could not continue. Now those responsible, both here on deployment and at home, had to bite the bullet and admit their failings. The inevitable temporary cessation of flying surprised no one, and was greeted with some relief by the aircrew in both carriers. *Glory* too, had been having a rough time of it. My earlier rest from flying was now to be enjoyed by all aircrew, and while I was not pleased for them, it made me less isolated. I was grateful that it had only been for one day's flying.

We sailed north for four days to the last of our Australian port calls, Brisbane, where we arrived on 8 August and would spend the next ten days. It was a lack-lustre arrival for two aircraft carriers – no flypast to announce our entry – and it was left to the RM band with the ships dressed overall to liven up proceedings as we berthed alongside.

For HMS *Glory*, not only would it be the last Australian visit, it would also mark the end of a very long deployment from the UK. She had left Ayr in April 1945 for the British Pacific Fleet equipped with Corsair and Barracuda aircraft, but arrived too late to see any action. Her air group would be re-equipped later that year with the current complement of Seafires and Fireflies, some of which were now transferred to *Theseus* to replace those lost. Now she was due to go home. We would be sorry to see her go. There had been some lively rivalry between the two ships, vying to outdo each other in the air and hosting parties.

Moreover, unlike us, their Captain, Couchman, was an old and bold aviator with perhaps a greater understanding of the airmen, although it has to be said that Capt Dickson, brought up with more conventional warships, had done his best to remedy his lack of association with naval aviation. With the assistance of a little instruction at a naval air station, he had become proficient in light aircraft. Then at his own expense he had acquired a Tiger Moth, got it on board and would occasionally fly it from the ship and land it back on board again. With his flying-helmet on and very long naval shorts, there was a touch of Biggles about his appearance. Nevertheless it gave him a basic insight into the deck operations business, more perhaps than he anticipated. Back in Trincomalee his engine had failed during a flight between ship and shore, forcing him to ditch in Malay Cove in shallow water. No problem. He put it down without apparent trouble and the aircraft was recovered to fly another day. All good experience and a feather in his cap.

Brisbane was the icing on the cake. Exceptional efforts had been made to transform the hangar into what it was not. The whole of the fire curtain separating 'B' hangar from its next-door neighbour had been hand-painted with a most impressive country estate scene, resplendent with large displays of flowers in the foreground. Lashings of bunting were everywhere, completely obscuring all trace of hangar walls. An artificial waterfall some twenty and more feet high led into the after lift well – the space occupied by the aircraft lift when down – and into a little stream over which a narrow bridge had been constructed. It was a remarkable transformation.

With this background shortly after the commencement of the now familiar 'At Home', the Captain appeared in a pony and buggy, accompanied by the Commander – Captain dressed in colourful top hat and tails, with a large carnation and wielding a lengthy whip. The Commander had drawn the short straw; he was dressed as 'm'lady', large silver wig, layers of clothes with collars in outrageous colours. The pony was led by the Sub-Lieutenant of the Gunroom, suitably dressed in riding-hat, jacket and, of course, jodhpurs, to a platform where a reception committee awaited. They too were dressed in turn-of-the-century clothes, led by the Master-at-Arms, putting on the style, who greeted the Captain as he disembarked with excessive doffs of the hat and other wildly exaggerated gestures. Bobbies, Sir Robert Peel type, with truncheons, controlled proceedings. By now the guests were overcome by it all and in fits of laughter. It was a complete success and a suitable finale to our Australian tour.

It happened to be Brisbane's Annual Show Week. We were invited to the local races, so I went with a few squadron chaps, anxious to recover some of my losses at the Melbourne Gold Cup meeting – which I did! Not much, but enough to enjoy a beer and a meal. I think by this time we had exhausted entertaining and being entertained. Apart from a large private tennis party to which we had been invited, and where I discovered the difference between my pretty average club efforts and the semi-professional standard of some of our hosts, I accepted only enough invitations to satisfy the honour of the wardroom

Strangely, although probably without significance, Cdr Robert Everett, the Commander Flying, or Air, as it now is, left the ship to return home, and was replaced by Cdr Ed Walthall, Staff Officer Air to the Admiral. In many ways I was sorry to see him go. He had commanded a front-line squadron during the war; he understood carrier operations from the pilot's point of view and had been understanding of the vicissitudes which had so recently beset the air group. He was a bit of a dandy, always well turned out, regulation half-inch cuff showing and invariably sporting a pocket handkerchief; it didn't meet with everyone's approval, but he would have been unperturbed by the opinion of others. Anyway, he went. Ed Walthall was another man. Quiet and of even voice, he fitted in without noticing he was there. I would come to know him very well in the future when we would again serve together, and his message of congratulations later on again, when I was promoted, was much appreciated.

Leaving behind Lt James with his broken leg in the local hospital, we slipped our berth on Monday 18 August, and to the accompaniment of the RM band playing 'Auld Lang Syne' departed Brisbane – and Australia.

Glory preceded us and was given three cheers and other ribald comments by some of the ship's company as we manned the side for her departure home. We had spent the last six weeks in Australia, and it had taken its toll. Now we looked forward to a period of rest and recuperation: but in New Zealand? A pious hope; they would not let us off that lightly. Still, there was nearly a week at sea before Wellington, time to catch up with squadron domestic chores, reports written, diary brought up to date and, of course, aircraft maintenance.

There are numerous tasks within a squadron organisation, all shared between the officers. One of my responsibilities was the Squadron 'Line' Book – a semi-official and more humorous account of squadron activities recorded with photographs, caricatures and other drawings, comments – anything of interest. I enjoyed doing it. One of the perks of being the author of the Line Book was an entitlement to photographs taken by the ship's photographic department for inclusion in it. Not unnaturally this also swelled my own private collection. In fact I was on very good terms with Lt Regan, the photographic officer, and he would good-naturedly respond to my particular requests for shots of pilots climbing in the cockpit, take-offs, landings, maintenance in the hangar, in fact anything of interest, such as squadron sporting activity, including those in the wardroom in the evenings! These, supported by appropriate, but not always flattering, comments found prominence in the Line Book.

And so on 30 August, with *Theseus* some sixty miles south-west of Auckland, the flight deck was a hive of activity. After doing duty as a floating cocktail bar, one could almost sense her relief to return to active service with the noise and bustle of aircraft engines, flight deck engineers operating arrester gear and catapults and the constant up-and-down of the aircraft lifts from the hangars below. We had left Wellington some two days before with mixed feelings, but were now on the brink of resuming flying operations for the first time for over a month. The ship had become operationally lazy.

Wellington had done us proud. We had berthed alongside Aotea Quay on the morning of 23 August to the rapturous welcome of a considerable crowd. If, by Australian standards, the heralding of our arrival had been a little more subdued, it was more to do with the New Zealand temperament and character rather than the absence of the traditional flypast to announce our coming. We were also without *Glory* and her escort, of course. But as we were to discover, the Kiwi is a different animal from the Aussie. The albeit friendly brashness is replaced by a quieter, more reserved character, not dissimilar from how we perceive our own.

Come the day, though, Wellington had proved just as testing as the Australian visits. For five days they showered the ship's company with invitations to everything and everywhere. A common theme throughout was their pride in their links with the 'home' country, After forty years as a Dominion in this year of 1947, they were to gain full independence from Britain, but to the majority it meant nothing to them. They were more British than the British and followed events 'at home' with extraordinary intensity; their knowledge at times could prove embarrassing!

For the aircrew especially, much as we revelled in the liberal hospitality which occupied most of our spare time, we were impatient to reach Auckland to put our hands to the plough and get flying again. We had been idle far too long, and the role of passenger did not suit us. The ship slipped her berth on the morning of 28 August, not only to the now familiar strains of 'Auld Lang Syne' but also to a spectacular display on the quayside by Maoris, dressed in colourful national costume, giving us their rendering of 'Po Ata Rau', the Maori Farewell – a tune familiar to us as 'Now is the Hour'. It brought a lump to the throat of even the most hardened 'old sweat'.

Two days later, with all aircraft ranged and engines started, we prepared to fly-off for a ceremonial flight over the city of Auckland. We would then continue to the RNZAF base at Whenuapai, from where we would operate for the next two weeks. Seafires and Fireflys formed up, flew around the ship to remind them they had an air group, then departed for the short distance over the city to display our skills – we hoped. After all, we hadn't had any practice for a month.

All went well, we started with the T and finished with eight pretty tight formation Vs, departed the city and, having obtained permission from Air Traffic, made an untidy rush at low level over the airfield at Whenuapai for which we suffered a little professional banter from the resident squadron after we had landed. But the natives were friendly, they had obviously been looking forward to our arrival, and for the next fourteen days we would want for nothing.

That evening there was a reception for us in the officers' mess, and there I was to meet a Sqn Ldr Selwyn Field and his wife Pauline. We latched on immediately, and I never looked back. It was Saturday, no flying until

Monday, we could let our hair down – and we did, ably assisted by our New Zealand hosts. It was the beginning of a very close relationship with the resident squadron and station officers; their married-quarter homes were open house to us, and we reciprocated by ensuring that they were always welcome to the ship, which was now berthed alongside in Auckland Harbour.

Before our departure two weeks later, the squadron aimed to achieve 200 flying hours, a not inconsiderable target. Weekends apart, this translated into twenty hours per day, and I made my contribution. In that period I personally flew twenty-seven sorties, frequently three times a day, and achieved a total of over twenty hours in the air. We were now back in our element doing what we did best. Oh, we were pretty good at socialising, too, but just lately the balance had been wrong.

I had now been adopted by Selwyn and his wife Pauline, and began to spend a lot of time in their company, either in their married quarter or elsewhere – they lived just off the base in a pretty bungalow residence of unusually attractive design, a far cry from the conventional MQs we were used to at home. Selwyn's misfortune was to have to fly to Suva in the Fiji Islands four days after our arrival, to serve in a detachment for a month, but before he left he made sure I would be well looked after – he left me his car and entrusted me with his wife! This was high-risk strategy by Selwyn. But he had no cause for concern. We enjoyed ourselves enormously while respecting his trust. It was a very pleasant few days.

It was also quite profitable – or could have been. 'There is a sort of gathering at the local club on Saturday,' said Pauline, 'it's in aid of a charity but they are usually a lot of fun.'

'That sounds good to me', I said. Then she added, 'If it follows the normal pattern, there should be a few gambling tables and cards to swell the charity's funds, nothing very extravagant, you can't lose very much.'

'Excellent, we shall go', I said.

For some reason which escapes me, but would, as it happens, subsequently prove useful, I had taken a driving test in Wellington and had a New Zealand licence. Consequently, with Selwyn's generosity I now had four wheels and very pleasant female company. Pauline was a vivacious, quite attractive girl, slightly older than me, besotted by Englishmen and their accent. I could do no wrong. She also brought me luck!

On the Saturday I drove her the four or five miles to the club for the charity affair, and we settled in to enjoy ourselves for the evening. It was a lively affair, the room bursting to the seams, plenty of activity such as sales of this and that and – yes – gaming tables, roulette, pontoon, etc. – seemingly well patronised. So I joined in. From the start I was 'Goldfinger' – the more I bet the more I got back.

Remembering it was a charity and I was supposed to be giving, not taking, I tried doubling each time I won. That was a disaster: it got worse, and I found myself with a considerable profit. Pauline was beside herself. A lot of her friends were there and I was being eyed with some suspicion. Eventually, I took out my original stake, put the whole of the remainder on the turn of a card and waited. To my everlasting embarrassment I won! That was the last straw. I turned to Pauline: 'Look,' I said, 'somehow I've got to off-load this. It's a charity and I simply can't take it.'

She protested, 'You shouldn't feel guilty.' But of course we hadn't come to take, but to give, so we decided that there would be a donation in the name of the Field family with the blessing of Selwyn. It was a tidy sum of money.

Two weeks passed all too quickly. On the Saturday before leaving, Whenuapai air station gave an Open Day in aid of 'Food for Britain'. This was a time of food shortage at home, and the New Zealanders, as others, were very mindful of the price we had paid in the recent war. By comparison they had hardly suffered. True to form the heavens opened just as we started up for the scheduled flying display. Low cloud and heavy rain threatened to force us to abandon the performance, but somehow we took off and were able to form up in time before the weather completely closed in. For the many thousands watching, they had their money's worth, and we in turn were treated with renewed respect, not least Capt Dickson: he had had his Tiger Moth flown off for the occasion and courageously flew it round the crowd in appallingly bumpy and very wet conditions.

That evening we drove down to the ship for a farewell get-together. Most of the Whenuapai people were there, and it seemed a suitable way of showing our appreciation. My lasting memory of Pauline is doing a hand-stand in the squadron dormitory on board, in front of half a dozen young officers after the air group party had finished. She brought the house down!

That was virtually the end of our Australasian tour. On Monday 15 September we would leave our New Zealand friends and fly back to the ship, taking with us a host of memories. I would keep in touch with Selwyn and Pauline for some time after that, but eventually the tides of time ran out, to be left with happy memories.

The rest and relaxation at Auckland had been a tremendous tonic. Two weeks of intensive flying ashore had us back in shape again, operationally ready for the rest of the tour. Now back on board, the flying programme, armament and other exercises had gone well for two days, until 18 September, when it seemed we were back to our old tricks again.

Towards the end of the morning sortie I returned to the ship early from a fighter direction exercise with an intermittent fault; the fuel gauge was fluctuating around the zero reading. This was annoying. I had only been airborne for thirty minutes and was reasonably confident I was not short of fuel. Still, I couldn't afford to take a chance; a fuel leak or siphoning was always a possibility, so I called the boss. 'If you are in any doubt,' he said, 'pack it in and return to the ship.'

So I did. The ship turned into wind to receive me, with HMS *Constance*, the escort, already on station, having listened to my transmission over the radio. I landed on, taxied forward, got out and reported the defect to the ACR (Aircraft Control Room).

The ship now decided to recover the rest of the aircraft. She was still into wind, the escort on station, there seemed little point in continuing the exercise for the sake of the remaining five minutes. I made my way to the 'Goofers' to watch. Seafires first, the CO made his approach, slightly high and a touch to starboard of the centre line. Correcting this as he crossed the round-down, he induced a little drift to port and touched down a shade heavy. The combination of drift and higher-than-normal rate of descent brought him to grief – the starboard oleo collapsed on catching a wire, and he finished up in an ungainly lopsided position with the mainplane on the deck. Poor Fraser, he didn't deserve it. The landing had not been all that bad, but the Seafire took no prisoners and the oleos would take no drift.

We now had a pause in the recovery programme while the aircraft was hoisted by the flight deck mobile crane and removed to the hangar. With commendable speed shown by the flight deck personnel, we were able to resume the land-on with little delay, and all remaining Seafires were recovered, followed by the first two Fireflys. Two to go. Big, burly Tom Stride, a back-row rugby forward, was next. He never seemed quite at home during the approach, and going from being low to being high there was an inevitability about the result. He cleared all the wires comfortably, and with smoke pouring from his brakes in a futile attempt to stop, he entered the barrier. Not a good morning's flying, but thankfully we were launched and recovered in the afternoon without further incident, and later that day departed New Zealand waters for Port Moresby. Or so we thought!

That evening all aircrew were called to a briefing. It transpired that the Foreign Office had contacted the Admiralty concerning developments in the Solomon Islands. It emerged that in and around the islands, there had been a good deal of unrest from the native population. Although a British Protectorate, the Solomons had seen no British military presence since the eviction of the Japanese, and the restlessness was spreading, threatening local British Administrators. Being aware of the naval task force in the area, Could we do anything? asked the FO – without, of course, provoking an international incident or exacerbating the situation.

What they wanted was 'gunboat' diplomacy with a light touch. Well, what could we do? We had a sizeable Royal Marine detachment on board, but the Solomons is an archipelago of hundreds of islands, and we had not been informed of any particular core of the unrest. So thoughts turned to the ship's primary armament, the air group.

Guadalcanal was a name familiar to us all, and this, together with the surrounding islands of Santa Isabel, Malaita and San Cristobal, would receive our attention. The plan was to carry out sustained flying over these islands to quell any thoughts of an armed uprising, and certainly to stop the present unrest spreading any further. What arms they had we knew not. The Japanese had not long gone, and the possibility of a sizeable arms cache could not be ignored. We would therefore take suitable precautions, not only against small-arms fire from the ground while flying but also for personal protection in the event of an unscheduled landing for whatever reason.

The Seafire cockpit is very small. When strapped in, arms and shoulders nudge both sides and the flying-helmet sits very close to the canopy. In other words there is little space for anything else. Personal protection, we were being told, would consist of jungle survival pack, knives and a 0.38 pistol, complete with belt and ammo. How on earth would we shoehorn this lot into our already cramped space? But we did. The pistol and belt shoulder harness was fed beneath the Mae West. We sat on the survival pack so that our heads were now hard up against the canopy, and put the knives in our overall leg pockets. It was not comfortable but at least reassuring.

For the next three days we beat the living daylights out of every large or small community we could find, flying at tree-top height in loose formation, making as much noise as possible. San Cristobal, Malaita and Santa Ysabel all received our undivided attention, finishing with Guadalcanal, where later we anchored off Honiara and gave limited shore leave to the local beach. During the whole time there were no signs to justify the FO's concern, but we did get a lot of friendly waving from the people we flew over – at least they looked friendly enough, and chances are that after the recent occupation by the Japanese, they were.

Four days later we were off Port Moresby, repeating the performance. Although not the subject of the FO's concern, the Australian government, which administered Papua New Guinea, was anxious that any rebellious behaviour in the Solomons should not spread. New Guinea had a history of tribal conflict, and it was close enough to Bougainville and the main islands of the Solomons group to warrant caution. As we flew over the interior of the island, mountainous in part but mainly heavily forested, it looked tranquil and untroubled by any untoward activity or outside influence – a picture of paradise, the home of unique butterflies and birds for which it was famed.

For five days we operated in and around the area without upsetting the native population by aggressive flying. There was time for shore leave to local beaches, which the troops enjoyed, but they were forbidden to venture further inland, and in fact there was little likelihood of any of the ship's company wishing to do so, since apart from Port Moresby itself, the coastal region was largely impenetrable, with dense jungle to the sea.

My twenty-second birthday had come and gone. I'd spent part of the day admiring Malaita Island from the air and almost forgotten the occasion. But the Squadron Staff Officer, 'Staffy', who knows about these things, quietly spread the buzz in the evening, and it cost me! But at duty-free prices it didn't exactly break the bank.

But that was more than a week earlier. We were now about to depart on our way north to Hong Kong via Singapore for the last stage of the tour. Before completing our final days' air operations, however, we had another 'funny'. We had successfully launched eight Seafires and the same number of Fireflys for a low-level strafing and bombing exercise, which in fact had gone surprisingly well. Towed targets and buoys dropped in the sea had been well and truly dealt with, and there was the sound of quiet satisfaction in the R/T patter as we returned to the ship. Ten aircraft safely aboard, including all Seafires and the first of 812's Fireflys.

Then John Elgar got himself in a pickle just short of the round-down. After I had landed and made my way to the island, I witnessed it from the safety of the ACR. He was quite clearly moving well across the deck from starboard as he took the 'cut' from the batsman. Then, as he caught a wire, about the fourth, he slewed further to port and moved dangerously across the deck to the flight deck edge. At that stage I was certain he and his observer were going for a swim. But he didn't. Somehow, with his port undercarriage and most of the fuselage and tailplane over the side of the ship, the aircraft tottered on the edge, saved by a projecting sponson, and was now swaying in the wind.

It was then that 'Pritch' Pritchett, the observer, showed his prowess as the 'fastest mover in the West'. Almost before the aircraft had come to a final stop, Pritch was out of the back cockpit, crawling along the fuselage to safety, to the cheers of the flight deck hands, apparently oblivious of the fact that he had caused the aircraft to rock dangerously by so doing. Lines were now attached to stabilise the aircraft, John was recovered from the cockpit and, with their usual efficiency, the flight deck party got the aircraft on the crane and forward of the barriers to allow the remaining Fireflys to land on.

No further air operations were planned during the passage north until disembarking to Kaitak airfield in Hong Kong – or more accurately Kowloon – in the latter part of October.

With a five-day passage ahead, thoughts turned to keeping the troops (sailors) occupied and entertained. Film shows were a regular feature in the for'rd lift well whenever ship's operations permitted. Sunday evenings were officers' evenings and the main film was always preceded by a Disney cartoon. For some reason, which I never discovered, the moment the captions appeared with the producer's name, Fred Humble, there would be an almighty cry of 'Good Old Fred' and then uncontrolled laughter. It never failed. It seemed then, as now, childish behaviour, but it made for an entertaining evening, often despite the quality of the main film.

But there had always been a strong tradition for the larger ships in the Royal Navy to provide self-entertainment of one sort or another during lengthy, often tedious sea passages. With a Royal Marine band on board, musical evenings, usually on the flight deck if weather permitted, were popular and well attended. But ship's concerts were the yardstick by which a ship was judged, and half-way to Singapore, 'Schoolie', the Senior Schoolmaster/Meteorological Officer who served as the ship's entertainments officer, put on a quite ambitious affair.

For almost two hours the ship's company enjoyed – or in some cases perhaps suffered – light-hearted sketches taking the 'mickey' out of some member of the ship's company or other, the more senior the better. There would also be very talented individual performances. In between would flow a wide and catholic variety of music from members of the RM band, who could turn their hand from Memphis Blues to Mozart with commendable skill.

Senior officers letting their hair down and making a fool of themselves on the stage in short sketches always brought the richest of ribaldry from the sailors. They loved it, the more especially, it seemed, when the object of their bawdy behaviour was directed at their own chief and petty officers. Schoolie could be very persuasive in co-opting 'talent' for his shows, but I thought he had met his match when it came to me. I was wrong: he got his man, and I took a small part in a sketch mocking Commander's Defaulters. It went well enough. From his reaction in the front row, the Captain thought it amusing, but I avoided eye contact with the Commander sitting next to him.

In the wardroom, early on in the tour, Jimmy Dundas, Lieutenant-Commander Flying (only he didn't – it was just his title), had taken to strumming the ivories after dinner. He was very good. In a short time this developed into a trio, with first Lt Tom Donald RM doing his stuff on the drums until I edged him out; I wasn't better than him but he could play the double bass and I couldn't. These were very enjoyable evenings and would continue until we returned to the UK, when Jimmy, with many connections around the London night-clubs, would continue to play with rather more professional talent than we offered. He was that good, and I was not invited!

The two-day stop at Singapore saw the departure of a large number of ratings who were due for demobilisation, and some who had declined the offer to 'sign on' earlier before leaving the UK now regretted that they had not done so. Formal 'requests' to extend their service fell on deaf ears, their replacements having already arrived in Singapore There was also a small batch of officers leaving for the UK, including John Butterworth of 812 Squadron, who had gone 'swimming' after his impressive accident in Melbourne. He was to fly no more.

It was now 12 October, and the disembarked officers and ratings would sail home in a rather scruffy-looking Dutch merchantman, MS *Sloterdyjk*, while we would proceed to Hong Kong in rather more comfort.

By 20 October the ship was off Hong Kong, and sixteen aircraft were ranged ready to fly off to Kaitak airfield, a mile or so from the outskirts of

Kowloon. This was now new territory to most of us, and it conjured up all sorts of oriental delights. It was 'new' in another way, for Kowloon was in the area of the 'New Territories', the area of greater Hong Kong situated on the Chinese mainland and very close to the Chinese border. Recent events being what they were, we would need to watch our step in the air to ensure no encroachment of the border. The natives were not friendly!

As dawn broke and the ship prepared to enter harbour to anchor, we flew off to Kaitak airfield, which had been an RAF base during the 1920s, but mainly for Fleet Air Arm aircraft, which it then controlled, continuing so to do until 1938, when the RN assumed responsibility for its own air support, thus correcting an anomaly which had existed for far too long and had cost the RN dear in the early part of the Second World War.

Along with Hong Kong Island, Kaitak had been occupied by the Japanese until 1945, but it was now home to MONAB No. 8 (one of the RN's mobile naval air bases). It would now support the air group's detachment ashore. Facilities were basic but adequate. Tents were erected to serve as maintenance offices and aircrew briefing areas, and, except when flying, the airfield was our home for the next two weeks. Although we would manipulate the daily flying programme to enable us to return to the ship from time to time, we slept and ate in a nearby building whenever we remained ashore.

Unlike present-day Kaitak, until recently a sizeable, and the principal, civil airport serving Hong Kong, in 1947 it was small with a runway made shorter by an approach over built-up Kowloon which extended almost to the airfield perimeter, necessitating a late, steep descent to the runway to avoid high-rise buildings. The local geography caused us some difficulty, with a high range of mountains just to the north, but nothing compared with the antics of the China National Aviation Corporation's daily run in its Dakotas. The uneven roar of their Pratt & Whitney engines would have us lined up outside the tents or stopping whatever we were doing, for they were odds-on favourites to misjudge the final approach and carry away yet another section of the boundary fence with their undercarriage. It said much for this ancient warrior of the skies that was the Douglas Dakota that the fence, not the undercarriage, invariably came off worst.

Kowloon was a bustling, sprawling town, less sophisticated than Hong Kong, but with plenty of interest. Goods of every description were beginning to flood into the area after the war, and the traders were looking for custom.

Tailors in particular were in a highly competitive market, and for the price of an off-the-shelf pair of trousers in the UK they would run you up a bespoke two-piece suit of excellent material in forty-eight hours, including an intermediate fitting. They had always been renowned for this sort of rapid service, largely developed from of the needs of 'passing ships in the night'.

It so happened, back in Wellington, which now seemed a lifetime away, I had been ashore with John Morton, with no particular purpose in mind, when we chanced upon an ironmongers sort of place. Wandering in, he sighted a lengthy roll of corduroy material.

'What on earth are you going to do with that?' I asked when the shopkeeper had pulled down the material from the top shelf.

'Oh,' he said, 'I'm told that in Honkers they will knock you up a jacket for the price of a packet of cigarettes – thought I'd try it.'

I needed little persuasion. The material was very good quality but what it was doing in an ironmonger's shop I couldn't imagine It wasn't expensive, and we both left with sufficient to make a decent jacket.

Now we would put it to the test. A few days after our arrival on the way to the United Services Club in Kowloon, we ventured in to 'Koh Lings', 'Tailors to the Royal Navy', as it was pleased to tell us. Mr Koh Ling greeted us at the door, and we sat down for the ritual of taking tea before discussing business. Indeed, if you were not to do business, one would still take tea as a matter of Chinese courtesy. We explained our requirements. Chinese tailors are excellent at copying, and John had thoughtfully brought an old hacking jacket of his for the purpose. It was also to my liking, sloping pockets with flaps, single split at the rear, etc. Mr Koh Ling looked approvingly at the corduroy material.

'You likee two splits at back? Much look better', he said.

'No thank you,' we said, 'how soon?'

'Maybe two three days', he replied. 'You fit tomorrow, I see.'

So we left, knowing that he would be as good as his word and that they would be ready for fitting the next day. They were, and by the third day we had two excellently tailored hacking jackets for a laughable price. Mine would last me a great many years until I grew tired of it rather than wore it out.

Our time at Kaitak was a relaxed affair. We occasionally tried to provoke the Chinese border guards by flying low, parallel and very close to the Chinese border, but they seemed unperturbed. Their own internal revolution

NCOs of 1837 Squadron Air Training Corps in 1943 during a visit by the Lady Mayoress. Author 4th from left.

Fairchild Cornell elementary trainer. 13 EFTS St Eugene 1944.

Aspiring naval pilots at St Eugine in 1944.

No 14 SFTS Kingston, Ontario in 1944 – Harvard advanced trainer.

Satellite airfield at Gananoque in the snow – author centre.

An amazing escape! One Harvard landed on top of another waiting on the runway to take off. Both pilots escaped.

'Premier' class escort carrier on which the author carried out initial deck landings in the Corsair.

The author flying a Corsair over Trincomalee.

891 Sqn Hellcat Night Fighter Squadron in 1945. Author back row far right.

The author with Sub Lt Bennet RNZVR and Mid Turner.

A Hellcat Mk2 newly equipped with radar.

Petty Officer Rogers fails to stop at the end of the runway and chews off my tail.
RNAS Nutts Corner 1945.

Sub Lt Warren RNZVR stalls during an ADDLS session narrowly missing the Batsman
and others before crashing on the runway.

HMS *Colossus* in 1946 off to Ceylon (now Sri Lanka).

A Corsair landing-on after an early morning pre-breakfast sortie.

HMS *Colossus* berthing at the South Mole in Gibraltar.

804 Seafire Squadron at Maydown in 1946 – author in cockpit.

HMS *Theseus* with 804 Sqn
Seafires and 812 Sqn Fireflies
ranged for take-off.

827 Squadron Barracuda landing
on *Colossus*.

Lt Peter Tod stalls on the approach
and is tragically lost.

Melbourne, HMS *Theseus* and HMS *Glory* 'open to visitors'.

Arrival over Sydney – author flying Seafire 136.

Theseus Air Group with *Glory* Air Group astern over Melbourne.

Lt Pritch Pritchard, observer, makes a rapid exit after his pilot landed across the deck.

A Seafire landing well to port, moments before hitting the batsman's position causing the death of one of his assistants.

Saved by the arrester wire from going for a swim!

The pilot misses all the wires and clears both barriers before causing mayhem in the forward deck park.

The aftermath of another pilot who missed all the wires, cleared both barriers, struck other aircraft and deck personnel before going over the side.

Air Group and ship's officers let their hair down on the way home to the UK after a mixed 'Showing the Flag' tour.

The author has a narrow escape after entering the barrier on HMS *Illustrious* during the DLCO's qualifying course.

Experimental trials on the Supermarine 510 aboard HMS *Illustrious*. The author stood on the aft gun turret to control the aircraft whilst being supported by another batsman against a fifty knot wind over the deck to avoid being blown over the side.

A navalised Meteor in which the author carried out a number of deck landings.

The loser in the contest for a future A/S aircraft for the Royal Navy. The author controls the Blackburn YA5 (GR 17) during competitive trials won by the Fairey GR 17, later to become the Gannet.

The embarkation of the RNVR Squadron from RNAS Stretton causes some excitement. Squadron Commander clears both barriers and lands on the forward deck park.

was more than enough to keep them occupied, and they could bide their time to reoccupy the New Territories – and Hong Kong.

Around the end of October, we became aware of the new government's policy regarding overseas territories. India had already achieved independence in August. Ceylon and Burma would shortly follow suit. In consequence of these national changes, the Admiralty anticipated events by withdrawing the aircraft carriers from Eastern waters and placing the naval air bases in Ceylon and Singapore into care and maintenance. This effectively curtailed our flying operations at Kaitak, and although *Theseus* would remain at Hong Kong until mid-November, it was decided that in the circumstances the air group should now prepare to fly on board as soon as practicable.

Accordingly, a few days later, on 4 November, the ship left her anchorage to receive the sixteen aircraft. Once on board it became clear that those would be our last deck landings and there would be no more air operations until we reached the UK to fly ashore. There was an air of sadness about it all. It seemed we were destined to finish as we had started, with a long passage and little to do other than make ourselves useful with ship's duties. Few of the aircrew were qualified watch keepers, but we could do duty as Second Officer of the Watch, which would count towards our watch-keeping time for eventual qualification. Highly qualified airmen we might well be, but for any sort of career prospects, the ability to con a ship at sea and carry out the seamanlike duties of a naval officer were essential.

We returned that evening to our anchorage to spend the next fourteen days. For us, the aircrew, it was an opportunity to see Hong Kong, which had been difficult while we were at Kaitak, and in fact we had had little inclination to do anyway. Kowloon may not have had the lure of the more glamorous Hong Kong, but it had much to offer, was on our back doorstep and boasted an excellent United Services Club, a most convivial place to relax at the end of the day or take part in the sporting activities which were available there.

I recall Hong Kong with little enthusiasm other than the magnificent view from the hills behind the city towards Victoria. A wonderful panorama taking in the Chinese mainland to the north, far beyond the New Territories, and then in the foreground the busy harbour bustling with activity, and then westward, numerous islands including the largest immediately to the west on which the future new airport, Chep Lap Kok, would become the centre for international travel, linked, as it would be, to Hong Kong Island by the ambitious road and rail system.

Shortly before leaving for the UK, on the Saturday evening, I happened to be ashore with John Ashworth and Bill Plews, fellow squadron pilots, to spend a last few hours and to have an early meal before returning to the ship. We had 'done' Honkers and were keen to start for home on the following Monday. It was, I suppose, about eight o'clock and we had just left the restaurant on our way back to the jetty when someone hailed us from across the street. It was the ship's Messman.

Wardroom catering in HM ships east of Suez had traditionally been the preserve of Chinese Messmen under contract, and indeed, many of the stewards would be Chinese, employed by the Messman They would go from ship to ship on arrival or departure, often exchanging ships at Aden or Ceylon. The system worked well since they could negotiate the buying of food at more advantageous prices than would otherwise be the case.

Our own Messman had done us proud, producing excellent food at a good messing rate, and it was he, Ton Ling (as good a name as I can remember!), who now gave a friendly wave from across the road. We exchanged a few pleasantries, commiserating with him on our imminent departure, and were on the point of leaving when: 'It's my birthday,' he pronounced, 'I'm having a few friends for dinner. I would be honoured if you would join me and my party.'

John looked at me and I knew what he was thinking; how do we get out of this without giving offence? 'That's extremely kind of you, but we have just left the restaurant after an early meal', I said in a voice both apologetic and perhaps unconvincing in declining his invitation.

But he persisted, and we accepted graciously and proceeded to accompany him further along the street to an establishment where it was obvious he was well known. We were shown to a room of considerable opulence, where we met his wife, other members of his family and a number of his friends, around twenty all told. Thus, an hour or so after finishing our last meal, we started again, but in quite different fashion!

There was a long, low table, and we sat on cushions on the floor; and for the next three hours, in slow order, we consumed untold delicacies punctuated by a selection of Chinese wines in the most convivial company, all under the constant attention of young waitress girls with an endless supply of hot towels. It was a fabulous meal, a banquet; and because of the unhurried pace and fascinating conversation, my digestive system did not rebel against being assailed again so soon after the earlier meal.

It was well past midnight when we made our farewells after an evening not to be forgotten. Ton Ling had already left his responsibilities in the ship and bemoaned the lack of opportunity in the future. There would be very few HM ships for the likes of him after we had gone, marking the end of many decades of service to the Royal Navy from the Ton Lings of this world and their forebears.

On 14 November we weighed anchor and got under way for the long passage home via all the usual ports of call, and the totally unexpected bonus of being home for Christmas. Except for some particularly severe weather in the Indian Ocean it was an unnoteworthy month at sea, but for some forty-eight hours at that time it kept us on our toes.

Before leaving Hong Kong we had embarked a number of very large crates containing aircraft parts, engines and the like, and these had been stowed and lashed down in the hangar. With the ship pitching heavily and rolling through thirty degrees and more, four of these had broken loose, causing havoc to the bulkheads and general mayhem. It was at this point that we discovered two ratings had been using the tops of the crates as sleeping quarters rather than the crowded mess decks, and they were now grappling for dear life to anything they could hold on to as the crates clattered from bulkhead to bulkhead.

The situation was serious enough to warrant a change of course to restore the situation and assess the damage, but for a few days life aboard was difficult and unpleasant. We went on to general messing as the galleys became restricted, and food was whenever you could get it. South-west of Ceylon the wind abated, the weather improved and normality was restored.

On 20 December, with the ship off Plymouth, we flew off for the last time and set course for Naval Air Station Ford in Sussex. *Theseus* would berth in Plymouth later that day prior to sailing for Rosyth for a well-earned refit. A few days before leaving the ship, the CO had asked us all individually to see him in his cabin for a chat about the future. He would discuss our performance in the squadron over the past year or so and suggest options or invite our views on the next appointment which he could recommend. After two barriers on landing – although I had now completed forty in the Seafire – I was mildly surprised but very pleased to be awarded an above-average assessment.

'What would you like to do next?' he asked. I hadn't really given this a lot of thought, and said as much, but then added, 'I would like another front-line embarked squadron', being the most obvious thing to do.

'Ah,' he replied, 'this is your third first- line squadron on the trot, isn't it?' I had to agree. Then he went on, 'I'm not sure the Appointers would wear that.' I didn't want a second-line squadron, and waited to hear what else he might suggest.

'You have had a good run, done well. As an above-average pilot I could recommend you for the Flying Instructors course at the RAF Central Flying School. What do you think about that?'

He saw my look of surprise. I hadn't given thought to this one. But then he added, 'Of course, you may not be selected, but I think you may have a good chance.'

That was it, then. I was pleased, I needed a change of scenery from front-line flying, and this offered an interesting challenge. But first, home and Christmas leave, picking up old ties again and looking forward to the future.

CHAPTER 8

Central Flying School

Early in the New Year of 1948, Frazer's recommendation bore fruit. My appointment from the Admiralty, in the rather quaint way I had become used to, said that I was to 'Repair on board HMS *Heron* for outside duty at RAF Central Flying School, Little Rissington to date 21 January.' There followed the usual thing about acknowledging this to Captain HMS *Heron*, copy to Commandant Central Flying School. Leave over, off I went.

I had had ample time to think about it over the leave period. I imagined it would be a culture shock to be going back to school again, but in fact that was not the way it was at all. My first introduction to what lay ahead came as I was standing outside Cheltenham station waiting for the service bus I had been told to expect to take me to Little Rissington.

'Are you going to CFS?' asked a character in RAF uniform, with two rings on his sleeve but looking as if there had been a third at some time.

'Matter of fact, I am', I said. 'Geoff Higgs', I added to introduce myself. 'I'm waiting for the station bus.'

'Tom Ashford', he replied. 'It looks as if we might be joining the same course.' As indeed it turned out to be.

The course, I discovered, was quite large, drawn from the various RAF Commands, Fighter, Bomber and Coastal, a number of foreign students from the USA, Australia, New Zealand and France, and six naval officers, two of whom had served in HMS *Glory* at the end of the war and accompanied HMS *Theseus* during the recent Far East deployment.

The general experience of the RAF contingent was staggering. On the whole they tended to be four or five years older than myself, and, judging by the wealth of campaign medals, had considerable operational experience. There was an almost embarrassing display of DSOs and DFCs adorning their uniforms, which in many cases showed signs of peeled-off rings on their sleeves as their wartime acting ranks had been reduced to substantive ranks; reduction from group captain or wing commander to squadron leader or flight lieutenant was not uncommon. But they were a lively lot, former experience was forgotten in this new challenge and we all moulded together very well in the little groups to which we were assigned.

The Central Flying School had a very long and distinguished history stretching well back into the early 1920s. In former days it always provided the official RAF aerobatic display team, and was renowned worldwide for the very high standard of students who passed through. The atmosphere was that of a university, and given the quality and experience of the typical students now being sent there, it was no surprise to find staff tutors and lecturers showing the greatest respect to their protégés for the next six months. If I was in awe of so much greater experience from the majority of my classmates at the beginning, I soon lost it. Backgrounds no longer mattered. We were all there to qualify as flying instructors.

After more than two years of front-line flying I was back at school, learning how to fly again; more accurately, it was an opportunity to polish rough edges that invariably creep in with the confidence of experience, to think more carefully about the business previously taken for granted. If you were to teach others, one's own performance had to be beyond reproach, and therefore we would now spend many hours flying with a fellow student, simulating the role of instructor giving tuition to a student would-be-pilot under training.

Tiger Moths and my old friend the Harvard would be used for these sorties, but there was the welcome opportunity to fly a variety of other aircraft for general experience. Quite early in the course I was initiated into the new world of jet and also multi-engined aircraft: in the former case, an opportunity to experience jets some years before they would be operated by the Royal Navy.

I remember the Vampire caused me considerable surprise on take-off. We had all been warned that the take-off run was long, but nothing prepared me for the leisurely way it accelerated and waddled and rattled down the runway, seemingly taking for ever to achieve any sort of lift-off speed. I was not the only one who would rotate the aircraft and rub the tail bumpers on the runway in an effort to get it airborne. But eventually it did lift, with not a lot of runway left. After the crisp get-up-and-go of propeller-driven machines, opening the throttle of the Goblin-powered Vampire produced a ridiculous response from the aircraft, giving more whine and noise than forward movement, and a tendency to believe you might have left the brakes on.

The Mosquito was something else. The twin Merlin engines fairly flung the aircraft along the runway; but if you weren't careful, it also took you sideways, threatening a ground loop. The two engines were not 'handed'; that is, both propellers went clockwise, and this caused the aircraft to swing violently when the throttles were opened wide at the start of take-off unless anticipated and counteracted with a bootful of rudder. It was a rapid learning process, and I found that for both take-off and landing – when the reverse would occur –leading with the appropriate engine greatly assisted directional control.

The stable of aircraft also included a Spitfire XVI in which, of course, I was completely at home. With a Packard Merlin engine and clipped wings, its performance was an improvement on, but otherwise not unlike, the Seafire XV. To complete the line-up there was the four-engined Lancaster. Unfortunately time did not permit full conversion to type, and I, as all others, had to be content with a familiarisation flight.

My recent good fortune with instructors – or in this case tutor – stayed with me. Flt Lt John Pinnington had the dubious pleasure of looking after me, and a more amenable, good-humoured fellow it would be hard to imagine. We clicked. Frequently during a Tiger Moth sortie he would say, 'Geoff, how about a cup of coffee?'

Quite early on I had discovered that this meant an unscheduled landing at a small airfield at Witney, near Oxford, which was used by a flying club. John had built up a friendly relationship with the air traffic controller there, and on these occasions we would land on a 'Green' from the tower, taxi over to the flying club premises, park and take coffee in the club restaurant. All very unofficial, but it was no secret, as one or two other tutors did the same. It became a pleasant diversion, particularly on cold winter mornings. As an alternative, when no flying was possible, we would retire to the local café at Bourton-on-the-Water, where the officers from CFS were well known.

It was an enjoyable and fulfilling six months. In the closing months, with the cricket season upon us, a number of us students played for the station eleven, which had a long-standing tradition of being included in the local villages' league. The cricket was of a surprisingly high standard, played with fervour and passion, typical village rivalry, no quarter given but plenty of beer flowing. Invariably, the local inn would do service as the pavilion, and I remember occasions when 'Next Man In' would be called, only for the transgressor to complain he hadn't finished his pint yet. I doubt if anyone who had the pleasure of playing village cricket in those days would regard it as anything but the epitome of that great English game.

Sadly, I fear, with the passing of time, it cannot be said to be played in quite the same spirit nowadays. Ruthlessness has replaced sportsmanship and rivalry between villages unlikely to reach the levels of genuine enthusiasm of those simpler days. Now they play for bigger stakes, players are likely to be recruited and offered inducements. It is still village cricket with the same traditions, but the prize at the end of the season is for the top two village elevens to play a final at Lords! Unheard-of in those days of yore; for me, though, the names Shipton-under-Wychwood, Moreton-in-Marsh and many others, such as Stow-on-the-Wold, will remain for ever etched in my memory.

The officers' mess at Little Rissington was 1938 vintage, one of a number built at that time to a very high standard. Two storeys with an imposing entrance hall, they put a strain on the RAF budget at that time, and were replaced thereafter with a simpler, single-storey structure of a slightly less lavish, but still very acceptable, standard which became known at the 'Thirty-Nine' type. Because of its rural location, Little Rissington was a favourite of the local Hunt for its annual ball, in common with many others up and down the country. They were ideal for events of this sort. The end of our course more or less coincided with the annual Mess Summer Ball, and so we had two very good reasons to look forward to it.

Now it so happened that we bunch of naval officers on this course, as our counterparts had done before us, considered it incumbent upon ourselves as the Senior Service to ensure we left in good style, leaving a good impression behind us. NOs on preceding courses had had their own particular way of stamping their character for posterity. Ours was a cart-horse!

For some weeks we had cultivated the friendship of a pretty hefty cart-horse – Neddy – in an adjacent field to the mess, feeding him with lumps of sugar and other delicacies to his liking until it was quite clear that there was a good deal of mutual affection. In a short time he would follow us anywhere, and the moment came when one of our number clambered aboard – successfully! No problem, he may not have enjoyed the experience, but he made little protest when a few more sugar lumps passed his way.

Came the night of the Summer Ball, and we would show these RAF types what we were made of. Half-way through the Reception process, Commandant, Mess President and one or two others in the line to receive honoured guests, up the steps and into the main hall came Neddy with Lt Bill Brewer aboard – to the great consternation of the Reception Committee. The more so because, at the crucial moment, Neddy decided to disgrace himself, and us, by performing on the extremely expensive and valuable carpet. They were not amused. We had rather overdone it, and next morning would be called to account before the Air Commodore.

'Mess capers are one thing,' he intoned, 'but you irresponsible naval people nearly ruined the evening.'

I suppose we had, and on reflection the next day could understand his anger. It cost us an arm and a leg for the damage done to the carpet and parquet flooring, but the reputation that lived after us made it all worth while.

After attending the Summer Ball, I drifted apart from my long-standing girlfriend for no good reason that I can recall. Partly, I imagine, the result of more or less continued absence over the last few years, with only the briefest of periods at home on leave; but principally, perhaps, because I realised that I was not ready for any permanent relationship at that time. At 23 years of age I was in a man's world and found it very agreeable. The opposite sex provided a more than pleasant diversion, but at this time I was loath to let it interfere with the more manly pursuits of sport and the odd pint afterwards, where the girls would not fit in easily.

At least that is how I saw life in my early 20s. Regrettably, I cannot recall having the courage to part from Betty with any sense of honour. I think I let things drift until she realised there was no future for her. But I was not proud of my behaviour; it was a blot on my character. Ten years later I had grown away from these laddish pursuits and met my soul-mate, and live happily ever after.

In due course we were passed out as qualified flying instructors, duly noted in the Navy List as such. We heard no more about the Summer Ball incident when we saw the Commandant before leaving, and in fact he wished us all well for the future. Its all part of life's rich pageant. I had now gone full circle from student to instructor in a little less than four years.

A week or so before the termination of the course, we each received our next appointment. Mine would be to RAF Syerston in Nottinghamshire, as would be a number of others from the course, including several RAF officers. I wondered whether I could improve on my original instructor, who gave me such a near-disastrous start those light-years ago.

CHAPTER 9

No. 22 Flying Training School, Syerston

Royal Air Force Syerston was where every aspiring naval pilot would carry out his training to 'wings' standard – if he survived that long. All-through training was a very recent innovation, replacing the former two separate Elementary and Service Schools which had existed for many decades. Now prospective pilots would start and finish with, in most cases, the same instructor. Beneficial, perhaps, for the student, but it placed considerably more responsibility on, and demanded more highly qualified, instructors, who would have to be selected with more care.

Syerston enjoyed the '39'-standard officers' mess set in an attractive position on the other side of the road from the airfield, a road which led to the nearest town, Newark, about six miles away. As lieutenants we shared a double room, and only the more senior squadron leaders or equivalent were allocated a single. Now, for some reason, not long after my arrival, I was asked to become Mess Secretary, and as such had the privilege of a single room – or cabin, as we still called it – a worthwhile perk.

It was a pleasant part of the country. The River Trent ran alongside the airfield, and the annual rowing regatta there attracted high-quality 'fours' and 'eights'. Syerston had always supported these events in one way or another, and invariably entered a crew. However, at this time we had more important things to occupy us – the business of indoctrinating our charges into the mysteries of flying.

I was appointed to 'A' Flight in No. 1 Squadron, one of four flights in two nominal squadrons. The OC 'A' Flight was Dave Keay, a South African; and joining with me from the recent CFS course were Dennis White and Keith Leppard. Dennis I had known for some years, when he had been our 'batsman' in *Theseus*, but Keith was new to me, although he had served in

94

HMS *Glory* during the time of our Australian tour. The Deputy Flight Commander and two others constituted the rest of the flight's instructional staff.

Shortly after arrival, we new boys would be checked out by the OC Flying Wing, one Wg Cdr Peter Broad, whose background was buried in the long-distant past, as was, it would seem, his concept of instructional technique. The check-out consisted of 'pattering' him through various typical manoeuvres as if he were a student under training, precisely what we had been practising for the last six months, but it transpired that his concept of flying was likened more to the era of Sopwith Camels and other First World War aircraft.

'Please demonstrate Maximum Steep Turns', he said; so I did. Half-way through the turn I demonstrated letting the aircraft's nose fall below the horizon, a common fault with inexperienced pilots.

'Now,' I said, 'just ease off the bank a little, reposition the attitude with the elevators and then resume the turn.'

All classical stuff, and I went on to describe the folly of pulling back on the stick to reposition the aircraft in the first instance. The voice in the front cockpit said, 'I have control. I will show you how we do it here.' He then proceeded into a Maximum Steep Turn, correcting the same error with the use of top rudder! And, of course, the aircraft juddered and protested its way round the rest of the turn in an alarming and uncomfortable manner, with me expecting the aircraft to flick into a spin at any time. Great Scott, I thought, what have I got here, and pondered how he could have survived this long.

What he had just demonstrated was very early string-and-wax aircraft methods from fifty years before, when their knowledge of aerodynamics and control systems was crude and elementary. There were one or two more rather quaint exchanges before we finished.

After landing I marched into Dave Keay's office. 'What on earth is all this about?' I asked. 'I've just spent six months being taught instructional techniques only to discover I've been wasting my time. I come here and find you do it differently.'

He laughed. 'Forget it', he said. 'The Wing Commander's methods went out with the Ark but we let him have his little say and then ignore him.' He went on, 'You teach here per CFS, as we all do.'

Well, not a start to give one much confidence; in effect a chief instructor at odds with his instructor staff, but I thought no more about it and got on with the task of initiating my new students into the world of night-flying; they were half-way through their course, I had acquired them from another instructor and they had just reached this stage in their training. Night-flying was not a feature of the earlier Tiger Moth syllabus, and this would be their first night-flying experience. From my point of view, as a first experience of instructing, it was a question of jumping in at the deep end. So for the next month or so I would spend more time flying at night than by day.

I had been given four students, all rating pilots, although within a few weeks I would acquire a Royal Marine lieutenant to replace one of these. Quite why he was transferred to me is lost from my memory; but from the beginning I sensed he was far from satisfactory for this stage of the course, and compared very poorly with the other students. First of all he had 'big boots', in short he was inclined to do things by numbers, in a rather clumsy fashion. He seemed to have little sense of feel and generally demonstrated a lack of empathy with the aircraft; there was nothing natural about the way he handled the aircraft, and I felt he was likely to be a danger to himself if he went on much longer.

Now I liked George Manuel, and for the next few weeks tried to improve matters with extra coaching and discussions, but eventually, as we were approaching the last three months of the course, I decided finally that he was not pilot material and should be taken off the course to return to the Royal Marines for soldiering, where he was better suited. A difficult decision, especially from an inexperienced instructor, but I took the plunge, referred him to the Flight Commander, who, quite content to accept my judgement, referred him to the OC Flying with the recommendation that his training should be terminated.

Dave Keay and I should have known better. In due course he was given a check flight by Wg Cdr Peter Broad, who subsequently declared that 'Lt Manuel was safe and about average', and that he saw no reason why he shouldn't continue. Surprise, surprise, but not to the Flight Commander or myself. But we had no choice. So I persevered with him, as with my other students, and eventually they were passed out, fully fledged naval pilots. They would now continue their flying training at RNAS Lossiemouth to operational standard.

The rub of this was that within a very few weeks of arriving at Lossiemouth, Lt Manuel would be considered unsuitable for further flying training. He was said to be unsafe and was recommended to be returned to the Royal Marines; which he was. There was also a bit of a backlash. Why, Lossiemouth wanted to know, had we not established this during his previous training, when we could have avoided time and expense? At least now the system had probably saved his life.

About this time, towards the end of January, we had been asked by the RN Football Association to enter the Air Command Knock-Out Cup competition, really to make up the numbers, since there were an odd number of eligible naval air stations. Well, we didn't rate NAS status in any sense, and certainly had only a fraction of the manpower. Apart from something over one hundred naval students on the course, there were perhaps twenty naval instructors. Could we field a respectable eleven out of that? Scratching around we eventually found ten who confessed to having kicked a football at some time or another, and would be willing. But where could we find the remaining one?

It so happened that the Senior Naval Officer at Syerston was my old Commander Air from *Theseus* days, Cdr Ed Walthall, and it was to him that we now turned, a most unlikely recruit, somewhat overweight and in his late 30s, with a dubious background of any sport, least of all football. But beggars can't be choosers, and there were no other volunteers, so in the bar one evening we cornered him. 'I'll make up the numbers', he agreed after a second glass of his favourite tipple. Thus prepared, we signalled to the organisers that we had formed a team.

The first round came and went. RNAS Bramcote, an RNVR squadron base, had fewer resources than ourselves, and in an undistinguished performance we just managed to beat them. Now to the second round. And whom should we meet? No less that the cup holders, RNAS Yeovilton. To cut a long story short, come the day, their supporters arrived in bus loads, adorned with their team's colours and rattles, enough to intimidate even the most ardent Syerston fan. Their team, beautifully turned out in yellow and blue shirts and stockings to match, made a striking contrast to the motley collection of gear we had managed to assemble. Not all of us had boots. Raiding the sports store, Ed couldn't find a pair to fit, and wore his plimsolls. There was an abundance of white naval tropical-style stockings, and I cannot recall more than four of us with the same-coloured shirt. We deliberately understated our gear to reflect the standard of our football, and, of course, there was no mistaking us for them on the field.

From the outset there was only one team in it, and their supporters let us know it with their derisory shouts from the touchline. In no time at all we were one down. But, for one or two of us who had played a bit before, and perhaps most of the team, the catcalls from the touchline started to irritate, and we began to resent the cockiness from the Yeovilton team and their supporters, and we determined to put together some sort of form.

Almost on the point of half-time, Stan Leonard, a more than good rugby player, received a long speculative ball from somewhere, sidestepped his opponent in the best traditions of a scrum half – which he was – and promptly put it in the back of the net. Stunned by this, the opposition went into a deep huddle at half-time. We, on the other hand, were more relaxed about the whole affair, but decided, nevertheless, that we would tweak their tails a little before conceding what we thought would be the inevitable defeat that would surely come after they had had their feathers ruffled just before the interval.

So we came out fighting, sometimes legally and sometimes not, depending on the skill and background of our players. Then, with little more than fifteen minutes remaining, still drawing 1–1, the ball came over from our left wing towards Yeovilton's goal. Ed Walthall, huffing and puffing towards the penalty area, got in the way with his knee as he was lumbering forward, and the ball was in the back of the goal. No one was more surprised than he – except the Cup Holders and the mass of Yeovilton supporters, who were beside themselves. Somehow, we survived the last minutes, and the Cup Holders were dispatched back to Yeovilton with their tails between their legs. They had lost to a scratch side who had made up the numbers! It was great fun, and later on in the bar, we gave Ed the other half of his favourite tipple.

Although I enjoyed football, my preferred winter sport was hockey. We had a very good hockey side backed by a Cambridge Blue and the Sports Officer, who had played for the RAF. Together with two Pakistani course officers, we had a team good enough to be offered a fixture against Cranwell. Cranwell, like their other service counterparts, would not normally deign to play station sides, but the preponderance of naval people at Syerston swung the odds. It was an enjoyable couple of seasons: the station eleven became affiliated to the Nottinghamshire Hockey Association, and three of us were invited to join the Notts Hockey Club after we had played against them. Later this resulted in all three being selected for a county trial, but unfortunately I was able to play in only one match before leaving the area on appointment; not that a second opportunity was by any means certain, anyway.

The second year of instructing brought another four students, one of whom, Lt Harry Julien, was an old friend. He had been in *Theseus* as an engineering officer during the Australian tour, and I was pleased to see him again. So we started again, this time flying Tiger Moths in the early stages, often four or five flights a day in an open cockpit in the middle of winter. At times it could be arctic. But it was a satisfying life, particularly watching the students' progress, sending them solo, taking a little pride perhaps when they were seen to be doing well.

The Admiralty, in one of its more generous moods, had authorised one Seafire to be kept on the base, ostensibly to keep the hand-in of the naval instructors. In practice there were only two of us qualified on type, but it was a great privilege to fly this as a diversion from the Tiggy and Harvard. Come the annual Battle of Britain Display in mid-September, I would demonstrate it to the public by carrying out aerobatics and other manoeuvres which they requested through the control tower. It raised a column in the local Press.

Wandering around after the flight, Dave Keay met up with me. He had been approached by a young woman who wanted to know whether any of the naval pilots had ever known her brother, who had been in the Fleet Air Arm. 'What's his name?' I asked, but he didn't know. So we retraced his steps and found her and her friend talking to Ron Crayton and Peter Cort, two of the naval instructors. I was introduced. 'Sadie Norcott', she said, and I knew at once. Four years had gone by since her brother, an instructor at Yeovilton, had been killed and I had attended his funeral. She was pleased to have met someone who had known him. It formed the basis of a short friendship with her and her friend Dulcie, who already seemed to be on good speaking terms with Ron. We would meet up in Newark at the White Hart, where Keith Leppard had made the acquaintance of the landlady's daughter, or at the more convivial Rutland Hotel just down the way. With three or four others, I think we earned a reputation for slightly riotous behaviour, but it was all good fun and taken in very good spirit by the two charming people who ran the Rutland.

Some months before this, I had acquired a dog, Duffy, from Peter Speed, an RAF friend from CFS days, who was now instructing with me. He had been given a posting abroad and was looking for a home for this delightful

Cocker Spaniel, which, of course, I couldn't resist, although I knew I was likely to be going back to sea again shortly.

Duffy was a very affectionate animal and found it difficult to be left when I went flying. The flight crew room was not a suitable place to leave him. Although by this time I had been appointed Deputy Flight Commander – which caused a certain resentment with Dennis White and Keith Leppard, who were both senior to me – I did not have a separate office, and so I couldn't ensure his safety. He howled, and only my status as Mess Secretary made it possible for him to remain in my room in the mess, where I had an understanding steward. But it became obvious that something more permanent was required. Thus my mother, who already had one spaniel, acquired another.

At the end of the year it came as no surprise to be told of another appointment. Eighteen months was the statutory time for instructing unless one specifically asked for an extension. Neither I, nor any other, would do so, and in any event it happily coincided with the end of the course, when all my students had gained their 'wings'. It had been an invigorating experience, rewarding and very enjoyable, but I would be glad to move on.

This time I was not asked; the Appointers had already pencilled me in to attend the Deck Landing Control Officers course at Henstridge, near Sherborne, and my appointment duly arrived towards the end of December 1949. Keith Leppard joined with me. It was a six-week course where all flying was done from Henstridge, but because of the lack of accommodation there, we would be based at Yeovilton and bus the fifteen miles to and fro daily.

It wasn't very satisfactory, but the nature of the DLCO training placed considerable demands on an airfield circuit, and this was simply not possible at Yeovilton, which already housed front-line squadrons and, in any event, was close to capacity. Henstridge did, however, boast a pretty basic mess, an old-fashioned Nissen hut, but it served its purpose at the time and we would lunch there daily.

Before I embarked on this new training I was faced with another significant decision in my life. Around the time of finishing at Syerston at the end of 1949, I was aware that the four-year Extended Service Commission which I had been granted in 1946 would shortly expire. I suppose I hadn't given this a great deal of thought, and certainly had not considered various options. Possibly Their Lordships would come up with a further extension, but on reflection, I think that I, and all those in a similar position to myself, were more inclined to live for the day and let the future take care of itself. So be it, we thought. But then the Admiralty announced sweeping changes in the officer structure, mainly concerned with rationalising some of the anomalies that had existed for decades which limited the opportunities available to specialists such as engineering and electrical branch officers. These were now to be drawn into the executive branch, with the prospect of wider opportunities.

'Air' was a different matter. They had always been regarded as first and foremost executive status, but in most cases at that time the 'A' was still displayed in the stripes denoting rank. This would now disappear, as would all the coloured strips between the rank stripes of the other various specialisations, purple for engineers, green for electrical, blue for schoolmaster and white for supply officers. Of course, it created a certain resentment with some, and for a time you could see a purple waistcoat just showing above the edges of a reefer jacket, or there would be an increase in the display of a white silk handkerchief in the top pocket of a supply officer.

At many naval air stations, and also at Syerston, where I was still at that time, there were ritual bonfires of the 'A' and much mourning. But it all sorted itself out in time, except that the various specialisations involved, with the exception of 'Air', never did see much benefit from the changes, and indeed, it is difficult to see how, if you had spent your time in the boiler room or some such, any other result could be expected. There was one section that remained aloof from all this, and that was the Medics. They continued to sport the traditional red stripe between their rank gold rings, presumably because they were classified as non-combatants.

From my point of view the more important announcement at this time was the offer of a Permanent, and of course pensionable, Commission, with full existing seniority. It came as a complete surprise. There had been no hint of this, and I suppose the most we felt might be offered was something similar to the RAF short-service 16/38 breakpoint, where you were discarded at the age of 38 or after sixteen years' service, whichever came first. So there was a lot to celebrate at that time, and the fortunate minority like myself spared not the partying.

The six-week Control Officers course passed with little of note – except for me, one almost disastrous incident during the embarked phase in HMS *Illustrious*. The primary purpose was to learn the technique for controlling aircraft onto the flight deck by the use of 'bats', simply tennis-racquet-type things, which you waved around to indicate to the pilot what you wanted him to do to complete a successful deck landing. But we would also fly the circuit patterns ourselves as part of the course, and carry out half a dozen deck landings in the process.

With my background I had, of course, been given the Seafire, and not the Firefly, to qualify, so off I would go to complete the requisite number with trainee batsmen controlling. No problem, I had arrived on board four times, each time being pushed back to the stern for the next one. Then on the fifth I somehow contrived to miss the blasted wires; at which point, with the barrier looming ahead, stupidly I started to brake. But I was still travelling at some knots, and the Seafire doesn't care for harsh braking at this speed; and unless you are fortunate, it is inclined to continue in anything but a straight line. So I managed to enter the barrier askew with the starboard wing first, resulting in the aircraft turning onto its back.

Then the fun started. The engine protested at this outrageous behaviour and promptly burst into flames ahead of me, still in the cockpit. By this time the Flight Deck Fire Party, with commendable speed, had unravelled the hose and was alongside the aircraft with the Rescue Crewman frantically trying to assist me out of the cockpit. Only he had gone to the wrong side of the aircraft! The little drop-down door of the cockpit is on the port side, and he had gone to the starboard side. By this time I had managed to open the door sufficiently to wriggle out and put a few feet between me and the gradually enveloping fire. But it was an unpleasant few moments. The fire was eventually extinguished, and I was subjected to the usual medical treatment, which I didn't need.

That completed flying for the day. Chico Roberts, the Squadron CO, had a word with me in the bar later on. 'Look,' he said, 'best thing is to put you on the first detail tomorrow, OK?' Well, I wasn't going to admit it wasn't OK, although the fire had made a nasty impression on me. So I said, 'Fine, not a problem.' And in due course I completed the rest of the landings without batting an eyelid, and qualified as a fully fledged Control Officer. Of the close on a thousand deck landings in many types of aircraft, the Seafire would remain the only aircraft in which I have come to grief. Three barriers out of fifty landings in the Seafire is not a great record, but then the Seafire is not a great carrier-borne aircraft, and its poor record throughout its time with the fleet speaks for itself. I also took some small consolation from the fact that all three barrier incidents were in Seafires with a belly hook, and the belly hook had accounted for the majority of all Seafire accidents during carrier landings during fleet operations.

CHAPTER 10

Back to Sea - HMS *Illustrious*

I was standing on the quayside at Portland harbour with my baggage waiting for a ship's boat, gazing at the numerous warships in the harbour and the Bill beyond when from behind, 'Hullo, where are you off to then?' I turned round to see a very tall, imposing commander, with greying hair and a pleasant smile on his face.

'Well, I'm waiting to get out to *Illustrious*', I said. 'I believe they are sending a boat for me.'

'Then we can go together', he replied. 'You look as if you are a new arrival, and so am I.'

It was Walter Lamb, and although I didn't know it at that time, he was the newly appointed Commander Flying wings and would become a very good friend.

After qualifying at Henstridge I had been appointed to HMS *Illustrious*, the trials and training carrier, which I viewed with mixed feelings. In fact it was to prove a significant event in my career, leading to an association with the world of test flying which I very much doubt would otherwise have been the case.

When I left Henstridge in early March 1950, the Korean War was beginning to gather momentum. One British carrier was on station in the area to support United Nations land operations, and I had hoped to be sent there to fill the available billet as second batsman in HMS *Ocean*. It was not to be. The Appointers, in their wisdom, sent a married officer rather than one of the other four of us, all unmarried!

HMS *Illustrious* was a fleet carrier with a considerable and enviable war record. She had also suffered much damage from enemy action, resulting in a prolonged period of repair in the United States. She, together with two others of her class, *Indomitable* and *Implacable*, were nearing the end of their service. But they were proud ships and would soldier on for another four years. *Victorious*, another of the class, had been selected for modernisation, and I would have the privilege of serving in her in the years to come.

Illustrious was a very happy ship. The Captain, 'Shorty' Carlill, and Commander, 'Buster' Graham, the Executive Commander, would both make admiral, and deservedly so; their nicknames reflected their stature. Cdr Walter Lamb turned out to be a breath of fresh air, wonderfully relaxed, nothing fazed him. He was a pre-war pilot and specialist air gunnery officer, but had steadfastly refused the opportunity to de-symbolise (the Admiralty's edict for all executive officers to qualify as watch keepers); thus he limited his own career opportunities, which was very much the Navy's loss.

It became a ritual for him and myself, together with Harry Burman, the other, and senior, batsman on board, to spend many leisure hours in the evening playing shove ha'penny. But this wasn't ordinary shove ha'penny. It was highly competitive, merciless stuff with an intensity that sometimes transcended rank, and if, or when, as he often did, the Commander joined in, then no holds were barred. But perhaps it was child's play compared to deck hockey. Both commanders were very big men, around six feet three and a corresponding weight to go with it. Now deck hockey can never be called a game of skill, but most of us followed a loose set of rules – barging your opponent over the side, for example, was considered bad form – but in Walter's and Buster's book anything went, and the medics often had a busy time.

One match I recall, when the stokers, who had some very substantial bodies, played the air department, was nothing less than sheer thuggery. The worst offender was the chief stoker, by a short head from Wings. Irrespective of where the rope puck was, the pair of them could be seen battling it out, shoulder to shoulder, long after either had last touched it. One stoker was seen clambering up the five-foot ladder from the port sponson with a bloody arm, having been deposited there by one of his own side in the general mêlée, which scarcely concerned itself with whose side you were on. Frightening and alternately exhilarating, it produced great bonding within the ship's company, but it was nothing less than miraculous that serious injury was avoided. Steel flight decks can be very hard.

But it was this sort of camaraderie which produced, arguably, the happiest and most efficiently run ship I have served in. The Chief Stoker, for example was a vital part of the flight deck engineering team, and his rapport with Wings and the air department, fostered by such things as deck hockey, ensured his team's total commitment to the smooth running of a flight deck, which, at times, can be very hectic, with tempers inclined to fray. He was quite simply the salt of the earth. He could do anything with his hands, and often a hammer, to provide temporary repair to flight deck machinery, often having to contend with a 35 kt wind over the deck.

Then the Commander, Buster Graham, representing the executive department of the ship, which in some carriers has been known to be at odds with its counterpart air departments, was never ambivalent towards what he saw as the primary function of *Illustrious*, and ensured that all departments worked together harmoniously. It made for a thoroughly efficient ship and hence a very happy one.

So I would spend the next twenty months in near-perfect harmony with my fellow shipmates of all ranks in a job which developed into an amalgam of tasks and responsibilities entirely to my liking. At the outset, Harry Burman, unassuming and somewhat self-effacing, declared his intention to lead a quiet life, and let me have my head. He had no wish to become involved with aircraft trials from Boscombe Down or the Service Trials Unit at Ford, but would happily do a stint on the flight deck – as we both would – to assist the Flight Deck Officer, and share the responsibilities for the annual training of the RNVR squadrons. Well, that was fine by me. Harry was married and had no great ambition to be First Sea Lord

The flight deck was the preserve of Adam MacKinnon, a senior lieutenant-commander and experienced wartime pilot, but now no longer active as a pilot. He came of wealthy Irish stock, or rather his wife did, and hence he benefited. He ran the deck and we assisted in addition to our duties as batsmen. We would become very good friends during our time in *Illustrious*, and I was sorry when he left after I had been in the ship for twelve months. He would go to his final job before retirement. Some years later on my way from Byfleet to the Leander Club on the Thames for lunch, courtesy of Capt John Stevens, an ex-captain of HMS *Leander* (all captains of HMS *Leander* were honorary members of the club), I diverted our small party a few miles to a hostelry where I knew Adam was mine host – but that's another story for the future.

The ship boasted one permanent aircraft on board, a Firefly, augmented as required by several others available ashore. The Ship's Flight was nominally the responsibility of a young sub-lieutenant pilot whose job it was to provide ship-to-shore duties for passengers, mail and ad hoc other requirements. At the earliest opportunity I qualified on type, and in addition to using one of them to travel to the various locations for duty, I would also give some of the young midshipmen under training the experience of taking off and landing back on the carrier, in the hope that they might be encouraged to think seriously of a future career in aviation. A little bribery does no harm, and I would wean them away from more traditional thoughts by telling them, 'The days of battleships and gunnery are long since gone.'

As a general utility ship, we operated mainly in the English Channel, using Plymouth for periodic leave periods, but generally spent weekends in Torquay or Guernsey. Both were highly agreeable for all the ship's company, and the officers in particular were made very welcome at the yacht clubs, a useful facility when waiting for the ship's boat to go back on board.

Early in May we proceeded north from our stamping ground in the English Channel to berth at Liverpool. As replacements for the Illustrious-class fleet aircraft carriers, two new 43,000-ton ships had been ordered during the war, the first of which, HMS *Eagle*, was shortly to enter service. The second, HMS *Ark Royal*, had been laid down within twelve months of *Eagle*, but had suffered delays for reasons which I suspect were due to lack of funding during the critical post-war years, and was only now, some four years later than *Eagle*, ready for launching at Liverpool.

Illustrious was given the honour of providing a platform for VIP visitors. It was a memorable occasion, flags flying everywhere, the place swimming with foreign diplomats and more gold braid than even Mr Gieves could boast. At the head of all this was the Queen Mother, who would perform the traditional launching ceremony after inspecting a guard of honour on the dockside adjacent to *Illustrious*. *Ark* entered the water, on time, without any hitch, always a good sign for a ship's future, and to the cheers and hooters of countless tugs and other vessels. For us, in *Illustrious*, it was a pleasant diversion from our normal activities in the Channel, although our deployment schedule would only permit us to stay until the following morning.

On the way south in the Irish Sea, I flew off to Culdrose, where we had planned to disembark two aircraft for a week while the ship was busy doing other non-aviation things prior to spending the weekend in Guernsey at St Peter Port. I had not at that time had an opportunity to carry out the necessary deck landing qualification, and so from Culdrose I followed the ship and flew direct to Guernsey airport for a few days' sunshine. I had no sooner got on board at St Peter Port than I was accosted by the Direction Officer, Lt Cdr David Verney.

'Geoff,' he said, 'I've got to get to Lee and Culdrose for a couple of days to check out some equipment. Wings seemed to think you might help.'

Well, it would ruin my plans to spend a few days in St Peter Port, and I hadn't had much free time lately, but I could hardly refuse, especially as he had pleaded his cause with Wings! So we sorted out his schedule. First to Lee for an hour or so, then to Culdrose. When he had completed his task there, back to Guernsey to check with the ship, then return to Culdrose for the night. On the Saturday I flew him back to Guernsey, where he apologised for ruining my weekend's sailing. But then, it was a happy ship and we all pulled together.

A few weeks later I made my first acquaintance with the test-flying world in the form of the Naval Test Squadron at Boscombe Down. It was then in the process of evaluating the GR17 specification for a new anti-submarine aircraft, and had reached the stage of looking at the deck-landing characteristics. One of the two contenders, a Blackburn concept, was not dissimilar from its Fairey opponent, but suffered through the non-availability of its planned turboprop engine, and was at some disadvantage with a temporary Eagle piston engine against the Fairey's Double Mamba.

This was of course an important contract, and the two companies would spare no expense in furthering their cause. It resulted in numerous invitations to dine here, there and everywhere, and in my role as batsman for the trials, I was naturally included. In this context, Fairey won hands down, but I doubt whether it had any influence in the final decision. They had a strong team led by a retired group captain, Gordon Slade, with Peter Twiss, an experienced ex-Royal Navy pilot, carrying out the flying.. But this sojourn to Boscombe whetted my appetite, and it wasn't just the extravagant dinners. There was something about the atmosphere which stirred the interest, and at that stage I was lost to the world of test flying.

But after a week at Boscombe I came down to earth. I now flew myself to the naval air station at Bramcote, the home of the Midlands Air Division, where its RNVR 1833 Squadron pilots were preparing for their annual deck-landing training period, always an occasion of great excitement! I spent three days putting them through ADDLS session after ADDLS session in their

Seafires, and came away feeling decidedly unhappy at their prospects. They took their flying seriously enough, but the RNVR atmosphere was more that of a highly select club where the social side of the weekends took pride of place.

The acid test came some weeks later. The best of the bunch flew four aircraft out to the ship, and I waited in some trepidation on the stern for their arrival. But there were no alarms; together we got them on board safely. But it was a brief lull before the storm. On his first attempt, the CO, looking good over the round-down, took the 'cut', but then, sensing that he was missing all the wires, pushed forward on the stick, bounced impressively and managed to straddle both barriers before finishing in an untidy heap the other side of them.

That set the scene for the day. Another pilot caught a late wire after slewing across the deck, somehow just managing to avoid going over the side, while a third was never in any danger of being in a position of landing aboard. So we sent him back to Lee. The rest of the training period of three days went much the same way. It proved to me that RNVR weekend flying was of limited value to the fleet, and it was not long before the concept of reserve air squadrons was scrapped.

Towards the end of 1950, *Illustrious* became due for a short refit, and would be docked in Plymouth for three months. Now I had no intention of kicking my heels for that length of time, pounding the deck as a watch keeper or whatever other duty might come my way. Besides, living on board when a ship is in dockyard hands is not the pleasantest of experiences, as I had discovered in *Theseus* at Singapore some years before, so I sought out Wings to discuss options.

'What had you in mind?'

'Well,' I said, 'I would like to be detached to perhaps a second-line squadron for some serious flying.'

'That shouldn't be a problem,' said he, 'I'll see what I can do.'

'The other little matter', I went on, 'is the question of the trials aircraft from Boscombe. I have only limited experience of jet aircraft from CFS days, but if I am going to control a variety of jet aircraft during the embarked phase, I really ought to have a better appreciation of their characteristics.'

'Ah,' he said, 'I'm beginning to get your drift, young Higgs. Are you making a pitch for a jet course?'

'Well, yes,' I said, 'and also to do a few jet deck landings when the Boscombe team come on board.'

Bless his cotton socks, he took it all very well. And to my mild astonishment, within a few weeks, there were signals flashing around between the ship, the Admiralty, and both Lee-on-Solent and Culdrose naval air stations, resulting in Higgs being detached to 771 Squadron at Lee, supernumerary for flying duties for one month from the middle of January, prior to joining 702 Squadron at Culdrose for a jet conversion course.

I could scarcely believe my good fortune. It was entirely due to Wings, of course. He must not only have had a good deal of influence in the corridors of power but also talked a good talk. Jet courses in those days were generally confined to pilots appointed to a jet squadron, and at that time, apart from one or two second-line units, there was only one first-line squadron, an Attacker squadron working up at West Raynham. Little did I then know that I would shortly make its acquaintance.

I was now to embark on a fairly busy period. In the middle of January 1951 I presented myself to Jack Welply, CO of 771 Squadron at Lee-on-Solent.

'What do you want to do?'

'As much flying as you can let me have in any aircraft available', I answered.

No. 771 Squadron was essentially a Fleet Requirements Unit, with the primary task of providing air targets for ships' radar, gunnery and any other requirements that came along. It boasted a variety of aircraft, such as the twin-engined Anson, Firefly trainer and Sea Hornets XX and NFXX1. So I amused myself for the next four weeks qualifying on the Anson and Sea Hornet, and flying numerous sorties in the Firefly, giving air experience to anyone who applied to Jack for a flight, and generally mucking about with warships in the Channel to calibrate radar and so on. It was a useful few weeks to get back into flying shape again.

The Sea Hornet in particular was a great bonus. I badgered and cajoled Jack and Tom Whittaker, who was in charge of the Hornets, until they found life easier to produce one and get me off their backs. After the Mosquito, its part stablemate the Hornet was extremely easy and delightful to fly. Its 'handed' propellers (rotating in opposite directions) eliminated the directional problems of the Mossie, and it was a lot quicker, well over 400 mph.

My short time at Lee was well spent. I managed to achieve a respectable number of flying hours, enough to put me in good shape to tackle the jet conversion course a week later.

Illustrious by now was well under way with her refit, and I called in to pass the time of day on my way to Culdrose. She looked in a sorry state with the dockyard hands clambering all over her, dirt and dust everyway, electrical cables hanging loose; and I looked with horror at the flight deck, with cranes and other items of machinery resembling the aftermath of several accidents. I was glad to leave them to it and be on my way.

At this time, February 1951, although I had landed there on several occasions in the past, the naval air station at Culdrose was new to me. I was a Yeovilton man – fighters – and Culdrose was home to the anti-submarine people. But for some reason, the Admiralty had decided to base 702 Squadron there, the Jet Conversion Unit, which seemed particularly inappropriate. However, politics were not my business. I was just pleased to be given the opportunity to convert.

It turned out to be very straightforward. Three dual flights in a Meteor followed by two solo, then twenty or so flights in the Vampire to complete the course. Nothing very complicated there, but I was jet qualified for the record and I now hoped to persuade the Boscombe chaps to loan me their modified Meteor for a few deck landings in the next trials period.

There were, however, several noticeable differences between operating a jet as opposed to the piston engine we had been used to for so many years. An upside was that engine management was simplified. Basically, there wasn't any. The pilot started the engine with outside electrical equipment, without the need to concern himself with priming carburettors of piston engines or Coffman starters, and then pretty well forgot about it – well, more or less. Oh, of course, the pilot still needed to monitor engine gauges, etc., but the modern high-performance piston engines had been gradually developed to operate efficiently at all altitudes, and this had meant the inclusion of two- or four-stage blowers and other refinements which occupied the attention of the pilot for much of the flight.

A downside was that fuel consumption could be embarrassingly high if flying at the incorrect altitude, particularly at low level. This meant that pilots and air controllers would need to pay much more attention to descent, circuit and landing procedures. Gone would be the days of all squadron aircraft descending into the landing pattern at the same time in the rat race of old. Now the tendency would be to spend as little time as possible in the circuit pattern, and in time, individually controlled approaches would be the norm regardless of weather conditions.

There were other idiosyncrasies of the jet engine, such as the somewhat slower acceleration during the early part of take-off, when the jet was at its most inefficient compared with modern piston engines such as the Centaurus and Griffon. In time, development of the jet engine would remedy this.

But there were two particular benefits with the introduction of jet-powered aircraft. The absence of a large and often long engine ahead of the pilot improved the forward view immeasurably; the cockpit was further forward and hence the approach and landing, particularly carrier landings, much simplified. There was a further and perhaps more important benefit. The absence of the need for ground clearance for the propeller(s) and the redistribution of the weight of the aircraft resulting from a further aft position of the engine, allowed the general introduction of a nosewheel configuration to replace the tailwheel. In turn the old 'bounce' tendency of many tailwheel aircraft was eliminated. The aircraft would now tend to pitch forward on landing instead of pitching up.

I said my farewells to the staff of 702, and would shortly be on my way. Len Jeyes had been my briefing officer and flown with me in the Meteor hops. He had a curious background for a naval aviator. Somehow, during the latter part of the war he had got involved with Special Operations during a detachment to the RAF. Arising from that he had converted to flying Westland Lysanders, and spent some time hopping across the Channel to land in remote areas of France and the Low Countries in support of SOE operations, dropping and picking up agents. He talked very little about it, but it must have been quite hazardous. He could never have been certain that these runs were not compromised; but he survived to return in due course to the Navy.

Leaving Culdrose behind me, I sallied forth to the Naval Air Fighter Development Unit at West Raynham near Norwich, beginning to feel a trifle nomadic – lacking roots. At NAFDU, Lt Cdr George Baldwin's unit was working up with the new naval Attacker fighter. George Baldwin's reputation went before him. One of the world's charmers, he'd had a brilliant war record and had looks good enough for a film star. I'd met him from time to time, and he now gave me a warm welcome. He also offered me free use of the unit's Vampire! So after a few days I shot off down to Lee to see a few friends, and then, at the end of the week, having completed the ADDLS training, I resumed my sporadic visits to my parent ship.

Illustrious was now out of dockyard hands and tied up at Plymouth, resplendent with a new coat of paint inside and out. She looked much better, and I was glad to be back on board for a few weeks. I liked Plymouth, or Guzz, as it was known in the Navy, and was able to sort out one or two old haunts. We had a lively gunroom in the ship, a trifle over full with trainee midshipmen from Dartmouth, but they were kept under some sort of control by Bruce Idiens, the Sub of the Gunroom. He and I were firm run-ashore partners, a relationship which had developed from our mutual interest in hockey, and in fact he had recently cajoled the Naval College at Dartmouth into offering us a fixture. We lost the match – Wings gave away too many penalties – but I think we won the social occasion.

I'm afraid our youthful spirits got the better of us during a run ashore later on. Bruce and I were unfortunate enough to meet a handful of midshipmen while we were out on the town one evening, having just availed ourselves of a little Italian and some excellent Chianti.

'Sir,' one of them said, 'we are just off to the Duke of Wellington (I think it was), would you take a drink with us?'

Well, I should have known that spelt trouble, but it seemed churlish to refuse, so I said to Bruce, 'Look, they are your charges, make sure they behave themselves.'

So we joined them for a convivial hour or so in the Duke. The Mids were as good as gold until it was time to go, when they felt they ought to leave their mark. Outside the pub were two barrels with nice brass bands, and it was one of these that attracted their attention. In microseconds the barrel was being rolled along the street and down towards the dockyard to the ship. Neither Bruce nor I could claim immunity; we had both been a party to the escapade – after the fact.

Back on board I felt obliged to confess all to the Commander, and added that I would be responsible for returning it the following day. He gave me a look that suggested I should have known better than get involved with midshipmen's pranks.

'Take the jeep first thing tomorrow and get it back', he said.

So I told Bruce to detail two of the midshipmen to come with the pair of us the following morning. In due course it was returned and we bowed low to the landlord, who took it very well. In fact, said he, 'When you next come in, have a drink on me, but please leave the barrel.'

They were harmless days, but not to everyone. On a quite separate and later occasion, enjoying a quiet pint in the same hostelry with Adam MacKinnon and one or two others, a number of Americans were there, a few of them showing signs of being a trifle rowdy. Nothing very much, but enough for the landlord to call them to order. Unfortunately the guilty few persisted and the landlord telephoned the American shore patrol office.

Within measurable time, two Army Patrol trucks parked outside and half a dozen patrolmen marched inside the bar, wielding truncheons, which they promptly, and indiscriminately, laid about any American uniform in sight. It was an unedifying sight, a brutal and typical example of American overkill. The transgressors and innocent were then bundled into the trucks outside, with the Patrol Chief apologising to the landlord. But neither I, nor those with me, were impressed by their sickening behaviour.

We had now reached the half-year point when annual trials and training were again upon us. I had a particular reason to look forward to the Boscombe trials and the prospect of deck landing again after quite an absence. There had been no real opportunity to deck land the Firefly. After all it was primarily the responsibility of the Ship's Flight pilot, Barbour, to carry out the general duties involving personnel and mail runs. Mine was to help run the flight deck and control the aircraft. But I felt a little frustrated at times and would remedy the deficiency as soon as practicable.

Meanwhile, and strangely in a way, I would now dive in at the deep end and deck land the Meteor, in which I had only three hours' flying time; and only half that solo, whereas I had accumulated a respectable twenty-five hours in the Firefly, mostly when detached ashore, but several flights from the ship and never an occasion to land back on.. Two solo flights in the Meteor was not accepted preparation to contemplate hurling oneself at the deck, but I knew the chaps at Boscombe would give me a decent run at ADDLS while I was there, and one or two of them had handled the 'bats' before.

So a week before the trials proper started, I manipulated a short period to work up with the navalised Meteor Mk III at Boscombe Down. I knew them all quite well by this time, and quite unofficially they had willingly agreed to assist with a few ADDLS sessions. Providing you have two good engines, the Meteor is a delight to fly and very straightforward; I did not anticipate any difficulty, and so it proved.

Meanwhile I had other responsibilities for the trials aircraft, which included the Vickers Supermarine Swift, a swept version of the Attacker and a derivative and contender for the RAF's new fighter programme. In some ways this was a departure for Boscombe trials, since it was primarily research into the use of swept-wing aircraft for carrier-borne aircraft, and as such would normally be the responsibility of the RAE at Farnborough.

However, there it was. Doug Parker was tasked with evaluating it, and it would prove a handful from his and everyone else's point of view. The landing speed was exceptionally high for deck landings; it had no refinements such as 'blown flaps' which would be introduced with the later generation of naval aircraft to reduce the approach speed, nor did the ship have the latest arrester gear equipment to absorb the higher entry speeds. In consequence, the wind speed over the deck would have to be of the order of 50 kts, and that entailed waiting for the day when we could anticipate a natural wind of over 20 kts.

From my point of view, I could imagine the difficulty of trying to hold my feet in 50 kts, let alone wield the bats. But we did. Standing on the after port turret with Harry holding onto me, I did my party piece for Doug Parker to do his. I am not sure any of us learnt very much from this exercise. The aircraft's control system and power response, while satisfactory for an aeroplane thrown together for research, was totally unsuited to the refinements required for deck landings. I don't think Doug paid too much attention to me; he had his hands full trying to get the aircraft onto the deck, but he completed fifteen landings without mishap.

The most hazardous part of the exercise was moving around on the flight deck, since if you were to lose you footing, there was a high probability of being blown over the side or, more likely, the stern! I remember saying to Doug afterwards, 'Next time you take the bats and I'll take a chance in the cockpit.'

The rest of the trials, which included the new Wyvern torpedo aircraft, went well enough, and in the middle of all this I achieved five deck landings in the Meteor, probably the easiest deck landings I had ever experienced, but it was useful to me to appreciate at first hand the greater anticipation required with the, then, sluggish response of the jet during the approach, compared with the piston engine. The refined and demanding affair of deck landing did not have the luxury of the latitude in touch-down point available with aerodrome landings.

A further week at Boscombe, and I was done with trials, since I would not be around when they next embarked. But they gave me a send-off present – a familiarisation flight in the Hawker Sea Fury, a relatively recent addition to the fleet, which I thought was a very nice gesture.

It was now nearly eighteen months since I joined *Illustrious*, and the time was nearing for another appointment. Where? I regarded myself as an experienced pilot, but where was it all taking me? I was qualified on most naval aircraft and a number of others. I had an Instructor's category which had given me the satisfaction of taking a batch of students from scratch through to 'wings'. In due course, perhaps a year or two, I would apply for the Empire Test Pilots course at Farnborough, but not yet. Besides, I would have to look carefully at the educational standards required.

So far I had coped with all that was demanded, but from talking to the Boscombe pilots I knew advanced mathematics, including calculus, and a high standard of physics were minimum requirements. The twelve months' study was said to equate to a post-graduate course, and I had barely scratched the surface at school for aspirations of that sort. But I consoled myself that in the last six or seven years I had recovered a lot of my earlier lost education and felt I could give a good account of myself. But first I had a job to do, here in *Illustrious*, for another six months. The future could take care of itself.

The remainder of 1951 was a mixed bag for *Illustrious*. Minor equipment trials and deck-landing training of new pilots gave way to a short deployment to the Mediterranean to participate in a fleet exercise, a welcome break after the sometimes dull routine in the Channel. The sailors in particular would appreciate the attractions of Main Street in Gibraltar and the more seedy bars across the border at La Linea in Spain, which offered rather more than the quiet and composed atmosphere of St Peter Port. And the 'Gut' in Malta was ready made for whatever took your fancy – and the sailors usually did! All harmless relief to the tedium of life aboard ship.

The fleet exercise, which included a number of foreign warships and aircraft, was not a great affair for us in *Illustrious*. We welcomed the more agreeable weather, of course, but I think we felt we were making up the numbers. However, it reminded us that we were first and foremost an operational warship, and exercise or no exercise, the ship's routine provided us with all the discomforts of a wartime footing, with general messing and darken ship at night, as well as doubling-up on watches. I flew interception and strike sorties as well as the mail run to the naval air station at Hal Far in Malta and to RAF North Front in Gibraltar. It kept my hand in and swelled my deck-landing count, but I cannot recall that the exercise itself made any great impact on any of us.

Then in November we sailed north for home waters, and I prepared to bid my farewells to this happy ship for my next challenge. I was to become an instructor at 767 Squadron, the Deck Landing School. Not a job I would have sought, perhaps, although it turned out well enough in time and stood me in good stead for the future.

I was very sad to be leaving my many friends in *Illustrious*; they would be missed. Wings gave me a well-above-average flying assessment, and from the report he gave me, he must have felt that we had all more than pulled our weight to maintain an exceptionally high standard in the primary function of the ship, the air department.

CHAPTER 11

Deck Landing School Chief Instructor

Towards the end of the year, after a short leave, I got off the train at Yeovil Junction to await transport to Yeovilton, the parent station for Henstridge. Since my last acquaintance with the squadron there had been little progress with facilities there, and we would continue to commute on a daily basis between the two. It was not an ideal arrangement with a number of buses having to make the nearly twenty-mile journey each way to transport maintenance and aircrew, which meant very early starts and long days.

But it was now that my previous twin-engine aircraft experience bore fruit. The squadron had been allocated a de Havilland Dominie to assist with the daily run between the two airfields, so my first task on joining was to formally qualify on type. No one else on the squadron could claim the distinction of twin qualification, and I therefore had the sole privilege of avoiding the tedious daily bus routine for as long as the current situation persisted.

Hardly had I dropped into the swing of the squadron's primary task when my past caught up with me again. The Captain at Yeovilton decided he wished to have more first-hand knowledge of flying. Unusually for an appointment to command a naval air station, Capt Paul had no aviation background, not as a pilot and not as an observer, and strangely, with only a few months left in his present job, he belatedly wished to rectify the situation; later on I would discover the reason. But now, having discovered there was a qualified flying instructor at 767, he asked the CO if I could be spared to give him a few lessons!

So for the next few months I would have a four-ring student. To some extent I had been hoist by my own petard. Only a matter of weeks after my arrival at Yeovilton, he had asked to be flown to Lee-on-Solent to attend a meeting with the Flag Officer. For some reason it fell to me. So come the day, strapping myself to the Dominie with him in the passenger seat immediately behind, we trundled down to Lee just after lunch, chatting away on the intercom. He knew I had been attached to 767 before, and now asked, 'What were you up to before that?' Innocently I confessed my time instructing new students at RAF Syerston – and that was to be my downfall! Perhaps I should have sensed his sudden interest. But it was a pleasant flight and I appreciated a friendly captain, and in due course I entered the circuit at Lee, landed and taxied over to a waiting car, in which he would be whisked off to his meeting.

It was mid-December 1951, usually dark by late afternoon, and the weather forecast at take-off from Yeovilton had not been particularly encouraging, so I hoped he wouldn't be too long for the return flight. With the dark gloom of winter descending ominously and the weather at Lee closing in, I got through to Yeovilton for their 'actual'.

'OK for the moment', I was told. 'But I wouldn't wait too long', advised the duty meteorology officer.

Capt Paul eventually returned, and I took off and made a rapid departure to the west just below an uncomfortably low cloud base. I had decided when I submitted my flight plan to opt for a VFR (visual flight rules) clearance, since I knew the area around the North Dorset Downs quite well, and with a relatively short flight in prospect it hardly warranted climbing laboriously through thick cloud to some unknown height.

The two Gipsy Major engines hardly gave an inspired rate of climb, and with cloud tops of around 6,000 to 8,000 ft I would have been calling for a QGH and descent as soon as I reached altitude. Then, before very long, the weather deteriorated and I was faced with the choice of staying visual, hoping the cloud base would not get any lower, or climbing above it with a very real chance that we would not be able to land at Yeovilton if the weather got below their limits. By this time Capt Paul was looking over my shoulder.

'Getting pretty grim, isn't it. Are we going to be able to make it?'

'It's OK, sir. I'm fairly familiar with the area', said I, feeling perhaps not quite as confident as I sounded.

With Sturminster Newton just to the north, I was now literally treetop hopping, and to complicate matters it started to rain. The cloud base was now down to about two hundred feet, and the visibility, despite the gallant efforts of the crude windscreen wiper, too low for comfort. My professional instinct told me to stop putting on the 'Ritz', admit defeat and climb out of it. If I climbed and we were unable to land at Yeovilton it would be inconvenient but otherwise of little consequence. I had a perfectly good diversion further north at Colerne, where the weather and landing aids were better.

But I was too proud to admit defeat and fail to get my passenger back to base, and confident in my ability and navigation and with only fifteen miles to base, I had done the worst part of the journey and was now over very familiar territory in the Henstridge area. Fortunately, shortly after pondering the situation, the radio, which had previously deserted me soon after clearing Lee, now gave contact with Yeovilton, where they advised a 300 ft cloud base, more than enough for the undemanding Dominie.

Shortly afterwards, I sighted the runway lights at my destination, and with my passenger visibly relieved, we touched down and cleared the runway. He had wanted more flying experience and I had provided him with an invaluable lesson on what to do, but perhaps not too often! And I told him so! That was his first flying lesson. He thanked me warmly later on in dispersal as I shut down, and much appreciated having avoided a long road journey from Colerne to Yeovilton.

Later, on reflection, I challenged my several decisions. Had I been foolhardy – imprudent? But no, I came to a resounding justification for my actions. At no time was I or the aircraft in harm's way. I always had a bolt-hole and was never out of my depth. It was part of my professional approach to flying to examine my reactions to the many difficult situations that came my way, and so it was now.

I would give him many more lessons in the future weeks, not in the Dominie, but in a Firefly Trainer. He never got further than handling the controls in the air at a safe height, and I was soon to discover the reason for his interest. On 1 May the squadron took part in a flypast over Yeovilton as part of a 'send-off' on his departure, not only as captain of the air station but also from the service.

A few days later his secretary sent me a batch of photographs of him and myself alongside the Firefly, with 'The compliments of Captain Paul' and the caption 'One for each of your girl friends!' and 'Thanks for the flying instruction which will be invaluable in the new civilian job' – he was joining Dowty, the aircraft firm!

Early in the New Year the refurbishment of accommodation at Henstridge was more or less completed, and we were able to transfer there permanently. It was far from luxurious: a collection of wartime Nissen huts, but infinitely preferable to the daily commuting run. It was a curious existence really. We ran a piece of Admiralty real estate solely to turn out Deck Landing Control Officers and retrain pilots who had failed with their deck landings at the completion of Operational Flying School.

Away from the more formal regimented and busy activity of Yeovilton, we settled in to a life in the country, very much our own masters, enjoying the atmosphere of a private flying club. There was no one else using the airfield to disturb our routine We were a relatively small outfit, fourteen or so aircraft, the CO and Senior Pilot plus the two instructors and four to six other pilots, so-called 'clockwork mice' who would take the lion's share of the 'mousing': their job was to fly the circuits and approaches under the guidance of the instructors to train the new 'batsmen'.

The squadron owned two slightly ancient motor cars, or, to be more exact, one was owned by 'Uncle' Bill Hawley, the senior instructor, and the other by one of the mice – Ted Pepper. Amazingly they were identical except for the colour of the leather seating. BSA saloons, vintage 1934, Wilson gearbox and fluid flywheel drive, luxuriously appointed interiors with thick pile carpet and silk handholds for the passengers. All very much in the 'Daimler fashion' from which they were derived. Old they may have been, but they provided the sole means of transport to the 'locals', and their reliability was assured by the care and attention of the local garage owner – or rather his son, about our age, a racing fanatic and mechanic *extraordinaire*. He lavished his care and skill on the two cars, making small parts where necessary, and rarely charged for his time. He became our first honorary member of the mess, a very sound investment

Not long afterwards I became the proud owner of my first car. Ted Pepper had become slightly short of funds and decided to realise some hard cash from his various assets, including his car. So I bought it for £100 on the never-never, since my finances were not all that great, either, and I was under a little pressure from Mr Gieves, the tailor, who 'wondered if it would be possible to make a small increase in my monthly allotments since my purchases were exceeding my monthly contributions'. Regrettably I had to reject his suggestion, but promised to review it in a few months! All very gentlemanly and friendly, such was the relationship between Gieves and his much-valued naval officer customers.

Not all creditors were as understanding as Mr Gieves. I recall the instance when a friend of mine was approached by his bank manager in terms of 'I am obliged to write to you, Mr Theobold, to ask if you would consider increasing your monthly repayments since your overdraft has now reached alarming proportions.' Somewhat incensed by this undignified commercial attitude, my friend, Lt Theobold, a somewhat eccentric character with a touch of South African in his family background, replied in the strongest terms explaining his system for financial control. 'It is my habit', he said, 'at the end of each month to place all my bills and overdrawn accounts into a pack which I then shuffle in the manner of playing-cards. Having given them a good shuffle,' he continued, 'I then cut the pack, and whosoever turns out to be the lucky one, I pay that month.' He hoped the bank manager would understand his system, but added, 'Should I get any more unpleasant letters demanding money, I shall simply exclude the bank account in future shuffles and transfer my business elsewhere.' This brought the immediate response, 'If only you would, Mr Theobold!'

But back to my recent purchase. My financial arrangement with Ted was, to say the least, somewhat loose. We agreed £25 a month – if I could afford it; if not, whatever I could spare at the end of the month. It turned out to be an amicable if protracted arrangement, and he would have been reappointed to Lossiemouth before the final settlement was made.

About the time of our permanent move to Hestridge the squadron received its first batch of Sea Furies to replace the ageing Seafires, and so now, every two months, we would receive a new course of aspiring Landing Signal Officers (formerly Deck Landing Control Officers) for six weeks' training ashore, to be followed by one week embarked in a carrier. My number of deck landings fairly rattled up, and by the end of my time with 767 Squadron I would have completed well over four hundred arrested deck landings, not counting the hundreds of 'touch and go' landings, which at times we found expedient to speed up the training.

To train new LSOs, we would deliberately introduce errors during the approach to the deck to check their reaction, but such was the expertise of the squadron pilots and instructors that any one of us could land safely without the aid of the batsman. Just as well, perhaps, because there arose an occasion during which I was supervising a trainee batsman when I needed to prompt him in the latter stages of the approach. He was more than a trifle hard of hearing and obviously hadn't picked up what I said. Undaunted, from giving the 'Roger' with both bats at arm's length horizontally, indicating all was well, he quite suddenly turned towards me with a quizzical look, and then, still committed to controlling the incoming aircraft, to my horror he put one bat to his left ear to hear what I was saying!

'What the hell was that signal?' said the pilot on landing, and I had to explain his difficulty in hearing.

'Well,' said the intrepid pilot, 'he shouldn't spend so much time in the night-clubs in London.'

The aspiring LSO in question was a well-known honky-tonk piano player, not only around the bazaars at naval air stations, and a very good one at that, but also in the better establishments up in the smoke in London; the Navy seemed to produce some very good piano players. We eventually passed him as proficient on the strict understanding that he wore a hearing-aid.

Shortly after this embarked period in HMS *Triumph*, we would have only a brief period ashore before returning again, this time to participate in a fleet exercise. Relatively recently, member nations of NATO had planned to hold a biannual large-scale exercise, an undertaking fraught with problems, not least with the French, who resented the dominating influence of the Americans, ignoring the fact that the preponderance of forces taking part would be from the USA. Anyway, despite initial difficulties and the sheer magnitude of the effort required to get together hundreds of warships and large numbers of maritime aircraft, 1952 was to see the largest assembly of ships and aircraft yet to take part in a NATO exercise to be held in the North Atlantic. The exercise was codenamed Mainbrace.

The British contribution was to include four aircraft carriers supported by numerous escort vessels and a number of submarines. There would also be participation by the Royal Air Force with long-range bombers and Coastal Command surveillance aircraft. HMS *Triumph* was to be one of the carriers taking part, and since she did not carry her own air group, we in 767 Squadron were assigned to her with fighters and anti-submarine aircraft. The exercise lasted ten days and was held in some of the foulest weather I have ever encountered at sea. *Triumph* was in CARGP2, consisting of two British carriers, two American and one Dutch, with the First Group, CARGP1 of three carriers, some distance away.

The exercise started well despite some communication difficulties, but by the third day, the weather and horrendous seas had begun to take its toll to limit the exercise programme. By mid-afternoon two of the carriers had ceased flying because of the state of their decks, which by this time were pitching and rolling alarmingly. *Triumph* had an advantage. She had on board the most experienced deck-landing crews, and we were reasonably content to continue flying for the time being, but then the third carrier stopped flying operations and we were left on our own.

It was late afternoon and I had been in the air in a Sea Fury on combat air patrol for just short of an hour when I heard the ship recall the two Fireflys on AS duty, the only other aircraft still airborne apart from myself. I then waited for my own recall for ten minutes or so, and then called the ship for the state of the deck. 'Not good,' they said, 'we are trying to find an improvement to the south.' With no diversion available this was ominous. The Fireflys had just scraped on board, but the ship movement had worsened and the deck was now pitching irregularly through twenty to thirty feet.

Another fifteen minutes, and the decision was made for me. I was now at the state where my fuel would allow the descent and one missed approach and overshoot if need be, and landing. So I called the ship and declared 'Bingo' (down to minimum fuel for deck operations), and they promptly turned into wind to receive me. Turning downwind, a vicious-looking sea below me, I could now see *Triumph* battling her way through waves and troughs, pitching and rolling beyond anything I had experienced before. I had one consolation. Bill Hawley would be batting me on and we also had voice contact with each other, a recent innovation we had developed, so he would be able to give me some indication of the rate of pitching movement.

On the final approach, from Bill's commentary, I tried to assess the frequency of the pitching stern. I needed to arrive just as the deck started to move downwards, and Bill would know this. What I didn't want was the deck to come up from its lowest point and hit me as I was about to touch down. I would also aim to land further up the deck, where the extent of the movement was minimised. It was now decision time. I arrived over the round-down, Bill signalling to continue, and we had it right. The deck had just reached its highest point, and I followed it down, hooked number four wire and stopped, very relieved.

Back on board, I unstrapped, got out of the cockpit and looked aft. Good grief, I thought, how did we manage it? One moment the stern was pointing to the sky and the next there was nothing but the raging sea to be seen. This was the last flying in the fleet that day.

In the autumn of 1952, the squadron was to move to its new base at Stretton, near Warrington in Lancashire. It was not a popular move, but Henstridge was to close down, surplus to requirements, and Stretton, then a base for the resident RNVR squadron, was grossly under-utilised. So with the Squadron Movement Order completed, stores and equipment loaded for transport by road and special train, Bill Hawley and I decided to take a leisurely train journey up north via London, and let the 'mice' fly the aircraft to Stretton. By the time we had tidied up things at Henstridge, and seen aircraft and ground party in the trucks on their way, it was late afternoon when we caught the train from Templecombe.

Arriving in London, we hailed a taxi. 'We want a nice quiet inexpensive hotel near the station to Warrington', Uncle Bill directed the cabbie. 'No problem, Guv, I know just the place.' And good as his word, he took us to a pleasant two-star hotel within walking distance of the station north.

It was September, and we entered the hotel to the sound of the opening overture to the Last Night of the Proms playing on the radio in the hotel lounge, where a large log fire welcomed us. We were both quite tired by this time, having started the day just after four o'clock in the morning, so ordered beer and sandwiches and settled back for the next few hours listening to the most memorable Last Night of the Proms that I can recall. Perhaps it was the long day or the atmosphere in this comfortable hotel, but the orchestra's performance and excellent programme, with all the typical fanfare of the 'Last Night', had a special touch about it. Regrettably, Bill would leave the squadron within a few weeks and I would replace him as chief instructor, with 'Tiny' (all of six feet three inches) Bowen, whom I had known from *Theseus/Glory* days, to assist me. The rotund frame of the one was to be replaced by the matchstick proportions of the other.

On arrival at Stretton, to my great pleasure I discovered that the Staff Officer to the RNVR squadron was none other than my old friend from *Illustrious*, Harry Burman. The Captain was one named Courage, a director of that well-known brewery, whose party trick was to feed unsuspecting young officers a little of the company's special directors' brew. To be fair, he gave you pre-warning – it was necessary – and he only served it in champagne flutes, which initially seemed a trifle stingy. But he was a fine host and regularly entertained the younger officers to lunch or dinner in his quarters.

The squadron was now to add the Attacker to its complement of aircraft, the first to arrive early in the New Year. That was fine by me. I had flown jet aircraft on two separate occasions before, at CFS and during my time at *Illustrious*, but such was the mystique of jets held by the Naval Higher

Command that, notwithstanding, I would have to do a refresher course which would last a week.

So in December, I got a lift down to Culdrose to complete a totally unnecessary week, flying twelve hours in the Vampire and Meteor, no matter that I was one of the very few to have actually deck landed the Meteor more than twelve months previously! The squadron would also need to have at least one other pilot jet trained. At that time I was the only one with any previous experience, and my tour of duty in the squadron was nearing the end, so two other pilots were nominated to complete the full jet course of one month, and they would arrive at Culdrose at the same time.

With my week's refresher almost completed, I had just landed from a Meteor sortie when there was a telephone call for me in the crew room: would I please go immediately to Commander Air's office. Almost simultaneously, there was a clatter of alarm bells across the airfield and I feared the worst. I was right: one of the two lieutenants from my squadron flying a Meteor had got into difficulties on the downwind leg in the circuit, when, apparently simulating an engine failure, he had gone straight into the ground from a thousand feet.

The Meteor was a difficult aircraft on one engine, the rudder control being just sufficient provided you kept the speed up and were very careful when lowering the undercarriage. This was a bitter blow. He had been with us in 767 Squadron for over six months, was well liked and had developed into a very capable 'mouse'. His loss was to have a marked effect on his counterpart and somewhat younger pilot on the course. They were extremely good friends and had been in a front-line squadron together before joining us.

I was now instructed to secure his cabin prior to taking an inventory of his belongings as soon as the immediate formalities had been completed. It was an onerous duty to go through a chap's personal effects, sifting out those things which it would be inappropriate to pass on to the next of kin, but the following day I embarked on this unpleasant duty, which fortunately, because of the short detachment for the pair of them, did not take a great deal of time. A similar procedure would take place back at Stretton for the rest of his belongings. That completed, I now prepared to return to Stretton in slow time by train rather than request an air lift. But I felt much compassion for the young squadron pilot I would leave behind, and gave him a few words of encouragement before I left.

Back at Stretton I lost no time in familiarising myself with the Attacker, the first of which arrived in mid-January. The Attacker was very much a stop-gap jet aircraft, whose usefulness was little more than the introduction of jet aircraft operations to the fleet. It was not a great aeroplane, having been derived in part from other types. For example, it employed a laminar-flow wing developed and produced for the Supermarine Spiteful, itself a development of the Spitfire. Around this time there was a proliferation of designs coming off the drawing-boards, most concentrating on swept-wing aircraft, but it would be some time before arrester gear and catapults in ships could accommodate the higher speeds associated with these aircraft. Thus the Attacker was stuck with a straight wing and a new fuselage which housed the Nene engine. For some reason the designer decided on a tailwheel configuration which made it difficult to manoeuvre on the ground without excessive use of the engine to swing the tail, unlike the piston-engine aircraft, where the slipstream from the propeller made the rudder immediately effective.

Despite its shortcomings, it proved a useful addition to the squadron in teaching *ab initio* control officers to appreciate the higher approach speed and flatter attitude during the approach, and it also gave us a nice toy to demonstrate on Air Days. Somewhat misguidedly, at the request of the Flag Officer Air (Home), I flew it to a USAAF base at Bentwaters for their Air Day in mid-1953. They thought it was a 'Wow', a 'Honey', and could scarcely conceal their admiration that the 'Brits' could make something like that fly. They were at that time considerably more advanced with their F86 Sabres, and their Navy was already operating swept-wing aircraft aboard its carriers. However, I like to think I gave them a demonstration which offset the difference a little.

The squadron seemed to be much in demand to take part in Air Days across the country, and we had a Sea Fury rigged up with RATOG (Rocket-Assisted Take-Off Gear) to provide a fairly impressive spectacle on these occasions. It would fairly leap into the air after the shortest of runs.

The SSAFA (Soldiers, Sailors & Air Force Association) authorities at Yeadon, Leeds, were unwise enough to request our participation in their Air Day at the end of May, and not being familiar with the state of their airfield, we proposed a rocket-assisted take-off followed by an aerobatic display, which they accepted. I arrived in my Sea Fury in the morning, together with

127

a Firefly flown by the CO and another pilot who had come up to watch events for the day. We had lunch and got into conversation with a Major Draper, a First World War Royal Flying Corps pilot of some renown, who related to us how he had recently been admonished and fined by the Stipendiary Magistrate in some borough or other in London for flying under Tower Bridge. He was at that time 72 years of age!

Shortly after lunch, and following the usual Air Display briefings about not flying too low or over the spectators, it came my turn in the afternoon programme, and I started up, taxied to the end of the runway and requested permission to take off. 'Clear for demonstration take-off' came back from the tower, but they could not have known what was in store, otherwise they might have had second thoughts. So might I! In standard fashion, I opened the throttle on the brakes until they began to slide, rolled forward about twenty yards and, with the stick hard back, activated the rocket gear. Swoosh, we leapt into the air at a nice steep angle and I thought, 'That's the best yet', very pleased with myself.

No sooner had I raised the flaps and undercarriage and prepared for the aerobatic stage of the demonstration than from the tower came an anguished voice complaining about the mess I had made of their runway! The rockets, slanted downwards from the aircraft, had fairly pulverised their Second World War runway surface. Anyway, I carried on as planned, and subsequently landed on what was left of the runway. They were right; it was not a pretty sight. Apparently, as soon as the rockets fired, some two inches of the tar macadam surface had simply rolled up behind me over a stretch of thirty feet and more. After this experience, we were careful to establish the condition of the runway surface before accepting further requests.

We had not been at Stretton very long when, in the wardroom one evening, I noticed a strange face at the bar, someone I hadn't seen in the mess before. There were not a great many officers there, and one tended to know everyone else, so I asked the barman who he was.

'That's Mr Booth, sir,' he answered, 'he often comes in with the Captain.'

So I wandered over to introduce myself. It transpired that he was an honorary member of the wardroom mess and lived a few miles away. Before he departed I learnt that he owned and was managing director of a fairly large company, which was clearly very profitable, judging by the new Bentley outside, and that he owned a large house with a tennis court.

'Do do you play?' he asked, and thus was the beginning of a close friendship for the remainder of my time at Stretton.

He would ring the mess to invite me to this or that tennis party with his wife Julie, and frequently with another pair, Bill and Helen Cherry. Helen was a well-known actress at that time, and both she and her husband were extremely good company.

Not long before I was due to leave for my next appointment, John rang me one Wednesday evening to join them the following day for tennis and dinner afterwards.

'Sorry,' said I, 'but I have work to do on my car before going on weekend leave.'

'What's the problem?' he asked. So I told him I had the cylinder head off and was fitting a new gasket. This was a fairly regular operation with my BSA; the engine was getting on a bit and there was always something that needed to be fixed.

'Now look,' he said, 'I'll send one of my chaps round tomorrow morning, I'm sure he will be able to fix it.'

He was as good as his word, and his 'chap', who it turned out was a skilled motor mechanic, arrived the following morning. He disappeared to obtain a new gasket, instead of botching up the old one, which – in my impecunious state – I was prone to do, and I disappeared later that day to be entertained. John was a very generous person and was very keen to show his appreciation at being elected an honorary member. He would frequently take one or two of us to one of the many pubs in the area for a quiet pint or two, and it was on such an occasion that I noticed something different about his car.

'John,' I said, 'you've changed your car, the leather seats were green before.'

'Ah,' he said, 'Julie didn't like the colour. Anyway it was nearly a year old.' He said this without boastfulness, but for the owner of a nearly twenty-year-old hack it beggared belief! I would keep in touch with this very nice couple for a long time after I left the area.

CHAPTER 12

HMS *Rocket* – 3rd Training Squadron

I had by now been forewarned of my next appointment and after a farewell party and presentation of a 'Mouse' tankard I left the Squadron to join the Anti-Submarine Frigate HMS *Rocket* in Londonderry to earn my full watch-keeping certificate and gain small ship experience. It was a sharp jolt to the system to go from a responsible flying job to being a 'green' member of the ship's company under training. But I was made very welcome, given the task of running the 'Boys' division and made deputy fo'castle officer, as well as running the wardroom bar to relieve the First Lieutenant, who was the previous incumbent of this task. My predecessor was 'Winkle' Brown, whom I did not know but whose reputation went before him. He had left the ship prior to my arrival.

HMS *Rocket*, a Type 15 A/S Frigate, converted from a fleet destroyer and capable of over 30 knots, she was equipped with the latest A/S weapon, two Limbo 3-barrelled DC Mortars. By the standards of the day she was an effective submarine hunter. We would spend five days at sea each week 'playing' with submarines and A/S aircraft from the nearby RAF station and after each exercise, would 'wash up' in the nearby shore HQ to discuss tactics. It was exhilarating and great fun and, for a 'new boy', very instructive. My only previous experience of small ships had been a week in HMS *Cockade*, in the Far East, when she had been attached to HMS *Theseus* as Guard Ship, but I had never been to sea in a submarine. This I now rectified and spent two days in one of the submarines attached to 3rd TS to experience the A/S world from the other side. Not for me, was my conclusion and my admiration for submariners rose considerably. They were a very happy bunch, lived in tight cramped quarters to work and sleep, and I learnt that when the exercises were closed on a Friday and the surface ships returned to port at high speed around late afternoon, the poor wretched submarines would be lucky to make port by seven or eight o'clock in the evening. By the same token, it meant that they would sail long before us each day to reach the exercise area.

I was to serve six months in *Rocket*, had been allowed a good deal of latitude in running various parts of the ship, learnt a lot and left with considerable regret. I had made many friends in the Squadron and at the Headquarters in Londonderry And so come the day of departure, after an extended liquid lunch at the nearby hotel – arranged without my knowledge – my departure by train from the station was quite a noisy affair. At that time I think I could have been persuaded to transfer my loyalties to general duties in ships rather than return to aviation, but the pull of my next appointment to the Empire Test Pilots School was too strong. Nevertheless it was a close run thing and who knows what the outcome might have been.

CHAPTER 13

Empire Test Pilots School

In mid-February, after a short period of leave, I drove my rather ancient motor car to the Royal Aircraft Establishment at Farnborough to join No. 13 Empire Test Pilots Course, one of five Royal Navy officers on a course of about thirty. There were students from the US Air Force and Navy, Australian Navy and Air Force, Canada, France, Italy, one of whom was the chief test pilot of the Italian aircraft manufacturer Fiat, and an Air Force officer from Thailand.

The chief test pilot of Fiat, Captain Bignamini, was an ex-Italian Air Force pilot who had served in the Second World War, spoke excellent English and was highly intelligent. He was always streets ahead of the lectures but never demonstrated any condescending attitude, listened carefully to note any differences in thinking between what was being taught and what he already knew. As a pilot he was probably about good or high average. During the war he had been shot down by a British aircraft off the Italian coast and parachuted to safety, subsequently to be picked up by an Italian vessel.

His Italian counterpart on the course, Trevisan, was a serving Italian Air Force officer of great charm. He was also an excellent pilot, and despite some language difficulty with some of the more technical expressions in the lectures, he overcame this by post-lecture discussion with other students. This was a high-powered course in every respect, both in the quality of the students and in the curriculum, which most of us would find very demanding, not only from the flying aspect but from the ground instruction, since it reached the highest levels of aerodynamics and other sciences. Even the most erudite of the students found some of the lectures difficult to hoist in, and would question whether the depth to which we were being subjected was really necessary

The staff, headed by a Group Captain, had long pedigrees in the world of aviation, and only the best scientists from the Royal Aircraft Establishment were appointed to the ground instructional staff to provide the students with the necessary background for the future work they would undertake. The students were regarded as the 'cream' from their various services, all well-above-average pilots with the ability to assimilate, translate and relate performance and stability results in the demanding world of the test pilot. At Patuxent River in the United States, where the US Navy conducted its own Test Pilots course, the sign above the entrance to its college read, 'Through These Portals Pass the Best Pilots in The World'. Of course, we wouldn't go along with that, but as with its Air Force counterpart, it ran a good second! We didn't need a sign. ETPS was rightly regarded as not only the oldest of its kind but simply the best.

The course was divided into syndicates of six to eight, with half attending morning lectures while the other half flew one or other of the numerous aircraft in the school's stable. They ranged from the humble Chipmunk trainer through several jets to the larger Valetta and Varsity and Hastings aircraft. They were all invaluable in demonstrating the various characteristics which we were required to report upon in simulated tests. Tests ranged from an evaluation of take-off and landing performance, through stalling and spinning and a variety of the more complicated evaluations to establish such things as stick force per 'g', manoeuvre boundaries (limits to which the aircraft could be put before it became unflyable), critical Mach number, asymmetric limits and many other tests which we might be called upon to make in our future jobs.

During the course I had my first experience of flying four-engined aircraft and several uncommon ones, such as a German Fieseler Storch, a high-wing monoplane which one could land on a sixpence and was used by Goering during the war, and another unusual one called the Bobsleigh, which was fitted with a sort of bed in the nose of the aircraft to evaluate the benefits to the pilot of flying in a prone position – more of this later. Then towards the end of the course all students were introduced to helicopters, although time did not permit qualification to solo standard.

Quite early on I found myself struggling with some of the lectures dealing with the more technical aspects of aerodynamics, where much of the scientific analysis required the application of calculus for resolution to determine rates of change and so forth. The dYs and dXs left me cold. I had not studied calculus at school, had little idea of its function and had to correct this fast. So through virtue of a friend of an aunt who was a mathematics lecturer at Bristol University I learnt enough to have an understanding and be able to apply it during the calculations we would make.

From then on it was plain sailing, if very intensive work. My cabin was between Nigel Ducker, Royal Navy as myself, and Tony Blackmore, an Air Force flight lieutenant, and between us we spent many hours burning the midnight oil. Tony had the advantage over us two Navy chaps. He was a university graduate with a Masters degree, struggled rather less than we did and was helpful during these long evenings. Later, on leaving the RAF, he was to become chief test pilot on the development of V Bombers at BAC.

Another student, Ivan Kincheloe, an American Air Force pilot of outstanding ability, had already been selected, on finishing the course, to join the X15 programme, the forerunner to the Space Program at Edwards Air Force Base. During his time at Farnborough, he bought two cars – a London taxi and a Vauxhall 16/98 which had in its lifetime raced at Le Mans. He spent vast sums having it restored to pristine condition – even to the extent of sending the wheels to a specialist to have them rechromed. On completion it was a splendid machine. The London taxi was bought with a different purpose: he wanted to drive it round New York honking the old-fashioned rubber trumpet-type horn on the outside, just to observe the reaction.

Coming up towards the end of the course, the Americans got wind of the arrival in London of the Harlem Globetrotters, who were doing a European tour and were to perform an exhibition of their incredible talent at Olympia. Irresistible to the Americans, of course, and Kinch offered to drive four of us to London in his 'taxi' to see them. Unfortunately, in parking in a narrow space with full lock on, he forgot that in these circumstances the back end went pretty well sideways, and to his great embarrassment, he damaged the mudguard and bumper! It was with considerable regret that we learnt later on that he had been killed in a flying accident in a F-104 which was used for continuity training but unrelated to the test programme.

About this time I decided that my much-loved and cared-for BSA saloon did not quite reach the image of a budding test pilot, and I started to look around for an alternative. I was now on maximum pay for a lieutenant, and a little more affluent, so my horizons were wider than when I had bought it – not much, but enough to make a difference. In the course of a weekend leave, I came across an advert in the local paper; a 1938 1.5-litre SS Jaguar was being offered by a garage off Blackboy Hill in Bristol, so I promptly paid said garage a visit and immediately bought it. I think it cost me about

£300 with the trade-in, and although 16 years old, it had been carefully restored and was in splendid condition. Thick, comfortable, green leather seats, walnut facia and trim round the doors, recently resprayed metallic silver with aluminium-coated spoke wheels, large silver headlights at the end of a long bonnet, it looked and felt what it was, a classic of its time. In due course I drove it back to Farnborough with some pride, and it would remain a treasured possession for some years.

The course was of eleven months' duration, which gave us the opportunity for numerous visits to industry, mainly those involved in aircraft or equipment development. They were always great occasions, with the various firms bending over backwards to 'sell' themselves, knowing that a number of us would be involved later on in their products, and would have some influence in decision making. Their hospitality was lavish, ranging from hired passenger boats on the Thames for drinks and dinner to the very best of fare at five-star hotels, where we would stay overnight.

Their conducted tours were always carefully arranged, and in some cases ended with their vintage aircraft being brought out for us to fly. This was great fun and much appreciated. It was also an expression of confidence in the course students since in every case these aircraft were unique: the Hawker Hart, Hurricane and Miles Whitney Straight from Hawkers, for instance, and the Fairey Junior at White Waltham out of the Fairey Aviation Company stable. To our credit none were broken or damaged, and I know of no occasion when these firms' trust in the standard of ETPS pilots on the many courses they entertained ever resulted in an accident.

The course concluded with each student having to conduct a 'preview' of a particular aircraft, much in the manner of assessing its acceptance for service use from the manufacturer. This was an extensive evaluation requiring five or more flights with a full report on each phase of the assessment. In effect it was the summation of all that we had learnt, and the pilots were supported by the scientific staff. My allotted mount was the Vampire V, which I put through the full test programme including stalls and spins, low speed and high Mach number performance, and so on. The final report would amount to twenty and more pages.

With all this behind us we prepared for the Graduation 'McKenna' Dinner for which ETPS was noted throughout the aviation industry. All the major firms' test pilots and many of the chief designers would attend, together with VIPs from the services and elsewhere. It was a very extravagant affair and invariably ended in the small hours with outrageous games in the officers' mess anteroom, but it was a fitting end to a great course, both academically and socially. The following day we would be presented with our highly valued diplomas and go our separate ways.

Graduation from the Test Pilots course gave the qualification 'tp', a highly regarded distinction that was added to the 'QFI' alongside my name in the Navy List. I would now go on leave in unusual circumstances, not knowing for how long. I had been earmarked for duty at Farnborough, but the Group Captain there, an unpleasant self-opinionated man, had little time for the Royal Navy and had vetoed any increase in the number of naval test pilots at RAE. There were two there at that time. Thus I was in limbo – or would have been had it not been for the interjection of Adm Sir Casper John, who had attended the McKenna Dinner.

During the course of the evening he had called me over and said, 'You will be going to RAE but we have to get rid of that b——y group captain there first. He doesn't want any more dark blue jobs in his establishment.'

Strong words about a senior Air Force officer to a more junior naval one. 'Don't worry,' he went on, 'I'll fix it. I'll have a word with my opposite number, Air Marshal Thomas, to give him the push.'

I never doubted the outcome, but I was surprised at the speed at which it happened. Casper John, then the Fifth Sea Lord, later the First Sea Lord, was not only very influential, he could charm anybody; and so he did. I received a telephone call shortly after going home for Christmas leave, confirming my appointment to RAE Farnborough. Gp Capt 'Snodgrass' was on his way in the first week of January, and I arrived two days later!

He was replaced by Gp Capt McKinley, who had been part of the post-war 'Aries' series of polar navigational flights in the Lancastrian, a converted Avro Lancaster. He was an outstanding officer in every way, and one with whom I would get on very well indeed. His house was open house on a Sunday after church, when he and his wife, an absolute charmer, would invariably invite any number of us for drinks. With his arrival, the spirit in the Experimental Flying Department rose considerably.

CHAPTER 14

Experimental Flying Department, RAE Farnborough and Bedford

RAE Farnborough

The Experimental Flying Department consisted of a number of separate flight organisations, each supporting the Research Departments, Aerodynamics, Structures, Radio, Met, Weapons and Naval Air. I was appointed firstly to the Naval Air Department but also to Radio Flight, which I joined with Flt Lt John Walker from the Test Pilots course. We would become very good friends, and later on I would be his best man at his wedding.

The Naval Department, commonly known as NAD, was the centre of all development involved with getting aircraft on and off ships, specialising in catapult and arrester gear design and any equipment associated with this activity. It had in its time been the forerunner of new techniques, steam catapults and much improved hydraulic arrester gear, and was currently involved in water spray gear for use at airfields, as well as aircraft carriers, the angled deck, and various devices to assist the pilot, such as the mirror sight and projector sight to replace the Landing Signal Officer. The scientists and engineers in NAD were dedicated people who tended to spend the better part of their careers in advancing ship/aircraft operation and compatibility. Their knowledge was invaluable.

Straightaway I inherited a 'nasty'. The Westland Wyvern, which had recently entered front-line squadron service, was experiencing an increasing number of engine failures at the end of the catapult launch during operations at sea, and as a result all catapult launches had been suspended until the fault could be found. This rendered the aircraft less than useful in its role, and understandably, the Admiralty had demanded the highest priority to resolving the problem.

My only experience of the Wyvern was a couple of months previously when I had scrounged a short flight while on the Test Pilots course. So I immediately set to work to fully familiarise myself with the aircraft, and more particularly the Python engine, an eight-bladed contra-rotating turboprop engine, a product from Armstrong Siddeley. The Wyvern had had a chequered start in life, requiring numerous aerodynamic modifications as well as prolonged development to achieve satisfactory engine/propeller/throttle response before it was accepted into the fleet. I made one handling flight, which included delivering the aircraft to Westland at Merrifield, followed by an air test and a short flight on another aircraft before getting to work on the catapult programme.

NAD was an unimpressive collection of buildings, which, with the adjacent hydraulic catapult and other bits of machinery, reminded me of a dockyard facility. Farnborough was still, at this time, the working location of NAD, but it was due to reduce to care and maintenance within the year, when all work, technical and flying, would be transferred to the RAE Bedford. Meanwhile there were still a number of outstanding test programmes to be undertaken, with the ageing BH4 catapult and the now obsolescent Mk 9 arrester gear with the Wyvern our first priority.

So early in January we embarked on a programme of investigation into the problems that had beset the Wyvern at sea. The most likely cause of engine failure had been traced to fuel starvation resulting from the effects of 'g' on the catapult, pointing to a malfunctioning of the recuperator, a system designed specifically to compensate for this very condition by supplying fuel from an auxiliary tank under air pressure when the 'g' effects interrupted the normal fuel flow.

This was clearly a high-risk flight test programme. The catapult was on a slightly raised platform and pointed directly down the 'Naval Runway', a short run of less than one thousand yards: all yesterday's technology for today's much faster aeroplanes, recognised by the much improved facilities shortly to be available at Bedford. But for the present it would have to do.

The test programme envisaged a series of launches, commencing at a lowish catapult end speed, gradually increasing in increments of ten knots to ascertain engine and fuel flow data, up to the normal carrier operating conditions. Thus could be determined the point at which the recuperator was unable to cope. We would then repeat the same conditions with another aircraft fitted with an improved recuperator which we hoped would prove the technical analysis and allow the engine to perform normally.

Quite early on it became apparent that the original recuperator was subject to malfunctioning at relatively low catapult 'g' forces, so we abandoned these tests and concentrated on the aircraft with the modified system. We hoped that there would be no engine failure, but as a safety precaution it was thought prudent for the pilot to make no attempt to get airborne but to terminate every launch by hooking the arrester wire about two-thirds down the short runway.

This all seemed straightforward. The aircraft was fully instrumented and each launch would be recorded and subject to later analysis. So far as I was concerned I would configure the aircraft for a normal launch, apply full power against the hold-back unit in the usual way, get shot off and then, as quickly as possible, close the throttle to 'Flight Idle', then to 'Ground Idle' and then lower the hook, but leaving it as late as possible to avoid undue wear on the crown before entering the arrester wire, all the time ensuring that the aircraft maintained a straight approach after launch to the centre of the wire. I anticipated no problem with this procedure at the lower speeds, but plainly, with the final higher end speeds, the time interval before arriving at the wire would be critical.

So with the two scientists/engineers, John Noble and Normal Holey, monitoring events, we set about the first day's programme. After three launches with the unmodified aircraft, we abandoned it for the rest of the trial and concentrated on the results with the aircraft and the larger recuperator. All plain sailing; the 'g' forces were well short of normal operating requirements, but we had made an encouraging start, and the handling of the aircraft into the arrester gear was no problem.

The following day was a repeat of the first, with progressively higher speeds. I had been working a little harder to manage the engine and get the hook down, but we were still short of the optimum conditions. So in order to make more rapid progress we agreed that we would increase end speeds by larger increments for the six launches planned for the third day, This would take us to the required ten per cent margin beyond normal ship operating clearance requirements

On the third day an unfavourable wind put it thirty degrees to starboard of the launch line. Unlike a carrier, we would have to live with that, but it meant an effective reduction in the 'wind on the head' that would have to be compensated for by increasing the catapult performance. It also introduced some control problems since the aircraft would tend to yaw markedly into wind immediately on leaving the catapult. I could have done without that, since the increased workload arising from the higher end speeds was calculated to be enough to cope with as it was.

However, we got off to a good start with the first two launches and were now not far short of the clearance requirements. The analysis of the results during the lunch break showed no malfunctioning of the fuel systems or the engine, which was encouraging. But from my point of view the time/distance gap was becoming critical, and for the short period from launch to arrest I had been working like the proverbial one-armed paperhanger! I had calculated that given a distance to run to the wire of approximately 300 yards and an end speed of over 80 kts, I would have approximately seven seconds after launch to get the engine back to ground idle, lower the hook and keep the aircraft straight. Given a second or so to recover from the effects of a 4 g launch, it was clear to me that the final launches would be touch and go to safely stop the aircraft in the wire. The Python engine – a turboprop – took time for the rpm to reduce from full throttle to Flight Idle, and to avoid damage to the engine it was not recommended that Ground Idle be selected until the rpm had stabilised.

We had now completed eleven launches and had reached the point where we could recommend a clearance for continuing catapult operations from carriers, subject of course to the retrofit of the modified recuperator.

But on the fifth launch of the day, our haste to complete the trial quickly by larger step increments of end speed nearly came to an untimely end, and caused some embarrassment. The end speed was up by five kts to an anticipated 90 kts, but the old BH4 catapult was anything but precise in these matters, and in the event the analysis showed close to 93 kts. This made it virtually impossible for me to hack the power in two stages, lower the hook and cope with the cross-wind to aim for the centre of the wire. Something had to go.

The launch was fine and I quickly got the throttle off to Flight Idle, but by then I was only just short of the wire, so I rapidly selected hook down; but by this time I was in the wire, and my attempt to kill the power to Ground Idle to avoid a too high entry speed was to no avail. At the full extension of the arrester gear, the wire snapped, the aircraft slewed to port and I sailed merrily on, heading directly towards SME (Structures Flight) hangars, uncomfortably close at a mere 200 yards away. With the engine rpm now back to Ground Idle, and a smell of rubber from the harsh braking that I was told was strong even as far back as the catapult, I resigned myself to an untidy end. I was now cantering over the grass. There was nothing more I could do except slew the beast as late as possible. And this I did, cheating the 'Gods' who had set out to have their fun. I finished up just measurably feet from the hangar, witnessed by some rather startled SME onlookers who invariably turned out to watch NAD capers off the catapult.

Prudence being the better part of valour, we called it a day. I had called a halt to any more launches at these higher speeds, and in any event we had done more than enough to prove the recuperator modification and satisfy the clearance required. As far as aircraft were concerned, I would appreciate a change of scenery. Back in the crew room, changing out of my flying-gear, I had a telephone call. It was from Robbie, Flt Lt Robinson, a former student from the course who had been posted to SME Flight. 'Hullo Geoff, this is Robbie. I didn't know you were that keen to join us.' He had witnessed the whole thing!

Radio Flight was responsible for the development of all devices and equipment designed to assist the aircrew from radio, homing and navigational aids as well as a variety of more obscure equipment then being thought up by the scientists which would be subject to pilot assessment. To carry out this wide spectrum of test evaluations, the flight was equipped with a broad cross-section of aircraft types. It would become commonplace for me to fly two or three different types in one day, stepping out of a Meteor or Hunter for the next flight in the four-engined Hastings before toddling off to NAD in the afternoon for catapult trials in the Gannet. It kept the mind alert. Fortunately there was little report writing involved. Recorders were widely used, and these, with post-flight discussion, also recorded, obviated the need for long written reports.

In the next few months I consolidated my multi-engined aircraft time, particularly in the Canberra, Hastings and Varsity. In between, the Hunter provided a little light relief with a homing trial. This involved ultra-low-level flying to home onto a device held by an Army major who would secrete himself in the depths of beyond. This system, appropriately codenamed Green Salad, would play a most important part in future Army support operations in the difficult terrain of Borneo and Vietnam.

The flight had for some time been given the task of conducting the early morning meteorological flight, primarily because we had the most suitable aircraft for the task, the Canberra PR7. And for some reason that escapes me now, I seem to have become No. 1 choice for this first flight of the day. I didn't mind at all – it was quite exhilarating to get off before the airfield was officially open, and poke up through the weather to send back the report for the daily met. briefing.

In due course, it produced a bonus. My familiarity and, perhaps, modest capability with the Canberra put me on the list of RAE demonstration pilots for Battle of Britain Days. I became No. 1 to fly the Canberra. In due course I would work up a routine for these occasions, and with 'Jimpy' Shaw, a flight lieutenant who was an exceptional aerobatic display pilot in the Hunter, we would do our party pieces on request at various RAF airfields.

Early in February I had another 'invitation'. I had just finished yet another 'lesson' in squash one evening with Johnny Walker, a more than above-average player, and was towelling down when he tapped my shoulder.

'Fancy another challenge?'

'Go on', I said.

'Well, I'm earmarked to fly an aircraft, either to the Middle East or Burma, in a month or so. It's a private thing, for Fairey Aviation, Fieldair, who are under contract to Defence Sales, to deliver a number of aircraft to several foreign air forces: India, Jordan, Burma and one or two others.'

'Very interesting', said I. 'So?'

'Well,' he went on, 'I've been asked to recommend another suitably qualified pilot, and I think I could tolerate you for a few weeks! Would you be interested?' At ETPS we had become very good friends, and I was pleased to be asked. Later on I would be best man at his wedding.

So in March I would embark on a totally unexpected journey – to Burma in fact. But first there were a number of mundane administrative matters to be settled. I didn't have a passport, would the Navy permit it, and what about leave? Would Vic Fourie, the Flight Commander, agree to losing two of his four pilots at the same time? We would normally be expected to stagger leave arrangements. I dealt with them all in order of priority. Vic gave his blessing, having consulted Wing Commander Flying and the Group Captain.

I next approached the Naval Staff, and here I struck a winner. 'Yes,' they said, 'no problem, we regard it as in support of government business, and the flying will be covered on the same basis as naval operations.'

'What is my status on travelling?' I asked.

'You travel as a civilian,' was the answer, 'no uniform.'

'Have you got a passport?' 'Don't worry', came the response to my 'No'.

'Pete Austin will fix that for you.' For which I was very grateful, since time was short and I couldn't wait the usual months. I knew Pete quite well. He achieved the impossible. I sent him photographs and he sent me a passport within three days!

In the meantime, I had flown with Johnny to Croydon to meet and be briefed by the Fieldair official responsible for the contract. So that side of the matter was dealt with and we would now await the final departure date. The details of the flight are more suitably covered separately in Appendix 1.

Back at the farm, the flying was varied and interesting. By the nature of things, test flights are generally fairly short, and it is not unusual to find the number of hours flown is far less than the number of sorties. Later on, with research aircraft, this would be even more pronounced. The mess life, too, was extremely agreeable. It was known as No. 1 Mess to distinguish it from the ETPS mess a few hundred yards up the road. Many of the senior scientific staff were honorary members, and together with contractors' test pilots who frequently stayed there rather than in hotels, the mess provided an excellent forum for harmonious working relationships.

On my return from foreign travels, I devoted more time to flying the Hastings which I had had little opportunity to do before. There were two main tasks with this aircraft at this time: a new experimental sonobuoy, and an experimental radio transmission system, single sideband. The former required a good deal of low flying over the Channel when I felt quite at home. However, my association with single sideband would eventually prove to be more productive and satisfying.

Unlike one or two other flights, there was no shortage of flying in Radio Flight at this time. Some of it was pretty mundane, long flogs up the Orkneys, for example, for some equipment trial or other, or bowling out over the sea for prolonged sonobuoy tests. But there were exceptions. During the Test Pilots course, I had flown an aircraft named the Bobsleigh, a light propeller-driven machine that had been fitted out with a 'prone' pilot position couch to assess the feasibility of reducing the effects of 'g'. It was thought that the horizontal flying position would enable the pilot to fly the aircraft nearer its design limits without suffering the discomfort associated with the more convention upright position. It was all very interesting, but there were a number of drawbacks.

Now in June I made a deal with Robbie. In SME they were conducting trials with a 'prone' Meteor, so I got hold of him in the mess. There was not a lot of work going on in SME at this time, and I had frequently offered him a second-pilot slot in the Varsity, so he owed me one. I reminded him of this and got my ride in the Meteor.

It was more sophisticated than the Bobsleigh in couch design, so that the head rested on a raised lip and the contour of the couch followed a more natural position for the body, with the legs horizontal to allow the feet to operate the rudder – a little like lying on the beach on one's stomach reading a book. The prone cockpit had been modified to provide a short 'stick' in front of the head with throttles on the left in conventional form.

With Robbie in the normal pilot's seat, we took off with me following him through on the controls to get the feel of this unusual way of flying. After getting the hang of it, I brought it in to land and was thoroughly disconcerted when I found my nose rubbing along the runway – or so it felt. All in all I thought it very uncomfortable, and while the birds might elect to fly like that, I thought it 'strictly for the birds'! There was an obvious advantage when manoeuvring in reducing the 'g' effect, but I could detect no other use for a prone system. It was difficult to keep a satisfactory look-out and the physiological after-effects on the body were unacceptable. I declared no further interest, and the trial died a natural death.

I was now beginning to practise my routine for the forthcoming Battle of Britain Air Days, subjecting my long-suffering navigator, Flg Off Betton, to a considerable amount of discomfort in the process. He took it all in good spirit. From take-off I hauled it up into a very tight 4 g turn to 300 ft and back down the runway at full throttle to pull another 4 g into a roll off the top of the partial loop, down the runway again, hauling everything off as I performed another tight turn, put wheels and flaps down for a very slow flypast, cleaned up the aircraft again, and another 4 g turn brought me down the runway at about 320 kts for a loop. Out of the loop I concluded with a 360-degree maximum-rate turn in front of the 'crowd' before landing. Bingo, that filled my allotted time. The Canberra was a big aeroplane to haul around the skies like this.

September display days were still a month away, and there was other flying to occupy my time. Early in August Vic Fourie left a message for me to see him after I came down from a test flight. 'Now what have I done?' thought I! But it was a pleasant surprise. A tropical trial involving a Vickers

Valiant in Ceylon was being held up through the lack of a vital aircraft component part, and they had signalled for an urgent replacement. Rather than risk dispatch by commercial aircraft, it had been decided to use our own resources, and the most appropriate was the Canberra – in particular the PR7 which we in Radio Flight owned. So we were tasked and I would crew it with a Flg Off Robinson as my navigator. We spent the rest of the day obtaining the necessary air traffic clearances and planning for refuelling stops in Cyprus and Bahrain.

Late that afternoon I had a telephone message from Gp Capt McKinley: could he ride the bucket seat and come out with me? I don't know what the response would have been if I had declined, but I much appreciated the way he put it; it was typical of him.

Early next morning we assembled for a take-off at 0430 which would allow us to make Ceylon in the day. The Group Captain brought a little pillow with him to allow him to sleep to relieve the boredom, and we departed on time up to the gunnels with fuel. Then it all went wrong. Safely airborne, I selected undercarriage up. Nothing happened! I reselected several times to no avail. Short of raising it by the emergency system, not desirable with a long flight ahead, I was stuck with an aircraft with a limiting speed of 190 kts. Meantime I had called the tower to report the problem, and with no fuel-dumping facility, resigned myself to a long flight, going nowhere, feeling very frustrated. The most I could do was to maximise fuel flow by extending the airbrake, but I was reluctant to lower full flap since this would have entailed flying for a protracted and uncomfortable period below 160 kts. I decided to leave the airbrake and flaps alone. It was also very dark, and dawn was some hours away. The Group Captain, very laid back about the whole thing, but obviously disappointed, now prepared to get his head down.

After an hour I had managed to burn off sufficient fuel to consider a landing, only to discover from air traffic control that fog was beginning to envelop the airfield. Dawn had almost broken, and as I returned to the airfield it was evident that the conditions, not the fuel, would prevent any question of landing for the time being. The Met Office was not hopeful for a clearance for at least an hour, so we considered an alternative. Blackbushe airport was the nearest diversion, but that would entail a journey of fifty minutes by road, and by that time the fog might have cleared sufficiently to land back at base. So it seemed prudent to remain airborne in the vicinity.

The time dragged on and Met were beginning to sound less than hopeful for an early clearance. We had now been in the air for over two hours and were very conscious of the need to get down, allowing the spare part for the Valiant to be flown out by alternative means. A spare Canberra had already been prepared with a spare crew.

Just after eight o'clock, I decided to attempt a landing, and asked for a controlled approach. Then I discovered I could not lower the flaps, as the hydraulic pressure had fallen below 1,500 psi. It was not my day. Fortunately the runway lighting at Farnborough was excellent, and with the help of a first-class controller I eventually managed to see enough of the lights at half a mile to touch down, and landed three hours and fifty minutes after I had taken off. But for the defective hydraulic system resulting in a recalcitrant undercarriage, I would have been well on my way to Bahrain by now, having refuelled and departed Cyprus.

I'd had enough of the Canberra for the time being, but a few weeks later we joined together for two Battle of Britain displays at RAF Tangmere and RAF Benson. Both displays went well and brought a nice Bravo Zulu to my Group Captain from his opposite number at Tangmere, who at the display briefing had been mildly surprised to find a dark blue job at the controls. His congratulations were received with all the more pleasure.

On the other side of the house, the Naval Air Department at Bedford was now up and running, mainly testing the new catapults and Mk 13 arrester gear, and from now until the end of the year this placed further demands on my time. Occasionally it was opportune to fly there in a Canberra or Varsity to conduct CR/DF trials with the Bedford equipment, carry out the required catapult or arrester trials in one of the naval aircraft, and then return to Farnborough.

I had now been promoted to lieutenant-commander, which put me in the odd position of being senior to my Flight Commander. This occasioned Vic Fourie to ask if this would create a problem. We had always got on very well, and he knew the answer, of course, but he felt he should clear the air. Then, almost as a mark of mutual respect, he recommended to Paddy Finch, the Wing Commander Flying, that I should captain a Hastings on an extended overseas trial in November. I was much chuffed by his confidence and told him so.

'Who would you like as 2nd Pilot?' he asked, but I hadn't given this much thought. The most obvious choice was Robbie from SME, who was used to 'heavies', so in the mess that evening I offered him the chance. We had flown together on many occasions in the Hastings and Varsity, and he now leapt at the opportunity.

In addition to Captain and 2nd Pilot, the crew would be the standard Hastings crew of navigator, signaller and flight engineer, the latter doubled up to cater for day/night flying. Then a team of six boffins – scientific personnel – led by a Senior Scientific Officer to conduct the single sideband trial, a system of communication by voice over vast distances by bouncing sound waves off the ionosphere in a fairly conventional way but producing a clarity unaffected by height or obstruction. This was 1955, well before satellites transformed everything.

We departed Farnborough in the early part of November for Karachi in Pakistan, stopping *en route* at Malta, El Fayid in the Canal Zone, Egypt, and then Bahrain in the Gulf. This was planned to provide communication tests at one, two and three thousand miles from base. At each stop we planned at least one flight, day and/or night depending on whether the transit flight had been made at night, in which case it obviated the need for another night test.

It was undemanding flying for the crew, but the boffins were working hard. On each stop, on arrival, I paid the customary courtesy call on the Station Commander to acquaint him with our test requirements, particularly as at meant opening the airfield for night-flying. There was never any difficulty, but at Karachi I met the 'oddball', the sort who considered aeroplanes were synonymous with the Royal Air Force.

The Group Captain there greeted me in a less than friendly way with, 'Yes, good morning', and then, 'What is a naval officer doing flying an RAF aircraft?' No offer of a seat in his office, or any other courtesy, which after a nearly five-hour flight raised my ire somewhat. I was inclined to respond, 'None of your business', as indeed it wasn't, but confined myself to, 'Sir, it is not an RAF aircraft, it belongs to the Ministry of Supply and is operated by the Royal Aircraft Establishment where no distinction is made between RAF or RN pilots.' And then added, to emphasise my irritation, 'Now if you will excuse me, I would like to attend to the needs of my crew and the scientific staff', and I departed in a huff.

I didn't come across many of his sort in the RAF throughout all my time in the service; most were quite the opposite, and I would spend many years at RAF-administered stations. But there was always this minority feeling at the relatively senior level, which seemed to stem from their perceived tenuous position as a separate fighting arm and their need to fight their corner to stay in business.

One flight only was planned at Mauripur (Karachi), and I filed for a take-off the following morning at four o'clock. After a long transit flight, I released Robbie from this one and put the Master Engineer in the 2nd Pilot's seat to assist with throttle control and other ancillary equipment. This was a not uncommon procedure at Farnborough, and as one of two flight engineers in the crew, he had not had a demanding transit flight. Moreover, they were used to the throttle procedures under the direction of the captain in the normal course of things when seated at their usual engineer's console.

I rolled on time, very dark, had lifted off from the runway and called for 'Undercarriage Up' to the flight engineer, which he did. Normal procedure, no problem; the captain required two hands on the control column at this stage. Then, with the airspeed settling down nicely for the climb, I called for 'Climbing Power' – standard procedure again. To my utter astonishment, he promptly closed all four throttles! We were then at about 300 ft, and with the airspeed now decaying rapidly, I grabbed the throttles, pushed them fully open, juggling with the control column at the same time to correct the ensuing loss of height. This was a bad moment. I had enough to do on a dark night, on instruments, without an incompetent engineer.

Strangely, he was a very experienced Hastings engineer, normally thoroughly reliable, and on the many previous flights with him in a variety of aircraft, he had had my complete trust. Now I wondered what had caused this moment of total irresponsibility. I think I had been too busy and too confounded to say much at the time, but after recovering the situation and getting the aircraft back into the climb I said, 'What the b——y hell were you thinking of? What were you doing?'

He looked very sheepish and muttered something about not having slept very well, and then, 'I thought we were landing.' There was nothing more to be said; I would deal with him when we got back on the ground. Meanwhile we had a trial to conduct.

Before we had left Farnborough, Gp Capt McKinley had asked me to give him a call from Karachi when we got there, so towards the end of the sortie I called Farnborough. It was then just after shop opening time, 8 a.m. there, and he came on the line. It was crystal-clear two-way reception, and he could scarcely believe that we were flying at less than 1,000 ft above the Indian Ocean, 3,000 miles away. Here and at the intermediate stops it was a highly

148

successful trial. In the fourteen days we were away, we had completed seventy hours' flying, half of it at night, all without incident – well almost!

My flying days at Farnborough were almost over. Both Naval Flight and Aero Flight would relocate to Thurleigh (RAE Bedford) early in January. In many ways I was sorry to be leaving Farnborough. I had enjoyed an intensive and wide variety of flying there that I could not expect to be sustained at Bedford, although, as it transpired, the next two years would require more of the test pilot's approach. Before departing finally from Farnborough, I collected a Wyvern for delivery to Thurleigh. It thus became the first and last aircraft that I would associate with my time there.

RAE Bedford

The RAE at Bedford consisted of a Wind Tunnel Site at Twinwood Farm – the airfield from which Glen Miller departed in 1944 to lose his life in an aircraft accident in unknown circumstances – and the newly constructed airfield at Thurleigh where all Research and Development flying took place. The latter was all that remained of a mid-1940 grandiose scheme to develop a National Aeronautical Establishment for the post-war period to replace Farnborough. In the event the scheme was radically curtailed in post-war austerity Britain.

I was now part of a small number of test pilots at Thurleigh who would continue where we left off at Farnborough, but in rather different circumstances. The airfield was a vast improvement in runway lengths and general layout, and with the soon-to-be-completed control tower it would attract a steady influx of national airline aircraft for instrument and general pilot training – a valuable source of revenue for the then Ministry of Supply to offset the huge expenditure of the aircraft research programme.

As pilots, we enjoyed the luxury of a new pilots' block with modern facilities, and about half a mile away, an officers' mess which had been built out of the remains of an old US Air Force prefabricated building. It was very basic, but in time we would turn it into a comfortable enough place for the unmarried officers to live. The post of Mess Manager was the preserve of a retired Army colonel who lived in the adjoining gatehouse; it was, in fact, nothing more than a single room and bathroom. He had recently lost his wife, and accepted the menial job of Mess Manager as a temporary expedient. He was a genial fellow, enjoyed the service atmosphere and, with two ladies from the local village, ensured a satisfactory standard of catering and cleaning.

Some months later, we would put his composure to the test. It happened that we had invited a senior naval officer from Ministry of Supply HQ to a dining-in night as a sort of inauguration of our humble establishment. We had an exceptionally fine evening and were pleased with the way things had gone. Wg Cdr Henry Larsen, OC Flying, as President, had seen the honoured guest off to his room along the corridor, and himself gone home to his married quarters.

It was then that several of us, by this time in good spirits, decided to modify the layout of the bar and anteroom. Both were small rooms, and for some time we had contemplated knocking down the dividing wall to bring the two together. Now, it seemed to us, was a good time to start! So, with enthusiasm and several large sledge-hammers, we set about demolishing the offending wall.

I suppose by the time we were in full swing, our guest had just about nodded off, and it must have been slightly alarming for him suddenly to feel the building tremble under the weight of our efforts with the sledge-hammers. Predictably, his curiosity got the better of him, and he shortly appeared in slippers and dressing-gown through the clouds of dust, smoke and flying bricks to discover the cause of his disturbed night's rest. Rear Adm 'Bigwig', the Deputy Controller Air at the Ministry, was clearly not amused, but in the circumstances took the only course open to him. Turning on his heels, and without a word, he retired once more to his room, reserving his ire for the following morning.

It was a very sorry sight the next morning, and a number of so-called responsible test pilots with large hangovers very shamefacedly faced a somewhat bewildered Mess Manager. But of course, after thirty and more years in the Army he had seen it all before, and with scarcely a raised eyebrow, organised a local 'brickie' to complete the demolition and make good the work of the amateurs.

Shortly afterwards, we had a nice letter from the Rear Admiral thanking us for our hospitality and expressing the hope that, as he had a very busy schedule, we would understand if he was unable to accept any future invitations!

Well before this, experimental work in the Naval Department had taken an interesting and busy turn. By mid-February we received the prototype DH.110 (later Sea Vixen), and very shortly after that the prototype N113 (later Scimitar). At the same time we were conducting a series of tests with a Sea Venom which had been modified with a system of 'Lift' augmentation by engine-blown air over the wing flaps. This boundary layer control system reduced the stalling speed by over ten knots, with the considerable benefit of a lower take-off and landing speed, and was the forerunner to systems incorporated in the later Scimitar and Buccaneer aircraft.

The arrival of the DH.110 for carrier operation clearance was a matter of some interest. Far and away the fastest and heaviest aircraft the Navy had ordered, it would stretch the new Mk 13 arrester gear and steam catapult to near their limits.

After a short briefing by the firm's chief test pilot and a handful of bumph to digest, I made a 45-minute handling flight on 14 February, followed by a similar one the next day. After the previous generation of naval aircraft it felt what it was – a big aeroplane. It was easy to fly, handled pleasantly enough, if a little sluggish for its role as an all-weather fighter, but of course this was the age of the air-to-air missile, for which it acted as the platform. It was not designed for the traditional close-combat tactics.

Over the next two weeks, the aircraft was put through a rigid programme of arresting proofing and catapult launches. I seemed to spend most of each day in the cockpit, but at the end of that period, apart from the two handling flights, my total flying hours amounted to a paltry forty-five minutes – nine catapult launches reaping five minutes for each launch and subsequent circuit. The aircraft performed well off the catapult, with no unusual characteristics, although initially I had some difficulty determining the correct position of the 'stick' during the catapult run. This was a 'first' for me and for the aircraft.

The arresting programme was tedious. Often I would spend the whole morning trundling down the runway at increasing speeds, where the deceleration into the wire would cause unpleasant neck whip-lashing. The cumulative effect on the body of a huge number of arrests, usually in a very short period of time, with a variety of aircraft during my time at Bedford would not be apparent until later in life.

In tandem with the DH.110, we pursued work with the 'blown flap' Sea Venom and arresting proofing with the Vickers N113, both shortly to be embarked in HMS *Ark Royal* for carrier trials. My one handling flight in the N113 before the arresting proofing was uneventful but exhilarating. I would come to know this aircraft well in the future, but the acceleration on opening the throttles surprised me. The 110 was quick, but this was an order different from anything I had flown before, and I had the distinct impression of being taken for a ride by the 22,500 lb of thrust. However, we settled down quite quickly, and this flight was the beginning of a long relationship where I never lost respect for its occasional spiteful tendencies.

If I had had any doubts about the volume and variety of flying after leaving Farnborough, they were quickly dispelled. The loss of each bridle that towed the aircraft during the catapult launch was both expensive and logistically unacceptable. Various schemes had been tried over the years without success. Now NAD had come up with another. After trials on the Bedford catapult with a Sea Venom, I flew out to HMS *Bulwark* in the Channel, where we would test it on their modified rig. It was successful but needed a more thorough trial with a variety of aircraft before it could be confirmed for general use.

The Sea Hawk also provided a little light entertainment about this time when we experimented with multiple RATOG (Rocket-Assisted Take-off Gear) take-offs with eight rockets, four either side of the fuselage. This was double the number currently authorised for use by the fleet. RATOG played a large part in carrier take-offs to cope with ever-increasing aircraft payloads, but it had always been treated with suspicion because of rocket unreliability. Asymmetric firing was commonplace, leading to wild yawing of the aircraft. The probability of failure with the use of eight rockets obviously carried with it considerable hazard. Fortunately, during the tests we never experienced more than a double failure on one side.

After completing the carrier proving trials with the DH.110 and N113, I handed over both aircraft to Boscombe Down pilots whose task it was to carry out the carrier qualification trials. So in parallel with their trials in *Ark Royal*, I took the 'blown' Sea Venom to the ship to put some numbers to the value of the new blown flap system. These would be invaluable in determining the benefits to the Vickers Supermarine Scimitar – production version of the N113 – when it came into service. There was keen interest in these trials from the many interested parties on board.

I demonstrated landings with and without the system in operation, and minimum launch speeds from the catapult, where they were able to compare the performance with the standard Sea Venom. Finally, with the ship steaming about thirty knots into a fifteen-knot headwind, I flew low alongside the port beam with full power achieving a speed ten knots below the minimum landing speed, gradually overtaking the ship by about twenty knots! Quite impracticable for any normal use, of course, but it was a simple demonstration of the value of the blown flap system.

Back at Bedford, I began doing some work with Aero Flight to augment the naval trials. There were at that time many interesting trials under way involving the Boulton Paul Delta, Short SB5, Avro 707A Delta, Handley Page 115 and other novel aircraft, including a Hawker Hunter with a blown flap system and a modified Gloster Meteor. The latter aircraft was an early research aircraft into deflected jet operation, and had been equipped with more powerful engines and bifurcated jet pipes to deflect the jet downwards through sixty degrees. This was a most interesting trial since the lower speed achieved was accompanied by a loss of control that had to be treated with some caution. At some point, also, height control was lost due to the thrust from the deflected jets being insufficient to keep the aircraft in the air. However, it was possible to fly the aircraft thirty knots below the standard Meteor. More could have been achieved if the jet deflection had not been fixed, but this would come later, with the Harrier.

All the research aircraft mentioned had been designed to investigate aspects of aerodynamic design incorporated in future aircraft. The HP.115 with its ultra-swept delta wing provided valuable data for the design of a new SST (Supersonic Transport) which eventually manifested itself in Concord. The Short SB5 incorporated a wing profile eventually used for the RAF Lightning. These were all very interesting aeroplanes to fly and I felt privileged to do so. The tally of aircraft types I flew in one month, never fewer that seven, in one month totalled ten.

None of them caused any real concern in the air, although in my last flight in the BP Delta, and almost my last flight at Bedford, I came unstuck and contemplated joining the Martin Baker Club for the first time. This aircraft was unique in having a control system activated by electrical impulses controlled by the pilot, and an extreme delta-shaped wing with no tailplane. It was subject to inertia cross-coupling, where the aircraft pitched and rolled at the same time, and in certain conditions it could be a handful. I was nearing the end of this last flight and had lowered the undercarriage when I discovered I could only move the control column to the left and fore and aft. My attempts to force the stick to the right proved fruitless; so I was stuck with going straight ahead or round in circles to the left. I now had to be careful in any slight turn to the left to maintain height and avoid the nose of the aircraft falling below the horizon, which would have risked a descending spiral without the control to reverse the turn.

At this stage I was also preoccupied with the cause of the problem. Was there a risk of the electrical system further inhibiting control movement? I was not to know, and meanwhile I pondered the question of ejection. But I was at circuit height when I lowered the undercarriage and was too low for comfort, so I contemplated climbing to a safe height, although I instinctively shied away from the safety of the runway just at this time.

By this time I had warned air traffic control of my dilemma, who in turn had alerted Tom Kerr, the senior scientist responsible for the aircraft test programme. He could offer nothing; it was a new experience for him, but he got some of his engineering chaps to do some rapid research into the system.

I now spent some time assessing various options. Most aircraft with a powered control system had a manual reversion alternative in the event of a power failure, although in the majority of cases you needed titanic strength to overcome the resistance of pistons and rods in the system. As a pure research aircraft, information on manual control did not exist. The system might have allowed it but no one had tried it; and the very design of this aircraft made it extremely hazardous even were it possible.

So I settled down to use what control I had to make a wide sweeping circuit to the left, aiming to line up with a short straightaway, taking particular care to avoid any situation that required a correction to the right to put me back on the runway centre line. I particularly wanted to avoid aborting the approach.

It was here that my carrier experience came to the rescue. I was used to tight approaches, rolling out just before touch-down, and that was what I now planned. With a shallow left turn to my selected point on the runway, I lined up with the centre line, touched down with only a minimum of straightaway (the point where the aircraft is rolled out of the turn to point of touch-down) and landed some hundred yards beyond where I intended, but content to have avoided a potentially serious situation. The fire tenders and ambulance, perhaps feeling cheated, were left to follow me down the runway.

The aircraft was now grounded and subjected to rigorous testing. But, as often happens with electrical problems, the fault could not be repeated, and it was written off as a transient one-off occurrence. And there the matter would rest, except that some years later, when I was relating the incident to a senior scientist who had been involved with initial manufacturer's trials of the aircraft, he described an identical happening at that time and was puzzled why this was not known at Bedford. But this was late in my time at Bedford. Much was to happen before then.

By the middle of the year 1956, we were well established in our new location and had wholeheartedly adapted to the local social scene – such as it was. Thurleigh was a bit out in the sticks but it had its compensations. Mess life had become very agreeable, with a number of us having a common interest in golf for relaxation, and a good watering-hole only a few miles away if we wanted a change from our own excellent bar.

It was by the good services of the captain of the Bedford & County Golf Club, himself an engineer at RAE, that the mess was granted honorary membership for up to six of us at any one time on the course. The captain, Mr Ronald Wall, was involved in the construction of the wind tunnels which had been brought over from Germany after the war, and I would get to know him very well – I would marry his daughter, who was employed as a scientist in Aero Flight.

For several of us, two in particular, Flt Lt 'Chunky' Webster and myself, the golf club would become a focal point of our social life. It was a convivial place to spend evenings after a round of golf, and with only one or two exceptions, the mess members were warmly welcomed. Through the Wall family, all of whom played at some level or other, we found a kindred soul in one Jimmy Hill, a low-handicap player who became a firm member of our Sunday-morning 'four', and with whom we would remain friends for many years. He felt privileged to be invited to our mess, and in turn would invite us to the Conservative Club for snooker and refreshment.

Coincidentally we had been accepted as social friends of the Wall family, and in due course I would form an attachment to their daughter Pat, both on and off the golf course. From the start we seemed to have common interests. There were always a number of mixed competitions in the area, and so we teamed up to form a formidable pair – or so we thought! I recall on one occasion our efforts resulted in a substantial win with numerous prizes for this and that, and the 'sweep' of a large sum of money which was promptly put behind the bar to provide drinks for our fellow competitors and, it seemed, all and sundry! Young and foolish perhaps, or exhilaration at being victorious. Whatever, it gave us satisfaction and pleasure, but such generous equivalence never brightened our door at other competitions, where we were not so successful.

As an alternative watering-hole to the mess, we had early on discovered an excellent country inn, the Wheatsheaf, at Keysoe, a few miles away. We became frequent visitors and soon established a firm rapport with the landlord and his wife, Geoff and Penny, who a little later would entrust us with running the bar when they wished for an evening off. We were hardly novices – we ran our own bar – but it amused the locals to be confronted with Webster or myself operating from the other side of the counter.

I was now more involved with research flying with Aero Flight than naval development work. It would be a few months before we saw the return of the Sea Vixen or Scimitar in their production form, although the demand for catapulting and arresting of one sort or another was always steady. But now, in July, there came to the Naval Department an aircraft I had not anticipated: the Short Sea Mew.

The Sea Mew originated from the need for a cheap alternative to the more sophisticated Gannet for A/S operations, and was conceived to operate from small, escort-type carriers. But the timescale was wrong, and it would soon be relegated to RNVR squadron status as a wartime back-up measure. Meanwhile it was to be put through the standard catapult clearance programme, only this time from the hydraulic catapult at Farnborough, which was more suited to the weight and speed of this aircraft.

Its arrival at Bedford in the hands of the firm's test pilot caused suppressed amusement in some quarters. To the uninitiated, perhaps, it represented a step back in time. Not remotely aerodynamic with a fixed undercarriage, it gave the appearance of a fuselage wrapped round the single Mamba engine, with a cockpit added as an afterthought. In fact it was nothing of the sort. It was a clever design for the job of A/S warfare for rapid production at a relatively cheap unit cost

I flew it to Farnborough the day after its arrival, and we started catapulting the same day. No time for niceties of two short handling flights which one would normally expect. I elected to stay at Farnborough rather than use the daily ferry service, and for the next two days we managed with little interruption to complete twelve launches at various weights and end speeds. She was a nice little old lady with no vices. Sluggish and ponderous, as its wing shape and general design would suggest, I had little doubt, nevertheless, that it would have acquitted itself well in the operating environment in which it was intended.

RAE facilities for proofing trials of its new naval aircraft. The Fouga Magister, a trainer, arrived in the early part of 1957, to be followed shortly thereafter by the Breguet 1050 – the French A/S aircraft similar to the Gannet. None of the French test pilots had any experience of catapult techniques, and after a handling flight in both aircraft I carried out the initial catapult launch of both aircraft with the appropriate firm's test pilot in the rear seat for experience. After several launches, they would go off by themselves.

Almost coincidentally with the arrival of the French aircraft, we had a visitor from the Blackburn Aircraft Company. 'Sailor Parker' was well known to us. He would drop in from time to time to pass the time of day, but now he had a more personal motive. Sailor was Blackburn's only test pilot, and the firm was in the process of constructing the new NA39, the Navy's new strike aircraft that would in its production form be known as the Buccaneer. Unfortunately Sailor was not a qualified *experimental* test pilot, and was aware that the firm was about to recruit a suitably qualified pilot to carry out the initial test flying. He felt he might strengthen his hand with his masters if he could claim catapult experience, and this was the purpose of his latest visit.

I had no authority to do so, but I arranged for some Sea Venom launches, sat him in the observer's seat and gave him a ride or two. For obvious reasons he does not appear in my logbook, although the following day I properly authorised him to accompany me, again in the Sea Venom, during some arresting trials. He was extremely grateful and showed his appreciation by taking a number of us, including the then Miss Wall to dinner at the Falcon Inn, a few miles away. This was not the first time. He had previously entertained us at this same inn on several occasions, always with most excellent hospitality. The landlord would later claim that we had cleared his cellar of his best burgundy, Nuits St Georges '49.

It was with great sadness that I learnt some time after I left Bedford that Sailor had killed himself during low-level aerobatics when, in performing a vertical manoeuvre, it would appear he encountered cross-coupling.

Now, in mid-July, the Scimitar arrived at Boscombe Down in preparation for the forthcoming carrier trials, so for three or four days I flew to Boscombe to work up with the two Boscombe pilots, who had their own trials to do. There was always a bit of rivalry between the two establishments, particularly where the clearance programmes had a sort of grey area.

However, it never affected the working relationship, and the subsequent trials in *Ark Royal* were highly successful.

Dennis Higton, the Boscombe scientist in charge of their trials, whom I would come to know well in the future, always waxed lyrical at the catapult minimum launches, and would later remind me, and others, how he watched with fascination the ever-decreasing end speeds and Higgs throwing up spray as he managed to get the aircraft to stagger just clear of the sea. He was right; they were exciting moments, particularly at the highest all-up weights, and required a deftness of touch with the controls.

I found the aircraft pleasant to deck land. Its biggest drawback was the excessive nose-up attitude during the approach, when it was easy to lose sight of the deck, and its tendency to rock forward after touch-down. The latter was only important during touch-and-go trials, when the tailplane control was barely adequate to rotate the aircraft into the take-off attitude before running out of deck. Altogether, in the week we had on board, my personal tally amounted to twenty-four landings, which I think must have been the lion's share.

I arrived back at Bedford from the ship to be confronted with an instrument rating examination in the Meteor with a chap from Farnborough. It was an annual requirement and only an irritating addition to an otherwise busy period.

The Sea Venom was always much in demand for one thing or another. It was an admirable workhorse for catapult and arresting data for the boffins, transport for all sorts of people between airfields and establishments and, of course, 'air experience'. All the pilots did their best to ensure that the boffins had first-hand experience of flying. After all, it was in our interests, and I was no exception. Along with a number of others I was able to provide Miss Wall, my future wife Pat, with a flight in the Sea Venom in the early part of August. She was not unfamiliar with flying, having experienced a number of flights in the transport aircraft, Marathon – usually with Wg Cdr Larsen, the OC Flying – and she also badgered her way onto a helicopter flight with my good friend Tony Thurstan and another in the Tiger Moth with the Security Officer, one retired Gp Capt Snaith of 'High-Speed Flight' fame.

The end of 1957 was now ominously in sight when I knew my time at RAE would be up. Including the Test Pilots course, I would have spent four years away from the Navy, which I knew would not bode well for my career prospects. It would be regarded as lost time, and although I would not regret it for a single moment, I realised I would have to pay for being out of direct touch with my chosen service. I was also ready for a change of scenery. There had been a number of personnel changes lately, including Bill Noble, the late OC Aero Flight, who had been appointed to a course at RNAS Lossiemouth, and also my good friend and golfing partner, Chunky, who had been posted back to the Royal Air Force.

I had missed Chunky these last two months or so, and my golf, with his absence, had not had quite the same bite to it. We had played much the same game – give it all you've got and slice it wide off the tee. Not perhaps quite an accurate reflection of our game, but we were both in contrast to the steady straight down the middle measured golf of our low handicap partner, Jimmy Hill. He would marvel at the length of our drives, but not always the result.

I would meet up with Bill again very shortly, but lost touch with Chunky on his return to the Air Force. It would be some time before his name would crop up again, and then in curious circumstances. Chunky was a local boy to Bedford, having attended Bedford Modern School, and his mother still lived there. He had many local friends there while he was at RAE, and many years later, I received a letter from a lady friend of his enquiring if I knew what had happened to him. She had heard he had gone to the USA, and believed that he had died there, but knew no more.

This was forty years on from Bedford days, but I promised to tap one or two sources and let her know. So I did, but there was an ominous block from the RAF personnel department, and it was only much later that I learnt he had been contracted to the US government with the blessing of the RAF to fly U2 'spy' planes for the CIA. That much seemed to be fact. Then the trail went cold, and I was unable to discover whether either of the two stories I was given was true. The first was that he had been shot down during a spying mission (over Russia?) or died in unknown circumstances in California. In due course I passed on this information to the lady in question.

One other incident occurred before I was to leave Bedford. It must have been about the end of August when late one afternoon I had a telephone call from Cdr Ken Hickson at the Ministry of Supply Headquarters. He was well known to me, an engineering officer who had served as a test pilot at Farnborough and Boscombe Down.

'Geoff,' he said, 'I've been asked to put forward a couple of names as potential test pilots to head up the Blackburn NA39 programme. Derek Whitehead at Boscombe has asked to be considered and I wondered if you would be interested.' He sounded a little diffident as if he didn't wish me to feel he was encouraging the idea.

Derek Whitehead had been on the same TP course as myself. An ex-Air Force officer, he had transferred to the Navy after the war when we were offering short-service commissions to pilots in the RAF who were surplus to requirements in the rundown. 'Block', as he was known, was a large, serious fellow whom I had first come to know at Central Flying School.

Sailor Parker, of course, was still with Blackburn at this time, and so far as I was aware, would remain there. My immediate reaction was, 'I can't do that.' It would be like a stab in the back to someone with whom I had become extremely friendly in the last few years. But that was a reaction I could live with; however, there were all sorts of other implications. It would mean resigning my commission and sacrificing a career that I had built up to the point of a middle-ranking officer and enjoyed. Then again, I knew nothing about recent developments with the proposed NA39, and with the post-war record of Blackburn anything the company touched was bound to raise a doubt or two.

It did not have an enviable record of success. I recalled its contribution to the Navy's GR17 specification in the early fifties, the YA5, which had turned out to be a fractured, phased development resulting in the aircraft, competing with the Fairey Aviation competitor, the Gannet, with the wrong engine because its turboprop engine was not ready at the time of carrier trials. Peter Lawrence, the company's chief test pilot at that time, had been most despondent at Boscombe and *Illustrious* when I knew him at that time. He felt very badly let down by the firm.

On a minor social point, during that period I never recall Blackburn offering any hospitality to any of us at a time when Fairey's Peter Twiss and Gordon Slade, the project and chief test pilots, were lavish and unrelenting in their hospitality. It was said later by someone more familiar with the firm than I that Blackburn did not encourage an entertainment allowance below board level! Not good PR, since much of the influence can stem from well below that level. How Sailor had contrived to feed us expensive Nuits St George I know not, but wouldn't be surprised if it had come out of his own pocket.

As an aviation company Blackburn was not a front runner. Much of its background had been as a sub-contractor, such as its version of the Swordfish, which it called the Blackfish. Any 'Swordfish' pilot would tell you he knew when he was flying a 'Blackfish', although the two were outwardly similar. The company's last contract with the RAF had resulted in the 'Beverly', a heavy transport to carry light armoured vehicles, but it was not a great success and was ordered eventually in very limited numbers.

Some of these thoughts flashed through my mind as I quizzed Ken about the prospects there and the package being offered, but he wouldn't be drawn.

'Sorry,' he said, 'I know no more than that there is a vacancy for a qualified experimental test pilot with two years' experience', and then added, 'Look, it's a very important decision, sleep on it and give me a ring tomorrow.'

So I did, and had a very uncomfortable night contemplating the pros and cons. The thought of a chief test pilot's job had its attractions, but the sacrifice of my naval career weighed heavily on me. I was also mindful of the fact that if I showed interest it could be a two-edged sword as far as the Navy was concerned. It could certainly be wrongly construed as to my future outlook in the service.

There was another ingredient in the pot to consider. Every now and then the Royal Navy, as with the other two services, found itself with the wrong balance of officers and their seniorities, and would offer favourable terms for a certain number to volunteer to leave. Failing the appropriate number of volunteers, the number would be made up by compulsory retirement. It was known as the 'Golden Bowler', but for those conscripted it was a time of uncertainty. A few weeks before the Blackburn business cropped up, a notice of redundancies had been issued by the Admiralty. For myself, I felt reasonably safe, although the number of officers around my seniority was quite large and I couldn't vouchsafe my future.

Notwithstanding, the following morning I rang Ken and, with some misgivings, asked him to put my name forward. I had concluded that on balance there was little to lose by having an interview at Holme-on-Spalding-Moor, Blackburn's base. In short time an interview was arranged there with Mr N.E. Rowe, the chief designer and managing director, known in aviation circles as 'NERO'!

Thus I flew to H-on-S M and was met at the airfield by Sailor. As someone who might take his present job, I found this distinctly embarrassing, although he was fully aware of the situation. NERO was an aircraft designer of long standing, although now regarded as a touch out of date with modern aerodynamics. He would shortly be replaced by a much younger but experienced Roy Boot. Anyway, he welcomed me well enough. We chatted about the progress of the aircraft, timescales and so on, and he volunteered that he anticipated a package that would include a salary of £3,000 per annum, use of a car (but only when on duty) and sundry other benefits. (Later on I would discover that it would *not* include membership of the directors' and senior management restaurant!)

After a tour of the factory and sighting, for the first time, the progress of the aircraft build, I raised a number of questions about the contract with the Ministry and the Navy and a number of other matters, which I think surprised him to the point where he might have doubted my confidence in the outcome of the programme. This was not so, but I think he had good cause to question my interest. I had not been exactly bursting with enthusiasm, and he must have sensed that my approach to the job and the firm was decidedly lukewarm.

The meeting was regarded as exploratory, without any question of a commitment at this early stage. We parted on friendly terms, Sailor accompanied me back to the aircraft and without a word to him about the interview I flew home to Bedford.

I wasn't offered the job. I think NERO knew my heart wasn't in it, and had I been invited to join them, I would have refused. Derek was offered it and took the post of chief test pilot with Sailor as his number two until he died a short while later. I would have much to do with Blackburn and the Buccaneer some time later on, and would work with Derek on the development programme. The more I saw of his situation, the more I knew I had undoubtedly made the right decision. He seemed content early on, but disillusioned when the development work was completed. In retrospect I ponder that I ever showed any interest in such a speculative future, however little. With the end of the Buccaneer development work, there was nothing else on the stocks at Blackburn. The company became absorbed into the Hawker Siddeley Group and its staff were dispersed or made redundant. At this stage, Derek left them and became an air traffic controller at an airfield in Kent.

Towards the end of 1957 I received my next appointment. I was to go to Naval Air Station Lossiemouth in Morayshire for the first-ever Squadron Commanders' Qualifying Course to be held. Bill Noble was already there and had had a sort of reintroduction to air warfare, but this was to be the first of the future formal courses to qualify for command, much in the same way that the submariners had traditionally selected their people for command, which they aptly called the 'Perishers' course.

Then in December I left the test-flying world for ever – or so I thought. Since joining the Empire Test Pilots School I had added another thirty-eight types of aircraft as 1st Pilot to my score, with the corresponding valuable experience. Ranging from fast, single-seat jets to heavy multi-engined transport/passenger aircraft, I felt competent to fly any aircraft in any situation. But I now had to turn my sights to and refresh my skills as an operational pilot, the primary purpose of a naval aviator, fighting aeroplanes, a far cry from the last four years.

Casting my mind back I knew I was a much better pilot for the experience, although it frequently crossed my mind that my position back with the Navy would not necessarily weigh this in my favour compared with my contemporaries who had gone the more conventional route in their operational flying appointments. I need not have had any such concern, as events would show, although the outcome would cause some resentment in certain quarters!

Before leaving Bedford I took the plunge and became engaged to Pat. My confirmed bachelorhood had come to an end! I was also awarded the Queen's Commendation for Valuable Service in the Air in the New Year's Honours List, which, as a good friend wrote to congratulate me, was a sort of poor man's Air Force Cross.

CHAPTER 15

Squadron Command Course and Scimitar Intensive Flying Trials

I was not then familiar with Royal Naval Air Station Lossiemouth. Other than discharging our students there from Syerston, I had only scant knowledge of its activities. It turned out to be a very busy place, with several second-line squadrons there and the temporary home of first-line squadrons during disembarked periods. Now I was to join 764 Squadron on the north side of the field for the Squadron Command course, together with a number of old friends and acquaintances, one of my recent ilk, Bill Hart, who had been on the same Test Pilots course as myself.

It was a small course of six experienced pilots; two had already commanded second-line squadrons, and all, apart from Bill and myself, had come directly from front-line outfits. One, 'Hoagy' Carmichael, the 'grandfather' of the course, I knew only by name and reputation. He had fought in the Korean War in 1953 as a fighter pilot and earned immortality in an unusual encounter. He was part of a strike operation in his piston-engined Sea Fury over North Korea and was returning to his parent carrier when – and here Hoagy would take up his story:

> I was sitting there, minding my own business, keen to get back aboard when, without any warning, a MiG 15 (Russian-built fast swept-wing jet) flashed across my windscreen about three hundred yards ahead, obviously not having seen me. Instinctively, without any time to get my gunsight to bear, I just pressed the gun button, more in hope than expectation, and got off a quick burst just as he crossed right in front of me. Then, unbelievably, he disintegrated, bits flying off everywhere. I couldn't believe it, I had unwittingly achieved the perfect maximum deflection shot. The last I saw was the MiG spiralling down out of control, minus many parts.

Hoagy would never take any credit for this. 'He just flew into my gunfire', he would say. But it created a bit of a stir back home; the Sea Fury was a fine aircraft, but was now superseded by the faster modern jet and really not a match for the MiG.

But back to the course. It would last just seven weeks, flying the Sea Hawk and concentrating on air weaponry and tactics. We would average three or four flights a day, usually of forty minutes' duration, firing guns at a drogue towed by a Meteor (often flown by my old BSA car friend, Ted Pepper), and discharging rockets and bombs at ground targets at Tain on the Dornoch Firth. We would usually operate in a flight of four, and for air-to-air firing, pilots were given colour-coded cannon shells to identify their hits on the drogue.

The Squadron Commander of 764 was an Irishman, not previously known to me, but it was soon apparent that he resented the fact that former test pilots without recent operational squadron experience were to be given command of first-line squadrons ahead of those such as himself. However, at the end of the day I think the TP acquitted themselves well on the course, and on a personal note I had the satisfaction of topping all the weapons results. At the end of the course I think it caused him to choke on his corn flakes to have to tell me this! However, hopefully, we were above letting petty jealousies interfere with professional judgement, and in due course recommendations went forward to the Admiralty for our next appointment.

With my background with the Scimitar there was always a high likelihood that I might be involved with the first Scimitar squadron to be formed. The Intensive Flying Trials Unit (IFTU) was already well under way at RNAS Ford, and I had had a visit about three weeks before the termination of the course from its CO, Cdr Tom Innes, another former test pilot! Tom, a wealthy Scot of the Innes clan, had not been on good terms with his Senior Pilot, another Scot, and decided he could not recommend him as Senior Pilot of the coming front-line squadron. He had therefore asked the Admiralty to reappoint him sooner rather than later so that there would be continuity from IFTU to the squadron. Thus there was a vacancy.

I didn't know Tom other than by name when he was a test pilot at Farnborough, nor he me. So he had turned up at Lossie for a chat and to see if we would 'get on'. We did. From my point of view it would mean sacrificing an appointment for immediate command of perhaps a Sea Hawk squadron, but the plan was that the bulk of the IFTU would be absorbed into the first Scimitar squadron to be formed at the end of May 1958, and that after a suitable interval of a month or so after embarkation in *Victorious* in September, Tom would hand over command to me.

I was happy with that, but then events took an unfortunate turn. He had hardly had time to return to Ford after the visit when I had a call from Cdr Des Russell, the chief tactical instructor at Lossie: 'Geoff, could you drop in on your way to lunch?' So I did.

'I'm very sorry to have to tell you', he said, 'that Tom had an accident last evening on his way home in his car – and I'm afraid it was fatal.' I was absolutely stunned. Then after a while, Des went on, 'I had a call first thing this morning and have been asked to take over the IFTU and proceed as Tom would have done, which means that as plans stand you would be my Senior Pilot in the new squadron.' He paused for a moment, and then said, 'How do you feel about it?' Then, typically, he said, 'Please don't feel embarrassed if you would like to consider it, but could you let me know by the morning.'

Well, I knew Des of old. He was an extremely nice person with the highest professional standards. He had already commanded two squadrons and as a pilot he had no peers. Having digested all this, without hesitation I said, 'I'm appalled to hear of Tom's accident and I must tell you I was greatly looking forward to working with him. But if you feel I can give you the experience you need as a Senior Pilot, for my part I don't need to give it a second thought.'

So that was it; Des went off to Ford immediately, and I followed as soon as I had formally completed the course. Armed with a certificate of qualification for squadron command, we all went our different ways. Bill and Hoagy were appointed to command of Sea Hawk squadrons and Eric Manual to Sea Venoms. Graham Rowan-Thompson, the youngster of the course, was appointed to a Sea Hawk squadron as Senior Pilot, and the last member was destined for command as soon as a vacancy occurred

I had not known much of Ford since those far-off days when we had disembarked there in our Seafires from HMS *Theseus* at the end of the 1947 commission. Curiously, the Captain at Ford when I arrived for the IFTU was none other than Ed Walthall, late of *Theseus*, late of Syerston and renowned for his goal against Yeovilton! It was nice to meet up with him again. The air station itself hadn't changed much in the intervening ten years. I was allocated part of a house (ex-married quarter) for accommodation, which was comfortable enough, but the houses were a little way away from the wardroom and lacked the togetherness of a normal air station wardroom mess.

The IFTU enjoyed a high standard of pilots, as one might expect of this type of unit, but the more important thing for me was the quality of the technical officers. Donald Titford, the senior mechanical engineer, was outstanding. He was above me in seniority, but for the moment that was of no importance. Donald was innovative, intellectually brilliant and, unusually, combined those talents with practical, effective day-to-day control of the work, always one step ahead. His opposite number, 'Rigour' Mortimer, the senior electrical officer, was arguably only a short head behind him. Despite enormous technical problems which arose from to time, he disdained any tendency to pessimism and would cheerfully work all hours of the day and night with his chaps to meet targets.

After a quick refamiliarisation with the Scimitar we settled down with a fairly relaxed programme for the next two months to complete the trials and, in off-duty time, to play a little golf at Littlehampton, where Des had bought a house in anticipation of his next appointment. Prior to being given a 'pier head jump' to relieve the late-lamented Tom Innes, he had already been appointed to a ship command to take place in December. Now he had been promised that would be fulfilled after a short period in the new squadron.

CHAPTER 16

803 Squadron in Command

At the end of May we moved the main elements of the unit to Lossiemouth to form the basis of No. 803 Squadron. The majority of the personnel stayed with us, and we were duly commissioned as an eight-aircraft squadron plus a Vampire Trainer for instrument rating and general transport use. Our work-up programme was very tight. We were already well into June, and in less than three months were destined to embark in HMS Victorious, a ship recently out of many years' refit with, as it would turn out, her own problems. From our point of view, the programme laid out for us would have tested most squadrons equipped with a new aircraft. But we had two other impediments. First the Scimitar was a complex aircraft, giving the maintainers headaches and sleepless nights. Fuel seemed to spill from everywhere, electrical problems were legend, and the logistics of the new servicing policy of replacement of component parts and not repair was a steep learning curve.

And then, to add to the intensity of the situation, we were told by the Admiralty to work up for an appearance at the SBAC Farnborough Air Show, which, of course, didn't mean just an appearance, but a performance that would do credit to the Royal Navy and its new supersonic aeroplane. Thus we had to work-up pilots who, with the exception of myself, had no experience of deck landing the Scimitar, carry out an air weapons programme to the operational standard required of an embarked squadron and, because the Scimitar was much in demand, we were obliged to fulfil commitments to support Air Days at Navy and RAF stations as well as the prestigious participation in the Farnborough Show.

I would myself undertake displays at Eglinton, Brawdy, Rosyth and RAF Turnhouse, as well as our own Air Day at Lossiemouth. This was a formidable programme, only made possible by the unstinting efforts of the maintainers to produce the aircraft required.

Behind all this was the more serious strategic role of the Scimitar, not then commonly known. Unofficially the Scimitar was just another strike aircraft, but to the privileged few it had a nuclear capability for which special training was required. *Victorious* had nuclear storage potential, and the Scimitar was the delivery vehicle, although at the time of embarkation only two aircraft were so equipped. For the moment this could be set aside, and in fact it was not until after embarking for the first deployment that we were able to devote any attention to this quite complicated programme. It would entail special techniques and a requirement for a fully instrumented range, as well as a decision to determine the most suitable pilots for the task

The SBAC Show at Farnborough was due to take place in the first week of September, and practice for this occupied much of our time in August. Most of us had some previous experience of formation aerobatics in flights of four, but the Scimitar was more of a handful compared with the Sea Hawk or Sea Fury for this purpose.

One of our problems was the reliability of the aircraft – or rather its unreliability. To over-commit ourselves would be foolish. We only had at that time eight aircraft in total, so we settled on employing six for the show and holding two in reserve. Up our sleeves we had one spare at Ford, which didn't belong to us but was promised if we got into difficulty.

It takes an awful lot of sky to carry out aerobatics in formation at high speed, and this can get boring for spectators if there is not something else to occupy their attention. So we decided on continuity as the main theme, and settled on a basic four for aerobatic formation with one other, me, carrying out individual aerobatics to fill in the time that the formation four rearranged itself for its next pass. The sixth pilot would be held in reserve for contingencies, performing other co-ordinated manoeuvres to ensure continuity. But we would first arrive over the airfield to start our display in a formation of six, very low in close formation, at maximum speed, Mach 0.98, well over 700 mph, with noise to match just to wake them all up.

Thus prepared, we faced the next logistic problem. It had been clearly apparent that we would have to find a more adjacent base to Farnborough during the SBAC week, and Ford took pride of place. Although not the nearest option – the RAF base at Odiham just down the road from Farnborough had its attractions – Ford had a number of advantages, not least of which was that it still retained the necessary Scimitar support equipment from IFTU days. It was also only a matter of ten minutes' flying time away and enjoyed similar weather to that of Farnborough, which meant that in the event of inclement weather we would be able to decide on an alternative bad-weather or low-cloud routine before taking off.

On 27 August we departed Lossiemouth for Ford to spend a week for final work-up and polishing of the display programme, and by the start of SBAC week on 1 September we were reasonably satisfied with our performance. We had to remind ourselves that we were first and foremost an operational front-line squadron, and not an outfit formed for displays, but we had done enough, we thought, to put on a good showing.

As it happened, the week went very well, and we were subsequently given highly complementary notices in the national Press and aviation magazines. Press notices prior to the show week had already warmed up spectators by photographs taken at Ford, and headlines such as 'Will They Overstep the Mach?' So we didn't disappoint them when we arrived from the Lappins Road end of the airfield in the west, very low, very fast, just short of Mach 1, enveloped in our little clouds of vapour indicating how close we were to breaking the sound barrier.

In the next ten minutes we would give a respectable display, alternating the formation four with my individual aerobatic routine, which I concluded with a simulated LABS manoeuvre – a low, fast run at nearly 600 kts before applying 4 g to pull up vertically in front of the crowd, invariably disappearing into cloud before rolling out at the top of the half-loop.

Landing back at Ford afterwards, we missed the evening entertainment each day, except for the final performance on the Saturday, when we drove our motley collection of cars back up to Farnborough for the concluding celebrations. It was quite a 'hooley', the officers' mess swamped with VIPs, test pilots from everywhere and others. By the early morning we were ready to go home. Breathalysers had not then been invented, which was fortunate for the majority who left the mess that night. I, however, was fortunate. I had taken the seamanlike precaution of ensuring that a chauffeur was on hand – Pat. She very nobly steered us back to Ford with the aid of directions – usually wrong ones – from Mike Maina. However, we made it without incident, followed by the others in another two cars.

With the show over we returned to Lossie and got down to the remainder of the armament programme, one or two Station Air Days and other matters for the three weeks before we were due to embark.

The persistent poor weather of the past few weeks showed no sign of abating as we prepared to fly to Yeovilton on 24 September prior to embarking the following day. With goodwill messages from the Captain and others, all eight aircraft departed in a cloud of spray down the runway, climbing to 30,000 ft, where the sun shone upon us. Just over one hour later we landed at Yeovilton, where we were to spend the night.

It was nice to be back at Yeovilton. It had been my first naval air station all those years ago for Operational Flying School, and my introduction to, arguably, my favourite aeroplane, the Corsair, and then again with 767 Squadron six years ago. It hadn't changed all that much; same old familiar, friendly wardroom and wartime cabin accommodation. It would remain the heart of naval aviation.

Meanwhile, HMS *Victorious* was tied up alongside Pitch House Jetty at this time, ready to sail early the following morning for a rendezvous with her squadrons in the vicinity of Nab Tower, south-east of the Isle of Wight. Apart from ourselves, 892 Squadron with Sea Venoms, a flight of four Skyraiders from 849 Squadron and four Whirlwind helicopters of 824 Squadron would make up the ship's complement of aircraft. The Skyraiders with AEW (Airborne Early Warning) were to provide air direction for the fighters, while the ASW role of the Whirlwinds was also to replace the more traditional 'guard' ship during take-off and landing operations. The CO of 892 was none other than Eric Manuel from the recent course at Lossiemouth, while Brian Stock with the Skyraider outfit and Jim Trevis with the 824 helicopters were both old friends of long standing.

The following morning, after a short photographic session for the benefit of the air station's records, we waited for our rendezvous time from the ship, which provisionally had been set for around 10 a.m. Then, slightly later than we had anticipated due to last-minute 'wire-pulling tests' by a Gannet from Ford, the ship signalled ready to receive. The order would be Scimitars first, followed by the Sea Venoms and Skyraiders. Jim Trevis, with two of his Whirlwinds, were already embarked, and one would be in position on the port quarter of the ship for the land-on. We had previously agreed that Des would take his four first, and I would follow with the other four at an interval of ten minutes. This would give the flight deck party time to sort things out on the flight deck. They were a new team, had not had a squadron on board before and their only recent experience had been with trials aircraft testing the ship's equipment.

Having seen Des lead the first four off to the ship, I called the tower and, on time, I taxied to the end of the runway and lined up with the other three in position when the control tower came up on the radio: 'Your take-off is delayed, return to dispersal for further instructions.' Over the R/T I ventured an enquiry, but there was no explanation, except that the ship had signalled a deck delay and to await further instructions. So I turned my flight back to dispersal, dismounted and reported to the control tower.

'We know very little,' I was told, 'except that there has been an accident and at the moment they cannot accept any more aircraft.'

So we were left in limbo, not knowing for how long or who or what had been involved. We were not to wait long. *Victorious* reported that she was dispatching three of the Scimitars back to Yeovilton to await further instructions, and almost simultaneously they arrived overhead requesting landing instructions. Then, as the returned pilots reported to the tower, the tragic circumstances of our first visit to the ship partially unfolded. It seemed Des Russell had landed successfully, but then, inexplicably, had gone on and over the front of the angled deck and into the sea. They knew no more than that the helicopter had immediately gone overhead the stricken aircraft, and did not know the fate of the pilot.

This was terrible news. We could not have had a worse start in the ship. Outwardly the other pilots from the first flight remained calm and unruffled, but I knew they must have been shaken by events, more especially since they would most likely have witnessed the accident and been about to carry out their first landings in the Scimitar. Questioning them revealed little more; they had entered the circuit on receiving an affirmative from the ship and Des had made what looked like a normal approach and, as far as they could tell, a satisfactory landing.

It was some hour or so later that the ship signalled a new rendezvous time, which gave me an opportunity to have a last-minute chat to the rest of the pilots before climbing into the cockpit for the second time, Leaving the next senior pilot to bring the remaining three, I departed with my flight of four and in due course called the ship requesting permission to join the circuit. With *Victorious* already turning into wind I lost no time in taking the flight down the starboard side, broke off to port in time-honoured fashion, joined the circuit and landed, shortly to be followed by the others at a reasonable interval. The separate section of three landed some ten minutes later. We were now all safely aboard, no further alarms, and in due course the Sea Venoms and Skyraiders followed suit.

The atmosphere in the ship was melancholy. I went straight up to FLYCO, the flying control position, where I was met by the Commander Air, Jimmy Richardson. He told me the sad news that Des, despite a good landing on the centre line, had come to the end of the run when the wire snapped and the aircraft had gone over the bow of the angled deck. He added that Jim Trevis in the helicopter had immediately put his aircraft over the top of the Scimitar, which remained on the surface for a good minute and more, but despite valiant efforts by the helicopter crewman, Des had been unable to escape from the cockpit and gone down with the aircraft.

A little later on, the Engineering Commander asked if he could address all the squadron pilots in the crew room. The reason for the accident, he revealed, was that the flight deck machinery control room had failed to change the setting on the arrester gear after the previous Gannet landings, with the result that, at the limit of the pull-out of the wire, it had snapped due to the heavier weight and speed of the Scimitar. For him and his engineering staff it was a personal tragedy, but he had been courageous enough to ask that he explain the circumstances to all the squadron pilots – which he did.

An unfortunate aside to all this was that the occasion of the first swept-wing aircraft to enter naval service coupled with a new ship had, with the encouragement of the Navy's Public Relations staff, attracted the interest of a large section of the national Press and a good number of VIPs. Inevitably, numerous photographs and yards of writing covered the front pages of the popular Press next morning, with scant respect to who the reader might be. One photograph, showing the Scimitar cockpit just above the water, with the helicopter and crewman above and Desmond Russell quite obviously doing all he could to escape, was particularly insensitive to everyone involved; but to his wife, who was more than likely to see it, it could have been nothing short of gruesome.

I had a brief meeting a little later with the Captain, visibly upset, and was then instructed to assume temporary command of the squadron pending further instructions from the Admiralty. Today I was 34 years of age. It was my birthday, and in all the circumstances, a more unwelcome birthday present I could not have imagined. Later that evening, a signal from the Admiralty formally confirmed my appointment in command. It had come a month or two before originally planned.

We flew the next day as normal, but then had a short break to deal with the inevitable Board of Inquiry instigated by the Flag Officer Air (Home). It was all pretty straightforward, the reason for the accident not in doubt. Appropriate measures to prevent any recurrence would be taken.

For me there was an irritating and unjustified comment by an over-zealous staff officer on the board to the effect that I, as Senior Pilot, should have issued instructions to squadron pilots to detach certain personal pilot equipment, such as the leg restraint straps, prior to landing. This apparently was a recommendation from the IFTU before Des and I joined it. But we had never felt obliged – nor needed – to follow all their recommendations, and this particular one was contentious, since it would have been virtually impossible to re-engage the links in the event of ejection, resulting in inevitable disaster for the pilot.

I was particularly incensed since I had not been called before the board while it was convened: with good reason. I had nothing to offer in the way of evidence, and I had assumed the board took the same view. Now to make comments *in absentia* – or perhaps more correctly *absente reo* – was shoddy practice. If this particular officer wished to question any part I might have played in the accident, he should have called me before the board.

In due course we received the board's formal report, and the Captain sought my advice and asked how he should respond. I told him the background, which he accepted, and together with a number of more technical comments from Commander Engineering on the state of the arrester gear, he referred them back to the Admiral. It was with some satisfaction that we learnt later that the Admiral, an aviator, with a somewhat more practical outlook, agreed our position and penned an internal memo with a slight dig at the staff officer in question.

By this time we were well on our way to the Mediterranean, where we would complete the work-up of ship and squadrons and deploy for the next three months. HMS *Victorious*, being newly out of long rebuild, had a number of new untried equipment such as Type 984 3-D radar, the steam catapult and a fully angled deck. All this needed to be integrated, personnel trained and procedures established.

We had left Gibraltar after a short break and embarked the Flag Officer Aircraft Carriers and his staff when we suffered our next setback. The launch of the Scimitar off the catapult required it to be rotated so that the tail-skid rested on the deck with the nosewheel in the air, and for this purpose about a foot of the whole length of the catapult track had been strengthened to absorb the considerable download exerted by the tail-skid.

Now, influenced by the presence and pressure from the Admiral's staff, we decided to run before we could walk!

There is always, in carrier operations, the need to expedite take-offs and landings in order to limit the time spent into wind and off the ship's desired course. Perfectly acceptable practice and competition between carriers to achieve the shortest interval between landings is the norm. Equally, no time is lost between the ship coming into wind and the first catapult launch. So on this particular morning, there I am, sitting in the aircraft in the 'praying mantis' position, ready to be launched and with the ship's head coming nicely round into wind, when, to my surprise, I am instructed to go to full power, the flag goes down and I am hurtled forward *still thirty degrees out of wind*! Inevitably, with the aircraft under the total influence of the catapult and no input from the pilot possible, the aircraft slewed into wind, resulting in the tail-skid sliding off the strengthened track.

For the less than two seconds of the launch this slight deviation was not apparent to me, of course, until, immediately on getting airborne, all hell broke loose. The Central Warning System bells clanged loudly in my ears and my attention was drawn immediately to a No. 1 hydraulic system failure. This meant I had lost the facility to raise the undercarriage, or lower the hook or flaps. In riding over the unstrengthened part of the track, the tail-skid was damaged to such an extent that a major hydraulic leak ensued. My mind by this time was very much in top gear, and when things had sorted themselves out and I was safely airborne, the ship and I had a little chat.

At this stage of our work-up, all flying was conducted with a diversionary airfield available, and fortunately we were not far from Oran in Algeria. So, suitably escorted, I made my way at very low airspeed, with the undercarriage and flaps down, to land there forty minutes later. Shortly afterwards the ship closed Oran and sent a maintenance party by air to carry out a temporary repair to the aircraft. Meanwhile I was picked up and brought back to the ship. For the rest of that day and into the late evening, Donald Titford and his chaps worked miracles, so that by the following morning the aircraft was deemed airworthy. I flew ashore in a Skyraider and brought it back to the ship. But unfortunately, that was not the end of the matter.

The ship's report back to the Admiralty caused the inevitable mutterings and 'what ifs' sufficient for them to suspend all further Scimitar operations from the ship, until the tracking could be modified. This was the greatest misfortune for the squadron. We had just begun to work well with the ship, particularly the radar directors, but now we were grounded until we reached Malta about a week later. The ship, too, was having its problems. The Type 984 radar was unreliable and the engineers were working overtime to keep things going. But no one was surprised after a seven-year rebuild.

It would be nearly two months before we resumed normal carrier operations. Before then the squadron disembarked to Halfar in Malta for a week prior to a further two weeks at the French naval air station at Hyères. I had meanwhile had discussions with the Captain, Charles Coke, on the possibility of lifting the ban by imposing certain restrictions for catapulting. As a result of a scrambled telephone call which he and I made from Malta to the Admiralty, I found myself dispatched by civil air to Whitehall for discussions.

The meeting was alive with senior 'brass', all making sure their yardarm was clear. Nothing would shake them. Caution was the keynote, and I returned empty handed. The ship would be provided with a modification in Malta dockyard, and until then the Naval Staff reluctantly agreed that, subject to carefully controlled catapult conditions, we should be allowed to launch up to four aircraft for the purpose of disembarkation to the naval air station at Halfar, with a similar dispensation for a previously planned visit to the French naval air station at Hyères.

In both places it was time well spent. The pilots were able to achieve sufficient flying hours to maintain efficiency, although personally my time was heavily bought up with administrative matters before and after the four days spent in London arguing a near-lost cause.

We had always planned to disembark to Hyères while the ship visited Toulon, so it was that on 24 September, almost a year to the day since that first fateful embarkation, we were given an enthusiastic and very generous welcome at this southern bastion of French naval aviation. We were also given a French motor car for the duration of our visit, a Citroen 2CV! Despite its odd appearance it was a wonderful experience. The French driver who brought it to the squadron dispersal happily demonstrated how it would ride over any rough ground by leaving the road and taking it over the bumpy grass airfield at speed without any discomfort. That set the pattern – from then on the shortest route was best.

The French can turn on the hospitality when they wish, and during our week or so there we wanted for nothing. The food in their mess was outstanding, accompanied, of course, by copious quantities of 'vin ordinaire'. The French work routine was strange to us; neither standard nor tropical routine as we knew it, but more shop-opening hours of, say, Gibraltar, Malta or most other Mediterranean ports of call. So we would crack off with first flights around seven thirty, pack up at midday and resumed at five for perhaps a flight or two. During the long lunch 'hours' and with some flying still planned, it was easy to fall into the trap of accepting the over-generous importuning of our hosts with the wine, but I relied on the common sense of all the pilots, and I never had an occasion to suspect that those due to fly in the late afternoon had violated the unwritten code of '*no drink before getting airborne*'.

A few days after our arrival, I was called to the ship, now alongside in Toulon, and asked to report to the Captain.

'Geoffrey,' he started, 'I hope I haven't disturbed your plans for the day at Hyères, but I had the Captain of the French carrier *Arromanches* to dine with me last evening, and he expressed a lot of interest in our angled deck and new catapult. So I told him I would be pleased to have one of my officers visit his ship to explain the advantages in more detail.' He went on, 'Commander Air suggested you should be asked and ...' He paused for a moment for me to comment.

This was uncanny, *Arromanches* was my first operational carrier, then named HMS *Colossus*, and I immediately told Captain Coke of the coincidence, adding that I would naturally be delighted to visit my old ship.

So he telephoned his opposite number – and within a very few minutes I was transported to my old ship and welcomed aboard by her Captain. My first impression was that she was a little elderly, as indeed she was, but the traditional dark grey paint of the French Navy did nothing to relieve this impression of obsolescence. Anyway, we went below to the Captain's quarters for a chat and the inevitable aperitif. He was intrigued with my former acquaintance with his ship, and pondered that twelve years and more had elapsed from that time.

What was even more astonishing was that his fighter squadron was equipped with the Corsair aircraft, the same aircraft I had been flying in this same ship all those years ago. The French Navy was some way behind us in its carrier aircraft, and had yet to introduce a truly high-performance jet fighter, although in the matter of ASW, with the Breguet Alize, it was on a par with the Gannet, both aircraft entering their respective services within a short timescale. *Arromanches* had been partially rebuilt and modernised a year previously, and fitted with an interim angled deck of four degrees, but this lacked the benefit to be derived from the full eight degrees of *Victorious* with the greater availability of deck parking space which that brought.

We wandered up to the flight deck, which was perhaps not quite as spick and span as I was used to, and discussed the new innovations now current in the RN carriers, including the new 'reflector sight' to replace the former 'batsman' to assist with landings, and I told him, also, of the way the flight deck space could be better utilised with a fully angled deck, as well as the more obvious benefit to the pilot. He was very proud of his ship, was due shortly to be relieved at the end of his time in command to report to the French Navy Staff; hence his interest in future developments. A little later, down below in his cabin, we had a light lunch, concluded our discussions, and I left to report to Capt Coke. It had been a most agreeable and, for me, quite nostalgic visit.

By the first week of December the decking had been strengthened and we were back in business without restrictions for the remainder of the deployment to the Mediterranean. We would spend Christmas on board, sailing for home in mid-January and flying off to Lossiemouth for a short period of leave.

On return I selected three pilots for LABS training and flew four aircraft to West Freugh, near Stranraer, where an instrumented range in Luce Bay had been made available for us. For the next five days we practised toss-bombing using 22 lb practice bombs, which had similar characteristics to the real thing. It was a pleasant sojourn, even in the winter conditions, and this new method of delivering a bomb to its target intrigued me; the more so since the results were surprisingly good and errors consistently small.

The next few months would see us alternately on board and at West Freugh until, in May, *Victorious* joined with HMS *Centaur* in preparation for Exercise Shopwindow, a demonstration of naval air power for the benefit of the Society of British Aircraft Constructors, the very same organisation we had performed for at Farnborough, only this time we would be on our home ground – at sea.

We had embarked the new Sea Vixen squadron to replace the Sea Venoms for this demonstration, and very shortly we would demonstrate how very dependent the modern aircraft is on well-planned logistical support. During a night exercise, one of the Sea Vixens had experienced a minor problem but

The launch of HMS *Ark Royal* at Liverpool in 1951 seen from the flight deck of HMS *Illustrious*.

The author departs RAF Bentwaters after a demonstration to USAF. *Photo courtesy of Master Sergeant David Meyer.*

HMS *Rocket*, leader of the 3rd Training Squadron in Loch Foyle.

The author with his SS Jaguar of 1938 vintage used whist at the Empire Test Pilot's School.

Landing of N113. (Scimitar)

RAF Mauripur, Karachi. The author with Flt Lt Robbie Robinson (2nd Pilot) and other crew members and scientists.

12 Squadron Command Course No 1 at RNAS Lossiemouth. From left: Graham Rowan Thompson, Bill Hart, Hoagy Carmichael, Eric Manuel, author and Geoff Perkins.

803 Squadron Farnborough Air Display in 1958. Forming up and then arriving at the airfield at Mach .98 to open the show. The author is leading the second section.

Squadron pilots at RNAS Yeovilton immediately before departing for HMS *Victorious*. From the left Cdr Des Russel, Mike Maina, John Beyfus, Peter Barber, Lyn Middleton, John Beard, Chuck Giles and the author.

The author landing a Scimitar aboard HMS *Victorious* in 1958.

HMS *Victorious* going alongside Pier 90 in New York, 1959.

A Scimitar landing aboard with the QE2 in the background.

A Scimitar in final approach to *Victorious*.

Scimitar 'touch and go' on *Victorious*.

The first use of the barrier by a Scimitar in anger flown by Sub Lt Westlake when the tailhook failed to lower.

HMS *Victorious* at sea.

NATO officers from SACLANT visit the nuclear cruiser USS *Newport News* for an impressive display of speed.

My host at the Society of Experimental Test Pilots celebration dinner, Captain John Young, an astronaut and Apollo 16 Commander.

Nos 3 and 6 Squadron's Engineers and Technicians who worked tirelessly in very hot conditions.

Greeted aboard USS *Lexington* by the Air Boss.

NAVAL AIR POWER

The author and Lt Cdr JA Taylor arrive at RNAS Lossiemouth after their non-stop flight across the Atlantic, the first by a RN aircraft. *(Flight Deck)*

On Monday, 4th October, Buccaneer Mk. 2 XN 974 (Commander G. R. Higgs and Lieutenant Commander J. A. Taylor, right) flew non-stop from Goose Bay to Lossiemouth in four hours and twenty minutes.

This 2,000 mile flight was an epic: not only was it the first Atlantic crossing in one hop by a Fleet Air Arm aircraft without flight refuelling, but it also gave a glimpse of our very considerable strike capability. No extra fuel was provided for the aircraft other than that available to regular front line squadrons, and the fact that 2,000 nautical miles were flown with ample fuel reserves, reveals an exceptionally large radius of action.

If one takes a pair of compasses to a chart of the Indian Ocean, adds a carrier's mobility of 600 miles per day AND a warning time of a day or two (plus the Buccaneer's flight refuelling capability), it can be easily seen that the Royal Navy's presence in that area, or any other area for that matter, is of the utmost military and political importance.

For what other reason is H.M.S. EAGLE, as we go to press, poised off the East African coast? And, let us note, she was there five days before the Prime Minister announced it on 1st December, having crossed the Indian Ocean in complete secrecy in six days.

Buccaneer Mk2 deck trials on HMS *Ark Royal*.

The author's wife
Pat receives the
SACLANT bowls
trophy from
Admiral
Dennison USN.

SETP visit to RAE Bedford, Bill Bedford, Hawker's Chief Test Pilot, on my right welcoming the SETP President.

The author with Lt Cdr Smith USN prior to his first flight in a Phantom Mk2 from NAS Oceana in 1962.

The author with Andrew Fyall, Project Officer, during the Rain Erosion Trials in Singapore during 1974.

A Scimitar launch from HMS *Victorious*.

RAF Tengah, Singapore after the Phantom flight during the Rain Erosion trials.

Post flight discussion with Andrew Fyall during Rain Erosion trials.

deemed it prudent to divert to RAF Station Valley, on Anglesey. Early the following morning I had scarcely awoken when the steward came to my cabin to say Commander Air would like to see me as soon as convenient. So I climbed my way up to the bridge to be told that Valley had no means of starting the Sea Vixen after its minor trouble, and it was proposed to strap a Palouste Air Starter pod on the inboard pylon of a Scimitar, and – of course – would I fly it to Valley?

We had never attached a Palouste to a Scimitar before, either ashore or afloat. Moreover, so far as I was aware there was no catapult clearance for it. It was shaped a little like a drop tank, but considerably heavier, causing the starboard wing to drop after the launch to a degree that surprised me. However, we made it safely to Valley, I parked close enough to the Vixen for the ground crew to connect up, and together flew back to the ship. I got my freebie from the Vixen CO in the wardroom bar later on that evening!

With only a short spell at West Freugh for LABS toss-bombing, we would be embarked for the whole of the three months from May to the beginning of August. The ship had been worked fairly hard during the early part of 1959, and at the end of May she entered Rosyth for a week's self maintenance before taking part in further intensive exercises.

A few days after entering Rosyth, late one afternoon with the day's work done, I was walking the quarterdeck, in time-honoured fashion, preoccupied with my thoughts, head down, taking a short constitutional before dinner, when the Captain appeared up the ladder from his quarters and joined me, 'hoping he wasn't intruding'. So we carried on back and forth for a while, chatting generally, when he paused in his stride. 'Would you please excuse me for a moment, I must just deal with a little matter that has come to my attention.' And off he strode to the head of the gangway where the Officer of the Watch and Quartermaster were stationed to monitor arrivals and departures – mostly officers, since the after gangway was mainly for their use.

In due course he returned, apologising for the interruption and expressing the hope that I had not been inconvenienced. He explained that while we were walking he had witnessed the arrival of an officer on board who had not been properly received – saluted by the gangway staff. So, as he said, he felt it incumbent to remind the Quartermaster of his duties! With that we carried on with our walk. I later asked the Quartermaster whether he had been admonished.

'Oh no,' he said, 'the Captain explained why he had come and was very nice about it, which did me more good than a telling off.'

To understand this apparently unimportant little episode, it would be necessary to understand the Captain – Charles Playfair Coke. An Edwardian gentleman of impeccable manners, quietly spoken, his attitude and approach to an ordinary seaman would be the same as to an admiral. His Edwardian manners were matched by the cut of his uniform, which more resembled the fashion of Adm Beattie and Jutland than the modern day Reefer jacket cut and buttoned very high, topped by an equally high white stiff collar and a cap invariably pulled low over his forehead. There was no hint of affectation; that was the way he was, the ultimate Edwardian gentleman.

A few days later I was invited to join him for a picnic, and armed with a large hamper we drove off into the hills behind Rosyth. He was a fascinating conversationalist. We talked of a mutual interest as water colourists and other matters. No 'shop', with the sole exception that I gathered he was a little disillusioned with the way the Navy was heading. On leaving *Victorious* a few months later, and after attending the Imperial Defence College course, he would retire, the first carrier captain not to be promoted admiral. But it was his own choice and the Navy's considerable loss.

Then, towards the end of June, the squadron complement of aircraft was increased to twelve. My maintenance team now numbered over two hundred, including a large number of senior rates; and I received another two qualified Scimitar pilots from the training squadron at Lossiemouth, giving me thirteen pilots to play with. Overall, this was quite a handful in a ship the size of *Victorious*. At 30,000 tons she was noticeably smaller than her contemporaries such as *Ark Royal* and *Eagle*, both well over 40,000 tons, and being some fifty feet shorter in terms of overall length, flight deck parking and hangar space had always been at a premium. The total number of aircraft now on board far exceeded the designed complement of twenty-three fixed wing and eight helicopters, but I had already been made aware of the reason for this: we would shortly deploy to United States waters and exercise with the American Atlantic Fleet.

American attack carriers at this time were in a league of their own in size and number of aircraft embarked. Variously of 60,000 tons or more, with a flight deck area of around four acres, they could easily accommodate sixty and more aircraft, depending on size. With our increased number of aircraft we were not about to be seen as the poor relations when we joined them for

Exercise Riptide in July; and we took some satisfaction in the knowledge that the recent inventions which they enjoyed, such as the angled deck, steam catapult and reflector sight to assist pilots when landing, all derived from the 'Brits'! We could also show them a thing or two with air direction, since they possessed nothing as sophisticated as our 3-D Type 984 Radar and Comprehensive Display System (CDS). Smaller is sometimes better, it is said, and we hoped to prove it.

With only a short spell at West Freugh for LABS bombing, we were destined to be embarked again for more exercises and visits to Aarhus in Denmark and Oslo before the ship departed for the USA. Shortly before our arrival in Oslo, I received a signal from the naval attaché there – none other that my old friend and CO from 767 Squadron days, Dave Newbery. He and his Norwegian wife, whom I knew from our squadron days, entertained three of us in great style during our stay, and we were able to return the compliment on board during the inevitable cocktail party.

We had occasionally operated without a diversionary airfield before, but now, if we were to continue flying while crossing the Atlantic, we had no choice, and accepted this increased risk for the whole of the week. Generally the risk is small, but a diversionary airfield takes the pressure off those occasions when either the ship's arrester gear becomes unserviceable or an aircraft suffers an emergency, preventing it from landing aboard. We had already experienced one occasion in the Bay of Biscay, out of diversion range, when a pilot could not lower the hook and was recovered into the specially designed nylon barrier: OK for the pilot but tough on the aircraft! However, there was no repetition during the crossing, and we managed a full day's flying for the six-day passage.

Arriving off the US eastern seaboard on 7 July, we announced our arrival! The Americans had requested that we test their coastal defence system as part of the planned exercises during our visit, and so at first light I led a flight of four Scimitars across the coast of North Carolina at very low level and high speed, to Greensboro, some one hundred and fifty miles inland, creating the most frightful racket during the flight and subsequent simulated attack, but succeeding in doing so totally undetected throughout the sortie. The Americans felt outsmarted and less than happy when we arrived a few days later in Norfolk, complaining that we had not given them notice of our arrival off their coast!

We now got down to the real purpose of our US visit, Exercise Riptide. This was a very large exercise involving the bulk of the American Atlantic

Fleet, in which we would be totally integrated. It lasted a full ten days and nights, culminating in UK and US aircraft cross-operating between carriers to test operating procedures. I took my No. 2 to USS *Saratoga* to land on her deck, but just as I was approaching this huge acreage, her deck was fouled and I had to take a 'wave-off'. My No. 2, following me, was more fortunate and landed; but then, for some reason not explained, the Americans had had enough of the Scimitar and wanted no more, so I went home in a huff. Later I learnt they had found the aircraft difficult to handle on their deck!

Later that day we entertained a large number of Congressmen, Senators, Senior Service Chiefs and Press on board to witness a day's flying, and, as it turned out, for me to distinguish myself again. As part of the programme I carried out a low-level, high-speed attack on the ship, culminating in a high (about 7 g) pull-up at close to 700 kts. Soon after the rotation, although it had been tested and cleared beyond this 'g', the hood parted company with the aircraft and my visor parted company with my helmet. For a brief moment I wondered what on earth had happened, and remember thinking that this was the first stage of the ejection seat firing. But fortunately it wasn't.

The immediate sensation was of a tornado swirling around inside the cockpit, and at this stage I was busy trying to keep my hands inside the cockpit and my eyeballs in their sockets. More by instinct I completed a roll off the top, and then, apart from articles of one sort or another which had gone over the side, I started to collect as much else as I could, maps and notes of one sort or another, while slowing to a more respectable speed. By now the ship was on the R/T: 'Nugget 201 (my call sign), you lost something from the aircraft as you pulled up in your manoeuvre. We think it has landed in the sea but could not identify it.' Then added: 'Can you comment?'

So I did, with the reply, 'I've gone back to open cockpit days – my hood left me.' Once sorted out, the return to the ship without a hood was really quite pleasant, and I landed without incident. Of course, our guests had had a ringside seat. They had seen the small explosion as the hood fired and probably thought it was all part of the show.

With Riptide over we got down to the real business of the three 'goodwill' visits we were to make. In Norfolk again for the 'wash-up', or analysis, of the exercise, I and a couple of others were invited to the home of an RN member of the NATO staff, Cdr 'Corky' Corkhill. He was somewhat older than me, and I knew him only slightly, and that mostly by reputation. But what I didn't then know was that I would come to know him and his wife very well within a year – I would relieve him on the staff in NATO and take over his house; the corner house on 53rd and Holly Road would be our home for two years. But that was in the future. We were now about to depart for Boston, Mass.

Massachusetts, of course, has strong British connections from the time of the *Mayflower's* arrival in Plymouth, and the Boston people turned out to be exceptional hosts. Our opening cocktail party to invited guests brought rich rewards to myself and two others – the ship's Navigator and the senior Direction Officer. In the course of our duties as hosts, we met a very expansive lady and her husband, who, it turned out, was a retired group captain RAF. She, the daughter of a former Harvard professor, and obviously well heeled, lived in Cambridge, a suburb of Boston, but also had a 'place', as she put it, out of town. To this we were invited to spend the weekend. It was non-stop entertainment: golf, boating and swimming on a nearby very large lake, and constant visits to her friends for this or that party, but mainly, I suspect, to show off her British guests. They were generous hosts in the extreme, and astonishingly, before leaving Boston, she arranged for one of her close friends, Clive, with whom we had played golf, to fly down to New York to entertain us there, clearly at her expense!

Arriving at Pier 90 in New York, he was there to meet us. He seemed to be a member of a number of clubs, obviously knew his way about town, and for four days we wanted for nothing. It was an extravagance beyond anything we could reasonably have expected, even from Americans. The first evening we dined at one of his clubs in a superb restaurant, high overlooking Central Park, before going downtown to Eddie Condon's, a fashionable but dingy establishment where, in semi-darkness, we listened to superb jazz and drank our host's expensive champagne. For two days he showed us New York, scarcely stopping for a moment except to invite him on board, where we could pause for a while and return a little of his generous hospitality.

We were not alone in experiencing the extraordinary warmth of the typical American. Others, including the sailors, would relate similar experiences. In Norfolk, Boston and New York, it had been undiluted and unstinting generosity and friendliness. We left in good spirits in early August for our return to the UK and leave for the ship's company.

By the middle of September we were deeply involved in an exercise Barfrost off the northern coast of Norway, making mock attacks against Norwegian airfields and towns, when the exercise gave way to a real-life drama.

The ship had lost contact with an AEW Skyraider that had been providing us with strike direction during our low-level simulated attacks, after reporting being an estimated 180 miles north of the ship but outside radar cover. As the aircraft continued to fail to report and no contact was made, concern mounted and searches were duly launched by all available aircraft. By this time, knowing the endurance of the aircraft, it was presumed to be down in the sub-zero waters near the Arctic Circle. For the whole of the day and into the night of 23 September, every available aircraft was scrambled for designated search areas, but without success.

By the following morning there seemed little hope of survival; then a signal was received from the Admiralty, passing a report from our naval attaché in Moscow that an aircraft had ditched alongside some Russian trawlers. The position given was some degrees west of where the aircraft should have been operating and where the search had been concentrated.

So the whole air group was launched again to locate the Russian vessel. I took my four 200 miles north in the general direction of the trawler's reported position, but despite an extensive search saw nothing. It was a wintry-looking sea, windy with heavy waves that restricted visibility to the point where, unless you were almost overhead a small vessel, it seemed unlikely that it could be spotted. We learnt later that the crew had been picked up by one of the trawlers and then transferred to a depot ship before being transferred to, and returned in, HMS *Urchin* of the Fishery Protection Squadron.

I had now been in the squadron for eighteen months and in command for a year. My time, I knew, was drawing near when I would be reappointed. The ship was due for another spell in the Mediterranean in November, but before that I had been lumbered with a task that rightly should have been the responsibility of the Naval Test Squadron at Boscombe Down – night carrier clearance for the Scimitar. When requested, the CO of the test squadron had reneged on the grounds that none of his pilots had current night deck-landing experience. We in my squadron hadn't either, but with pressure from the Flag Officer, were committed. I therefore 'volunteered' myself, holding John Beard, my No. 2, as a reserve.

It seemed to me prudent to carry out a few launches from the Bedford catapult before the trial in the ship, so after a session or two of night MADDLS at Lossiemouth, I flew down to my old stamping ground and renewed acquaintance with a number of old friends. They were all very kind, welcoming me warmly, and in due course I completed a session of night launches and returned to Lossiemouth before going out to the ship in Lyme Bay on 19 October.

Over the next four days, despite an almost total lack of wind, I flew five night sorties with a total of nineteen landings, various overshoots and 'rollers' (landing with the hook up) before calling it a day. This was more than enough to 'clear' the aircraft for night operations – if they ever became necessary.

The aircraft was not an ideal aircraft to land on board at night. With its high nose-up attitude on the approach, the deck would disappear in the latter stages, and on the dark moonless nights when I flew, with the exception of a destroyer stationed ahead of the carrier with masthead lights showing to provide a rudimentary horizon, there were no other reference points for guidance to the deck. The reflector sight provided height discrimination, but otherwise was of little help. It resembled flying into a dark hole. However, there were no mishaps and we made our recommendations to the Admiralty.

There was an amusing story I came across later on reading Adm Sir John Treacher's book *Full Throttle*. In the course of the last sortie there was little natural wind, the ship was making a healthy thirty knots straight towards the coast and we were keen to achieve one more landing, when the destroyer ahead signalled an anguished 'I can hear the dogs barking.' Clearly worried at his close proximity to the beach, he was much relieved when I landed on, the ship altered course and the dogs could no longer be heard!

After a busy month in the Mediterranean exercising closely with the American 6th Fleet, we turned for home, and on 12 December I left the ship for the last time to fly to Lossiemouth and relinquish my command. Shortly beforehand, I had been given advance notice of my next appointment – to the Royal Air Force Flying College at Manby for an Advanced Air Warfare course lasting six months. But I had more important matters to see to before that.

CHAPTER 17

Goodbye to All That

Pat and I had now been engaged for two years and had decided to marry when my time in command of 803 Squadron came to an end. So with my old friend, Bill Noble, lined up as best man, we tied the knot at Berrow church, the local parish church to Pat's parents' home. It was a highly successful occasion, attended by the usual array of family and friends and a number of officers from the ship. So ended an over-long bachelorhood that proved in every way to be a propitious time to make this momentous change. By the end of December, with a new wife and with leave coming to an end, I was given another huge boost – advance notice for promotion to commander. This was splendid news. Apart from anything else, it meant a considerable increase in pay at a time when it was most needed.

Somehow or another we had acquired a dog, Rinty, so with the car up to the gunwales, with luggage in a precarious state of untidiness and animal under Pat's feet in the well of the passenger seat, we set off at a nice steady rate for the far reaches of Lincolnshire – in particular Mablethorpe, where we had arranged temporary accommodation for the duration of the course.

We had coasted along quite nicely and I was congratulating myself that the cases, bags, pots and pans and so forth were still much where we had crammed them on starting off when, travelling along a narrow road through a small village, a young urchin, without any hint that he was about so to do, suddenly dashed out into the road only yards in front of us. I braked hard and the wretched boy came to no harm; but the chaos inside the car was another matter. It thoroughly frightened the poor dog, who by that time had been sleeping peacefully, not to mention Pat, who found a frying-pan and sundry other articles flying about her person in unrestrained glee, or so it seemed. Order restored and cursing little boys for evermore, we proceeded for the remainder of the journey, settled in to our new temporary home and looked forward to whatever 1960 might bring.

In a number of ways this was a turning point in my career. Most obvious, of course, was the responsibility I had now acquired on my marriage. Gone would be the carefree days when I had only myself to consider. We were now a team, and consultation and agreement would replace the more insular approach of the bachelor lifestyle. At 34 years of age it was high time I settled down and thought more of the future; never afraid of a challenge, I looked forward to it.

But from a career point of view I faced a different prospect, and within a few weeks it would manifest itself all too clearly. With promotion my operational flying days were over after sixteen years, and as if to reinforce the point I was now forewarned of a staff appointment that would follow the present course at Manby, but not until I had completed the statutory Staff College course. The Navy had never placed much emphasis on staff training, in direct contrast to the Army and Air Force, where qualification at a staff college was a prerequisite for promotion. But in the last few years we dark blue chaps had suffered a few reversals in the cut and thrust of Whitehall shenanigans, particularly with the Air Force, and decided that if we couldn't beat them on equal terms we had better join them.

So, hardly had I started at the Flying College when I was telephoned by the Admiralty Appointers. 'Ah, Geoffrey,' Ian Robertson intoned, 'we have been considering your next appointment; how would you like a spell in the States after the arduous business of running 803?'

Then, before I had time to answer, he went on, 'Charles Evans, whom you know, of course, is going to Norfolk as Deputy SACLANT (Supreme Allied Commander Atlantic), and Ray Lygo, his Staff Aviation Officer, whom you also know, was pencilled in to accompany him for an operations staff appointment there. Well, Ray feels with his seniority as a commander that he ought to go to sea next, so the Admiral has suggested you in his place.'

The die was cast. After Manby, we would go to good old US of A, where I would attend the Armed Forces Staff College course in Norfolk, Virginia, lasting another six months, before taking up my appointment on the staff of SACLANT.

For a newly married and promoted commander it seemed heaven sent, and in due course so it would be. But first there was a little matter of spending six months with the 'Crabs', as the Air Force was commonly known by the Navy.

RAF Air Warfare Course

The Flying College was one of the élite educational colleges of the Royal Air Force. It was established to prepare senior officers for high command, and

189

was very much a 'gentleman's' course attended by group captains and senior wing commanders. For some time one naval officer of commander rank had been included, but I now broke the tradition. I would not make that rank for another six months.

The Commandant of the college, Air Cdre Teddy Donaldson, had earned moderate fame as a member of the RAF High-Speed Flight some years previously when it established a new world record in the Meteor. Later he became the *Daily Telegraph's* Air Correspondent. During the course he invited a number of students and their wives to dinner, for which his gourmet table was renowned. He was proud of relating to you how he would first shoot and then prepare jugged hare in his rather special way. Pat and I were privileged and thoroughly enjoyed the evening.

But his more notable achievement during the six months we were there was to protect one of the Air Force officers from court martial. An extremely experienced wing commander, who had commanded a Canberra aircraft squadron in the not too distant past, was careless enough to attempt to land with the undercarriage up. Realising his error when very close to the runway, he was, nevertheless, skilful enough to succeed in hauling it back into the air as he felt the underside of the aircraft touch the ground. So off he went again, to land properly this time, with the undercarriage down.

But of course he had severely damaged the aircraft's structure, and current RAF regulations were that an 'undercarriage-up' landing was an automatic court martial offence. The Commandant knew this, of course, but to his everlasting credit he decided, before reporting it to higher command, to deal with it himself. He gave the offending officer a formal admonishment, which he recorded, and by his action, rendered a CM impossible, subsequently reporting to the Air Ministry that he had dealt with the matter himself. This was his last job, and perhaps he had nothing to lose by incurring the wrath of those higher up, but his stocks with the course members soared with this decision.

We worked in syndicates, and for the flying part of the course, which was equally divided between flying and studies, I was teamed up with Gp Capt 'Mac' McLean, a much-decorated Australian; it was a most happy experience and he became a good friend of Pat and myself during the time we were there.

The studies were closely oriented towards the then current 'Cold War' problems, and the college was used by the Ministry of Defence as a sort of 'think tank' to assist in its planning. It was a fascinating period, with often considerable sustained argument before we presented our solutions to the directing staff. Not unnaturally, the old chestnut of submarine or V Bomber delivering nuclear weapons was much to the fore, but I was a lone voice.

A number of visits of one sort or another broke the routine, including a four-day tour to Europe visiting two American Air Force bases, where they both excelled themselves with air displays and then, in the evening, barbecues enough to feed the five thousand. We wound up the tour with a couple of days in Paris, alternating between NATO Headquarters – then in Paris, but later in Brussels when the French divorced themselves militarily from the Alliance – and the 'Crazy Horse' night-club, an establishment, it seemed, that was well known to the majority of the course, particularly those having served in the Second Tactical Air Force.

Of some special interest to me was the time in the air, when we were required to perform the duties of navigator in the Canberra while another student flew in the front seat. With only one exception, we were all pilots with varying backgrounds, and those single-seat 'jockeys' like myself had always relied on our own 'pilot navigation'. Others, such as the bomber and coastal pilots, had had the luxury of a navigator, and it was unlikely that those pilots had ever had recourse to operate the navigational equipment themselves. Now we would all be turned into competent navigators, able to operate effectively all the navigational aids available, and soon we would be put to the test.

As a sort of celebration at the end of the course a visit to Malta was programmed. Some would travel in the college's Valetta and the rest would fly the four Canberras to the RAF base at Luqa. Mac and I drew a lucky straw. We would take a Canberra. I would trust him to get us there with the aid of the Decca navigation system that, by this time, was 'old hat' to us, and he would rely on me to navigate him home. The Flying College enjoyed an enviable reputation throughout the Air Force, and the Luqa Station Commander and his chaps laid on a fine programme of entertainment for the two days we were there. A fitting end to an academic course of some distinction, punctuated by sufficient flying – nearly one hundred hours – to keep our feet, metaphorically speaking, on the ground.

I had already been notified of the travel arrangements for America, but was ready for a short period of leave to sort things out, not the least of which was the laying-up of the car and arranging for Rinty to be looked after in our absence. Lovely dog that he was, part Collie, he had caused a local farmer at Mablethorpe some consternation by rounding up his chickens after escaping from the house. We paid for the damaged or distressed chickens, but I wasn't surprised later on after we had left him with my parents that he proved too much of a handful, and a new home was found for him – on a farm!

CHAPTER 18

Back to America - US Armed Forces Staff College

Well, it was for me, but for Pat it was not only to be her first visit but also her first abroad anywhere. These were the days when, for the majority, abroad meant the Isle of Wight or Isle of Man, or even Scotland! Hard to imagine now with packaged holidays to just about everywhere and cruise ships of mammoth proportions carrying four and more thousand passengers to wherever your imagination takes you.

But for us, in 1960, it would be the RMS *Queen Elizabeth* to Pier 90 and New York. I was no stranger to this, either. In 1944 I had made the same voyage in the same ship to exactly the same pier in New York, though in vastly different circumstances. Then she was a rather drab grey troop ship, continually subject to the threat of submarine attack, and comfort was at a premium; but now she was resplendent in the traditional red and black, the hallmark of Cunard, and we would travel in relative style, enjoying five days at sea and reflecting what life would be like in the 'States'. Then again, it seemed only yesterday that I had looked out at the Statue of Liberty in HMS *Victorious* on our way to our berth at the same Pier 90. I was getting to be an old hand.

It was hot on our arrival in New York, very hot, but there was a Good Samaritan to ease our way through the formalities and relieve us of baggage and any other problems. Mr MacStoker from the UK Mission to the United Nations had been helping the arrival and departure of British Service officers for many years, and his knowledge and influence was a byword. So it was that having made sure that we knew the departure time of the train from Pennsylvania station, he wisely advised a boat trip round New York on the First and Hudson Rivers to relieve the heat, and said, 'Leave everything else to me.'

On arrival in New York I had received a message in the ship from my Boston friends of nearly a year ago. Drop everything, it said in effect, and come straight up to Boston with your new wife to stay for a while. I had forewarned her of the date of our arrival, but hardly expected her not to understand that that would be quite impossible, so I telephoned her. 'I have first to report to the Staff College', I said, but added that we would take an early opportunity to visit and would telephone from Norfolk when we had settled in and the dictates of the course allowed.

I detected an increasingly wintry American lady on the other end of the line as we talked, obviously not used to being rebuffed in her plans, and by the end of our conversation she was clearly offended. Later, from Norfolk, I telephoned on two occasions, but it was evident that the association, which had been warm and almost outrageously generous, was a thing of the past. To scorn the advances of a rich American lady was unheard of.

My predecessor at SACLANT and the Admiral's secretary, Edmund Berry, had thoughtfully arranged accommodation in Norfolk at Tallwood Street, a ranch-type house perfectly suited to our needs for the duration of the Staff College course, after which we proposed to move out of town.

We settled in to our new home aided by typically friendly and great-hearted neighbours. In short time, with their help, we became proficient at barbecuing almost everything – American style, which meant monstrous T-bone steaks, ribs and chicken any way you like, and of course the inevitable burgers. But their generosity went beyond this. They owned a useful boat for water skiing. The Norfolk area is a wonderful place for water sports, and soon we were both able to more than hold our own on the skis. It was a splendid introduction to the laid-back American way of life, and from here on we were to make the most of it.

Norfolk was not a particularly attractive town. Understandably, almost totally devoted to the needs of the US Navy, it lacked a sense of permanency, which reflected its ever-changing population with ships' crews away for long periods. But it was pleasant enough, if indiscriminately overburdened with signs and gaudy placards on buildings, streets and any spare space in archetypical American fashion but so alien to that in the UK.

From Tallwood Street the Staff College was on the other side of a busy railway leading out of town from the main naval base. Not a long journey, but not infrequently I would be held up by the passage of a goods train – not just any old goods train, but one that frequently consisted of several hundred wagons of considerable size. Counting them was good therapy when pressed for time to make the first lecture, knowing that it might be fifteen minutes or more before the gates would open to admit the ever-lengthening queue.

So I commenced the second half of 1960 in continuous studies, but now devoted more to tri-service plans and operations, much of it directly related to the Far East theatre, particularly Laos. Vietnam was yet to come. I think that we British – apart from myself as sole naval representative, there were two or three Army and Air Force officers on the course – viewed the forthcoming prospects with a more detached outlook than the Americans, who accounted for the bulk of the students. Mainly half-colonels or equivalent, it was evident they considered their careers depended on their acquitting themselves well, and consequently they were bemused by the more relaxed attitude of the foreign element, which included representatives from other NATO countries as well as ourselves.

Everything was done with typical American thoroughness and more than a degree of overkill, with little thought to expense. As an example, a visit to the US Army at Fort Bragg tied up the better part of the local police force, which would precede the coaches in which we travelled, stopping all other traffic in order that our progress would be unhindered. Outriders on motor cycles accompanied every coach. The sense of importance was tremendous; but perhaps not nearly as impressive as the live display of guided weapons and other armament at the Army base. Live ground-to-ground rocket missiles disappeared down range for scores of miles, while ground-to-air missiles attacked and destroyed drone air targets flying overhead. As a demonstration of modern weaponry it was unsurpassed, but more important was the fact that it was all laid on solely for the staff course, although VIPs from this or that political party had been invited. The cost must have been astronomical.

Extravagant as that was, a few weeks later the US Navy and US Marine Corps laid on a full-scale opposed amphibious assault exercise in North Carolina which was nothing short of a mini 'Overlord'. The forces numbered many thousands, air, land and sea, countless ships and assault craft, very realistic landings with the use of live ammunition and a considerable number of tanks and aircraft in support of the ground troops. The landings were opposed by a combined US Army/Marine force of considerable strength, giving the whole exercise an uncanny sense of realism. No half-measures with the Americans.

Just occasionally lectures on sensitive national subjects would be labelled 'US Only' or sometimes 'US/UK Only', the latter reflecting the special relationship between the two countries, when even the students from the Commonwealth countries would be excluded. I don't recall that this caused resentment. It was common practice in most countries, and on one occasion, when 'US Only' applied, it gave the rest of us the opportunity to fly to New York for a two-day visit, first to the United Nations Assembly to witness a session with Mr Kruschev in full flow during a debate on the Cuba crisis – but with both shoes on! – and then the following day to the US Army Academy at West Point to talk and lunch with the cadets. We were clear winners over the boring old lectures to which our American students had been subjected in our absence.

During the course I made particular friends with a USN commander, Bud Gear. He buttonholed me one day: 'Geoff, did you ever know a Dickie Reynolds in the Navy? He was in one of your carriers in the Med when I was in Saratoga, and I got to know him very well.'

Well, of course, Dick was an old friend from Boscombe days in the early fifties, and I gave Bud a bit of background of our relationship. This cemented a friendship which went beyond the staff course. Pat and I got to know him and his wife Sally well, particularly as, a little later on, both wives would produce children – Sally twins – at much the same time. Sadly, within a few months of his appointment to command a Vigilante squadron on leaving the college, he was killed landing on board a carrier.

At the end of the year I had had my fill of defence studies, and was pleased to be awarded the diploma before moving on to my appointment with SACLANT. For two weeks I would overlap with 'Corky', with whom I had been in frequent contact for the last six months and therefore there would be a pause before moving into his house. This was in any event fortuitous, since we had been told that the owner, a retired American admiral, was to sell the house on its being vacated by the Corkhills. However, he was persuaded to change his mind, and we departed from our temporary hotel in Norfolk to move into 5301 Holly Road, Virginia Beach, a house of some character, in an area with a number of other Brits. The ocean was a couple of blocks away, with a wonderful sandy beach as far as the eye could see.

CHAPTER 19

SACLANT, Norfolk, Virginia

After twelve months' continuous studies I was very keen to return to a job to earn my keep. The benefit of the two excellent courses I hoped would be apparent in the future, but from the miscellaneous gossip about town, the appointment at Supreme HQ Atlantic was unlikely to tax me to any great extent. Not that it would lack interest – far from it – but much of the maritime policy and decision making was laid at the organisation next door, CINCLANTFLT, the Commander-in-Chief Atlantic Fleet, the corresponding American command, wholly staffed by American officers.

Adm Dennison shared responsibilities for both NATO and national commands. American dominance of NATO had long been a thorn in the flesh of a number of member countries, but the reality was that 'he who paid the piper called the tune'. Very shortly the French would find their position too invidious to remain a military participant and would reduce their role to a political one. Proud France; one suspects they had never quite recovered from the ignominy or humiliation of needing US/UK forces to re-establish their national boundaries after invasion in two world wars; and then, within measurable time, having to call again on the US for assistance in their fight against the Communists in their attempt to re-establish their former colonial position in French Indo-China.

Come what may, I settled in and began to enjoy a complete change of lifestyle. I shared an office with an American of Polish extraction, Cdr Jan Jablonski, and divided responsibilities for operations and plans, which was our primary role. Pleasant enough, he seemed to find it hard to relax, almost as if he was afraid he might reveal a national secret during the course of our work or in conversation. Consequently we never socialised out of working hours. He was not typical, however. Most of us, including the chaps from other NATO countries, were made very much at home by our hosts, and slotted in very well together.

Norfolk, a huge naval complex and the main base for the American Eastern Fleet, also encompassed a sizeable US Marine force based at Little Creek. Its importance to us, however, was that it included a very good golf course, one of three excellent service-run courses in the area to which we had been invited as honorary members for the length of our stay there – all at no cost. Any one of them would have done credit to the best of British golf courses, and one, in particular, Sewalls Point, boasted a clubhouse of Colonial design that would have rivalled the best in Surrey or Berkshire.

The Brits at Virginia Beach included representatives of the Navy, Air Force and Marines, and with a few Canadians, plus a sprinkling of Americans from SACLANT, the atmosphere of friendliness and interdependence in the community was very agreeable. It was high living. We were able to enjoy a maid for house chores, petrol was unbelievably cheap and hence the urge to travel was easy to satisfy without concerning ourselves about the cost.

Socialising, too, was never a problem. British officers on the staff had access to duty-free liquor and beer transported in bond from the British Embassy in Washington. Monthly orders were placed with the designated 'barkeep', and in due course picked up from the secure store in headquarters. There was no limit imposed other than the obvious one that it was for personal consumption and not to be resold. Strictly interpreted, it should not have been available for entertaining foreign nationals, but I believe that had been the basis for acquiring this concession from the Foreign Office in the first place: that is, that we should not be inhibited by cost from returning the customary lavish hospitality of our American hosts, whose rank-equivalent income generally was much above ours.

In June 1961 we became proud parents of a baby boy, whom we named David. It gave an added dimension to our lives without, it would seem, curtailing any of our activities. Around this time I was due for leave, and we had provisionally planned to tour eastern Canada. So come September, with a small child, scarcely three months old, and threatened by a hurricane 'Esther' that was forecast to hit the Tidewater area, which included Norfolk and Virginia Beach, we sallied forth by car, inland towards Charlottesville in order to avoid the storm on our way north. It is never wise to venture much off the beaten track in the States when looking for overnight accommodation, but needs must: we had no wish to get tied up with 'Esther' and our options were limited this late in the day. Then, with the day drawing to a close, we were in luck; we arrived at Gordonsville, Va., a 'one-horse town' boasting just one hotel, 'The Old Oaken Bucket'. It slightly belittled its name, as it was comfortable, cheap and met our every need.

Two days later, despite pouring rain and poor visibility, we crossed the border into Canada to spend a couple of days at Niagara to do the town and the Falls. If David had known, he might have screamed his head off, but he was asleep, and, totally protected by oilskins, we took him on board the *Maid-of-the-Mist* for the never-to-be-forgotten boat trip around and under the awe-inspiring American and Canadian Falls. Niagara then was virtually unspoiled, no crowds. Later it could boast the tallest building in the world, although, in truth, it was no more than a large spire atop a modest building.

Travelling east along Lake Ontario, we spent no time admiring the questionable charms of Toronto, preferring instead to hasten towards Kingston and the Thousand Islands. A nostalgic visit to my old training ground at Kingston airfield was in some ways disappointing, although quite what I expected after seventeen years is hard to fathom. The old hangars were still there, uncared for, and the control tower, but instead of bustling activity with dozens of training aircraft and half-trained students, there could be seen only one private monoplane and a rather tired-looking character emerging from a wooden hut, bent on going about his business. However, it was all part of life's rich pageant. I was glad to have returned, but we had better things to do than live in the past. Gananoque, the 'Gateway to the Thousand Islands', beckoned.

It was well named. A few miles beyond Gananoque, where, all those years ago, we had been detached to a satellite airstrip during our flying course for two weeks, to carry out armament practice, lies an area of outstanding beauty. It was 24 September, and full of anticipation for the following day we checked in to the Jothwi Gardens Motel on the edge of the St Lawrence River. Tomorrow would be my birthday and we were about to make the most it.

The quite remarkable over fifteen hundred islands of one sort or another that scatter the St Lawrence in this area range from little more than a rock to much larger islands of immense size, many of them of several acres with magnificent mansions and pseudo-castles. The whole area is navigable, and the boat trip we took lasted for several hours of unbelievable scenic beauty. We could have spent a whole day wallowing in this delightful scenery, but time waits for no man. We had much to look forward to by way of Ottawa, Montreal and Quebec before we left Canada.

Our schedule, loose as it was, would not permit in-depth exploration of these historic cities, and so, with minimum fuss, we checked the Parliament Buildings and Château Laurier in Ottawa and continued on our way to stay the night in Montreal. If you have seen one you have seen them all, it is said. And so it was with Montreal, a busy commercial city of great interest, but with a long journey ahead of us and a small child, it was an indulgence to be forgone. We were now, of course, in French Canada, Quebec Province, where it was not unusual to find only French spoken. My French had always been less than rudimentary, but now Pat found that even hers did not extend to 'a packet of razor blades'.

Not only the language but the atmosphere was different, less cosmopolitan, a suggestion of not being part of the rest. Unlike Montreal, Quebec itself was charming. The buildings, unmistakeably so French in style with their green roofs and iron balconies, cried out to be different from other Canadian cities. So bravely leaving David in the care of a lady at our lodgings, we explored the more interesting parts of this fascinating city until, eventually, we happened upon a furrier's establishment, which we left with rather fewer funds than when we entered. But it was worth it; Pat looked very chic in a splendid fur coat with mink collar: not perhaps quite as acceptable today, with ever-changing prejudices, but very fashionable then.

There was one more thing we had to do: take an aperitif at the Château Frontenac; so we did. Like taking tea at 'Raffles' in Singapore, or a pink gin at the 'Rock' in Gibraltar, it has to be done, one more to chalk up. At all events it was very enjoyable and gave us that little extra chuck-up before departing from Canada on our way home through New England.

Now we were in magical country. Driving south through the White Mountains of New Hampshire in the autumn Fall is an experience not to be missed. Punctuated by occasional lakes and streams, the trees, an almost unbelievable mass of colour with their leaves yet to fall, present a vista on a crisp, clear, sunny morning that defies description. As if to remind us that this was New England, now and then we would come across a small town with an English name: Dover, Manchester and, inevitably, *Bristol* would be some such. It was all a fitting end to our travels before braving the chaotic traffic in New York.

By the time we had fought our way around north Manhattan, New York, through eight lines of traffic, always seemingly having to cross numerous lanes to get to the one we wanted, and later on, taken the ferry across Chesapeake Bay at the entrance to the Hampton Roads on our way to Little Creek and home, we had travelled a little over three thousand miles. Not a mammoth journey, but one that gave us an appetite for further and longer ventures in this huge and fascinating country.

SACLANT was full of surprises, not the least of which was a conversation I had with my Admiral, Charles Evans, when he called me to his office to get updated on the work I was doing in the Ops/Plans Division. He lived a relatively quiet life, with little real responsibility except to represent the UK in this NATO organisation. He acquitted himself well in this role, and with his fiery red beard and very British manners, the Americans loved him. He was not unused to America and its people, having served in Washington some years earlier, when he had made many friends.

It was now that his time in Washington bore fruit. While we were chatting in a general sort of way, he suddenly switched the conversation. 'Have you thought of keeping your hand in flying while you are here?' he asked. Well, this came as a bolt out of the blue since I was unaware that any facilities existed for this sort of diversion from the staff work. But now, with perhaps our time together in *Victorious* in mind, he had obviously given it some thought. He received a very enthusiastic response from me, of course, and with that he went on to explain that he had friends in high places in the Pentagon, and in fact the present admiral responsible for air matters on the Navy Board was an old friend of his from when they were both commanders in Washington.

'Leave it with me,' he said, 'I will see what I can do.'

I thought little more about it at the time. We were in the middle of a NATO maritime exercise and I was watch keeping in CINCLANTFLT's Operations Room, in itself unusual since the Americans were generally reluctant to permit foreign nationals to enter their 'holiest of holies'. However, about two weeks or so had passed when Charles Evans rang me.

'I think you should be hearing from the Captain at Oceana within a day or two offering some flying. Don't raise your hopes too high, it may be only training aircraft, but it's a start.'

Well, this was great news. Naval Air Station Oceana was just down the road, and quite near both HQ and home. Shortly after this, I had a telephone call from Captain, NAS Oceana.

'We've had high powers at the Pentagon instructing us to afford you some flying. I don't know what it's all about but come and call on the 'Air Boss' here to discuss it.' I thanked him, and in a day or so went to see the 'Air Boss', the American equivalent to our Commander Air at an RNAS. After the inevitable coffee, he drove me to VA-43 Squadron to meet the its CO, and I arranged a provisional date for the first flight.

From here things went from great to outstanding. I arrived to fly on the first morning to discover they had allocated a special named car space, was introduced to and greeted by all the VA-43 Squadron chaps in the crew room, then issued with all the gear one needed – two of everything – and promptly briefed for my first flight by, of all people, Lieutenant *Bristol!*

This set the scene, and after a couple of familiarisation flights in the Grumman F9F 8T, a swept-wing, high-performance aircraft, we switched to instrument flying and general air traffic patterns.

I travelled out to Oceana as often as my duties at SACLANT would sensibly allow, and after the several flights in the F9F, I was passed to the other side of the squadron, ATKRON FORTY-THREE, and switched to the delta-wing Douglas A4B and A4D, the USN's principle attack aircraft at that time. I regarded this not only as an expression of confidence but also a considerable privilege. It was a very nice aircraft to fly, a touch lazy in lateral response, but seemed to have no vices. I was fortunate in having as the Ops Division boss at SACLANT HQ a Captain White, who had not only already expressed his wish that I should take whatever leave I needed to see his 'wonderful' country, but that I should now take advantage of the opportunity to fly as often as I wished, provided I kept up with my work. I had no problem with that.

However, my opposite number, Jan Jablonski, showed some irritation at a Brit being given the opportunity to fly American aircraft while he, an American Navy pilot, had no such authority. 'Off again', he would say as I left for an afternoon spell of flying. Poor fellow, he couldn't conceal his pique and I couldn't resist tweaking his tail.

'Why don't you lobby someone in high places at the Pentagon?' I asked him one day, knowing full well that no such individual approach would be tolerated through their chain of command. However, after a time he accepted my absence with equanimity, and even enjoyed my comments about the day's flying when I later returned to the office. Up to the time I left I don't think he ever understood how Charles Evans could possibly influence the naval authorities in the Pentagon, and when, almost at the end of my time at SACLANT, I was authorised to fly the McDonnel F4B Phantom, the USN's latest and most potent fighter/attack aeroplane just entering squadron service, he went almost apoplectic.

In between the less than onerous duties on the staff, there was an abundance of time for socialising in one form or another. Quite early on I had joined a four for golf, and every Sunday morning. Wg Cdr Ken Murray and Ed Griffiths, a major in the Royal Marines, together with a USN captain, Ed Waring, would trundle off to the Amphibious Base at Little Creek where we were honorary members of their golf club, a demanding course with considerable water hazards.

Ed Waring was as laid back as anyone I ever knew, but this concealed a highly intelligent and deep-thinking personality. He lived only a block away from us and had taken to picking me up in his car on our way to golf. Time keeping meant little to him. He would always arrive late, still munching his breakfast. But he was a great character and great friend. Later the four of us would enter as a team in the Norfolk district league and come a commendable second from top, largely due to our two low handicappers.

Unfortunately, the demands of one young son took precedence over golf for Pat, but there was some consolation when she turned out to be a natural 'bowler'. Tenpin bowling was a very popular social occasion in which we enthusiastically took part. SACLANT ran several teams to compete against each other, and this regular activity was not only most enjoyable but highly competitive. From humble beginnings we learnt fast, but it was Pat who would be the 'spare' ace and, later on at the end-of-season dinner, justly deserve the honour of receiving from Adm Dennison a handsome trophy inscribed with 'The Most Improved Bowlers'. We ignored the *double entendre*!

Earlier in the year, as if to retaliate against John Glen's spectacular event in orbiting the earth in his spacecraft, Mercury Friendship, a catastrophic storm descended upon the Tidewater area, carrying away everything in its path. Houses were reduced to matchwood and those built immediately on the seashore fell into the sea or onto the beach. Waves of twenty to thirty feet flooded the adjacent roads, leaving cars wallowing in the wake of floodwater rising four feet or more.

Our house on 53rd Street was on a slightly higher level than the immediate beach area, and we were fortunate in escaping the flooding or any serious damage, but for a short period we would have unexpected lodgers. Our good friends, the McNeilles, a British family and colleague at SACLANT, suffered severe flooding to their house near the beach, and would see their car immersed up to the roof in floodwater. The unexpectedness and speed of the tidal wave had left them insufficient time to take even the most elementary precautions.

Incredibly, many of the houses that had fallen into the water or onto the beach when the piers or sandy foundations had given way would be subsequently raised and their wooden structures rebuilt. In areas of persistent hurricanes and violent storms the Americans are seemingly well used to the aftermath, and just get on with the task of shoring-up and general restoration with little fuss or delay. More importantly, however, the disruption to traffic and hence commercial and other activities such as schools is often considerable.

On these occasions the local radio would make periodic broadcasts announcing the temporary closure of schools and other establishments. Apart from the need to discourage non-essential road traffic, these broadcasts were intended to permit the essential recovery services to get on with their work unhindered. Previously, while at the Staff College, and in Norfolk on the fringe of Hurricane 'Donna', I was unaware of the need to listen in to the local radio, and had conscientiously fought my way to work, only to find the college closed. In a stroke went the long-held naval discipline in which I had been inculcated that death, dismissal and retirement were the only acceptable reasons for not going to work!

It was about this time, May 1962, that we were introduced and encouraged to enjoy the world of camping. Some of our good friends at this time were the MccGwires, a British couple with a young family. Mike had been my predecessor at the Staff College and taken me under his wing to show me the ropes on first arrival. Highly intellectual, he had elected never to specialise as a navigator, gunnery officer or whatever, and was hence one of the rare breed known as a 'Salthorse', a euphemism for 'jack of all trades, master of none'. But that had been his choice. He would have excelled at anything he turned his hand to, and had at some time before coming to America been the assistant naval attaché in Moscow, where as a Russian linguist and interpreter his talents would have been more than useful in the intelligence world. Later, on leaving America for his next appointment, it was to the submarine depot ship *Maidstone* as executive commander, a job he disparagingly referred to as 'hotel keeper'; but that it certainly was not. I would next meet up with him in the Ministry of Defence some years later when he was a staff officer in the Naval Intelligence Division before eventual retirement. He was, perhaps, far too clever for the confines of the service and, perhaps, one or two very senior officers.

With his encouragement and the loan of his tent, we drove off south for a loosely planned holiday in Florida and the southern States. Most sensible Americans avoid this southern area at this time of the year, May and June, but it was Hobson's choice, and we had become accustomed to the heat and humidity of Virginia. The excessive heat in the south would eventually turn things into a camping/motel holiday, but in three weeks and 4,000 miles we managed an overview of the northern part of Florida and the southern States as far as New Orleans, which had a particular attraction for me.

From early days I had been passionately fond of jazz music, tempered in more recent years by a broader, more catholic taste, perhaps, in the more serious form; but nevertheless still a devoted follower. And what better place than the home of 'Dixieland'? New Orleans boasts a unique establishment called 'Preservation Hall', which, as it names suggests, is an old, somewhat tatty building, wooden floors and benches, where one can indulge in the purest of traditional jazz from a group, perhaps of six or eight old-timers of vintage years. Their names were legendary in their world of music, and if any one of them was under the age of 70, you had an off night. Mostly in their late 70s or early 80s, they would occasionally run out of steam a little, but there was always someone else to fill the gap. It was an unforgettable experience, a dream come true from my earliest youth when, as a 16-year-old, I had been hired to play the drums in a small outfit. Regrettably, nerves had got the better of me on the day, and I had let them down. But that was a long time ago.

On arrival in New Orleans we had forsaken modern hotels to stay on St Peter Street in the heart of the French Quarter, where after eight in the evening the street was alive with marching bands and a noise level from every bar and restaurant to be heard for miles. The atmosphere was electric. We stayed for just two days before heading home across the twenty-four-mile-long Lake Pontchartrain Causeway, a road bridge said to be the longest bridge in the world on the north–south New Orleans Expressway.

Time in America was now running short. Another six months and we would be looking for a sailing date, but then our friends, the MccGwires, persuaded us to follow their example and travel west for one last holiday. Protests about not subjecting David to more prolonged travel fell on deaf ears.

'Leave David with us', said Mike and Helen. 'He'll have lots of company and he's too young to miss you for a couple of weeks.'

The seed was sown. I had some leave left, and with Capt White's approval I turned it into seventeen days – enough, we thought, to get to the Rockies and the Canyons. So in late August 1962, armed now with our own tent and camping gear, and with some misgivings about leaving David but no doubts that he would be more than well looked after by Helen and Mike, we set off for an ambitious journey that would take us by way of Chicago to South Dakota and the Badlands on the first stage to Yellowstone National Park and the Tetons. In two-and-a-half days we had averaged eight hundred miles a day, taking turns driving and sleeping on the road, but to complete our itinerary and maximise the time in the West, it was both necessary and worthwhile.

It was not a journey for the faint hearted. After just over two weeks we would have travelled nearly 7,000 miles through central America as far as Salt Lake City, Grand and Zion Canyons and numerous other places of incredible interest, regretting only that time curtailed our stay in many of them. On our way south from Salt Lake City, the road runs through the Navajo Indian Reservation, an area of desert devoid of any visible means of support, typical of the general pattern of the American contribution to the indigenous Indian tribes. Living in mud huts, their survival depends on sinking wells for water, a capacity for weaving hand- loom rugs and making silver work which they hope to sell.

If Zion Canyon was stunning with its red cliffs, Grand Canyon was breathtaking in its hugeness. Camping at the top of the South Rim, the panorama down to the Colorado River and beyond was awesome, and the sunset later on indescribably beautiful. It happened during the course of the evening that we met and got talking to another young English couple, who, it transpired, had just emerged from walking to the bottom of the Canyon and back up again – a distance of sixteen miles. Having discovered earlier that the traditional mules for the descent were fully booked for three days, we were now inspired to follow our new friends' example and walk. So we did.

Starting out very early the following morning to avoid the heat of the day for the return journey, we made good time to the bottom, grateful to paddle in the river to rest weary feet. Conscious of the need to get most of the way back to the top before the main heat of the day (it was still only about nine o'clock), we lost no time in commencing the ascent, first to Indian Gardens, a sort of oasis half-way up, before continuing the rest of the way. It proved very hard going, but we looked in much better shape than the party travelling in the reverse direction on mules. Already clearly saddle-sore, they had scarcely scratched the surface, and might well ponder their mode of transport later on. By the time we reached the top, weary, thirsty, but undaunted, we had walked for around twelve hours over some of the roughest ground, which even the mules found challenging. We were both pleased and proud to have met the challenge.

Now we had one last call before departing for home. Col Bob Kraus, a fellow student at Staff College, insisted we spend a day or two with them at Colorado Springs on our way home, so we left Mesa Verde National Park to make the short diversion to the Air Force College where Bob was instructing. It was nice to see him and his wife again, but in truth we were almost too tired by this time to enjoy their more than kind hospitality. But they understood and were pleased that we had taken the trouble to call on them after such a gruelling journey.

We arrived home on 7 September after travelling for a day or two through pleasant but boring Kentucky, miles and miles of unrelieved plain country, to retrieve one young son from the MccGwires. He seemed more than content with his foster-parents and their children, and it was a while before he realised who we were.

By now we felt we had taken to heart Capt White's exhortation to see his wonderful country, but it hadn't been all play. Exercises and operations consumed much of my time. During one exercise I was privileged to embark in the USN Cruiser *Long Beach*, a new state-of-the-art nuclear-powered vessel, to witness its remarkable performance. To illustrate its acceleration, the Captain wound on full ahead from near stop to achieve well over 40 knots with a surge and time that would have done credit to a high-performance racing-car: most impressive, particularly when this was combined with the ability to stay at sea for very prolonged periods, only inhibited by other logistic considerations.

A NATO exercise involving SACEUR (Supreme Allied Commander Europe) forces required Mike MccGwire and myself to travel to Paris for several days to integrate and agree force levels and other planning matters with our opposite numbers. It was a welcome diversion from the daily routine and an opportunity to see how the other half lived. The Command at that time was coming to terms with the impending withdrawal of French forces from NATO, which would shortly result in SACEUR moving to Brussels. In the meantime French participation in NATO exercises was always in doubt until the last minute, a situation the French seemed to revel in as an opportunity to wield the big stick with the other member nations – the Americans in particular. That aside, we enjoyed the visit. Mike knew an inexpensive hotel off the Champs Elysées, inevitably named Hotel Bristol, where we stayed and thus remained well within our limited budget. After four days we flew back to New York and home.

In January of the new year 1963, I left the office one morning for Oceana and a couple of flights in the Douglas A4B, mindful of the fact that they were likely to be the last I could fit in before preparing to return with my family to the UK. It had been an enormous privilege to fly with VA-43 Squadron over the last several months, and I was sorry it had come to an end. Then, as I was about to depart from their crew room, the Air Boss arrived. 'I've got a little surprise for you, a departing present.' Then added, 'VF-101 across the other side have offered you a ride in an F4B if you can get out here the day after tomorrow.'

I could have fallen through the floor. The F4B Phantom, a Mach 2 fighter/attack aircraft, was just entering USN service, and apart from one other squadron on the west coast, VF-101 was the only outfit so far equipped. It was a tremendous opportunity and such an expression of confidence in me personally and my flying that I was lost for words. I know not how it came about. I had had no direct contact with 101, and could only assume that the Captain Oceana had obtained authority from the appropriate staff in the Pentagon. But I was not about to worry about the details, and duly presented myself two days later across the other side of the airfield to the Squadron 'Boss'. One hour later, having studiously gone through the relevant performance notes, emergency procedures and other matters with a USN lieutenant-commander whose name now escapes me, and more regrettably, failed to record in my logbook since he bravely rode pillion in the navigator's seat with me, we both walked out to the aircraft, carried out the external checks and got strapped in.

The Phantom is a big aeroplane with a large pilot's cockpit, but I felt at home straight away. I had been well used to American-style cockpits and their layout from my early squadron days. I started up, taxied out to the end of the runway and lined up for take-off. I was about to experience reheat, or 'afterburner', as the Americans call it, for the first time, and having pushed both throttles to the first gate, rolled forward about a hundred yards, went on to slide them both forward into reheat. The acceleration was both immediate and astonishing, and with a slight tweak on the stick we were airborne and climbing at a very steep angle. My friend in the back, working the radar, spoke to me for the first time.

'How was that?' he asked. Then suggested, 'Take it out of afterburner and we'll swan around for a little while you get used to the feel.'

Good advice: things had happened very quickly and I was nudging close to Mach 1 in the climb before I reached a reasonable altitude. Shortly afterwards, having gone through the usual performance bits and pieces, stalls, single-engine handling at low speed and so on, I climbed to 40,000 ft for the planned high-speed run south along the coast to Cape Hatteras and beyond.

Unlike subsonic aircraft pushing through the sound barrier, when the controls get stiff and generally ineffective, and the aircraft pitches and bucks almost out of control, going through Mach 1 in the Phantom caused only the slightest tremor to indicate passing through the speed of sound, and we rapidly accelerated to Mach 2. Finally, around Mach 2.2, we seemed to have stabilised and I throttled right back. I was running out of sky, or rather fuel, so with a voice in my ear from the back cockpit giving me a course for base, we trundled gently back.

I called local control for permission to land, entered the circuit and touched down, deploying the tail 'chute as the wheels touched the runway. Wonderful: the whole flight had been exhilarating, no snags, no problems, a thoroughbred to delight any pilot.

Walking back to the crew room I expressed my thanks to my 'navigator'.

'My pleasure', he replied, adding, 'I'm sorry we can't give you a return trip but I gather you are off back to UK very shortly.' Well that was nice, but I knew very well that only one flight had been authorised, and within a few weeks we would be on our way home.

A little over two weeks later, clutching a typically over-the-top American SACLANT testimonial to my 'dedicated, etc., etc. contribution to NATO', we said goodbye to all our friends and departed for New York and, once more, Pier 90, where we were to sail in RMS *Sylvania* for Liverpool.

During our time in America, and in common with most Brits, we had bought an English car, a Humber Hawk, and had it shipped over to the States on the understanding that, provided there were enough miles on the clock to show 'reasonable' use, there would be no duty to pay on return to the UK. But arriving in New York there was the inevitable dockers' strike, so the car became a bit of encumbrance, and together with all our heavy baggage it would be left behind to be shipped as and when. But it didn't spoil the voyage home; *Sylvania* enjoyed single First Class accommodation only, and five days' relaxation put us in good shape to meet the families in Liverpool, and provided, for me, time to contemplate my next appointment.

A month or so before my time in America was up, the naval Appointers had written offering several options for my next job. I lost no sleep making a decision – it was no contest; although perhaps I should have been more aware of the effect the choice would have on my future career. Among the options was one to the Naval Staff in the Admiralty, an obvious career move, but I had just had two years' staff work and wanted a break. In any event one of the alternatives was one that brooked no refusal: an opportunity to die for, command of the Naval Test Squadron at Boscombe Down, perhaps the most-sought-after flying job in the Navy.

CHAPTER 20

A&AEE Boscombe Down

So, after attending debriefings at a number of defence directorates concerned with my time and work in the States, and a short refresher course at Lossiemouth flying Hunters, in May 1963 I found myself once more at the Aircraft & Armament Evaluation Establishment, Boscombe Down, where, thirteen years earlier, I had first been smitten by the test-flying world.

Giving Mike Crosley, my predecessor, no time to delay his departure, reluctant though he was, I got the chaps together and got down to business. A number of them were well known to me, and from my Bedford days Denis Higton, the senior scientist responsible for that side of the house, was a trusted and much-valued friend. There was much to be done.

In the course of the next few months, the Buccaneer Mk 2, re-engined with the Spey, would replace the Gyron Buccaneer Mk 1 and would require full evaluation. A much more potent and powerful aircraft, it would prove a winner and remain in service with both the Navy and the Air Force for many years to come. All being well we were due to take it to *Victorious* for initial carrier qualification day and night clearance trials at the end of July, so there was little time to spare.

One particular trial involved flying with the canopy removed up to a maximum speed of 550 kts, a trial which I suspect had been introduced after my Scimitar experience of four years before. There were no particular problems. The buffeting was quite acceptable, but since it had been removed before take-off we were unable to say whether the canopy would cause any damage to the aircraft in the event of its being lost in flight.

On 31 July I landed on *Victorious* for the first time since December 1959. It was a strange homecoming. I had no feeling for it now, contenting myself with a job to do, forgetting the past. In the next ten days we would achieve the full range of tests required, up to a maximum all-up weight of 44,000 lb, with the lift augmentation on and off, concluding with a night deck landing assessment. I left the ship very satisfied, having personally achieved another eleven deck landings, including two at night, and flew off to Yeovilton before continuing to Boscombe. We were not due to go to sea again until the following February.

Meanwhile, as a family we were now well settled into a married quarter only a short step from the airfield. As Senior Naval Officer as well as being CO of the squadron, I had the use of a car and driver who would collect and return me in the mornings and evenings, and being the most senior of the four test squadrons' COs – the other three being commanded by wing commanders – I also assumed responsibilities as Deputy Superintendent Flying to the Group Captain, Mike Giddings.

In no time at all, it seemed, we were approaching the time for the next series of carrier trials. This time the main task involved the Sea Vixen Mk 2, fitted with an auto-throttle for the approach and landing, a great step forward in reducing the work load on pilots during carrier landings. We would also move a step forward with full clearance of the Buccaneer for first-line service by an assessment of approaches and landings on a single engine.

So in the first week of February, with a full team of aircrew and scientists, we embarked in HMS *Hermes* for a full two weeks. On this occasion I opted for a Sea Vixen to the ship, and over the following period made over fifty approaches and touch-downs, using auto-throttle to control the speed down to the deck. With the exception of some slight difficulty just over the ship's round-down, where turbulence confused the auto-throttle speed sensor, the trials were a complete success. Only the natural prejudice of front-line squadron pilots, who were reluctant to entrust electronics to the equation of deck landing, limited its use later on.

The Buccaneer single-engine evaluation was largely uneventful, but the approach and landing needed very careful monitoring to avoid creating a difficult and perhaps irrecoverable situation. Due to the bleeding-off of power caused by the lift augmentation (blow system), this had to be left off to ensure sufficient power to the remaining single engine for a satisfactory approach and, more importantly, the ability to overshoot at any stage, including an actual touch-down/missed-wire situation. These were matters that could not be properly simulated ashore on the runway. For a number of reasons we would finally recommend a rather higher approach and landing speed than we had anticipated.

Before these events, in November to our great delight we had added to our family a daughter, Catherine. Gone now were all thoughts of camping holidays. Instead we acquired a medium-sized caravan, and in the many months to come made full use of it for holidays and often for weekends in the New Forest, a wonderful way of relaxing after a busy week, just mucking about with the ponies and generally enjoying the great outdoors. In those days the New Forest was unregulated, and it was possible to pitch camp anywhere within reason, much in contrast to the organised and restricted sites available nowadays.

The test-flying pressures continued unabated. Something or another always seemed to be added to the expected programme, frequently the result of an incident or other happening in front-line service that carried with it a deadline from the Admiralty, usually yesterday!

One such was the need to clear the AEW Gannet for a carrier landing in the event of failure of one engine. With the help of HMS *Eagle* we knocked this one off in four days, which took the wind out of the sails of the Admiralty when we reported. A month or so after that we were back in *Eagle* for more Buccaneer work, to assess the minimum catapult launch speed for a variety of configurations. This was 'old hat' to me. I had laid claim to fame in this territory with the Scimitar many years before, and Denis Higton would frequently 'dine out' relating the story of roughing-up the sea with my jet pipe exhaust in that aeroplane.

Flying often had to take second place to the work of the 'office', which occupied much of my time. With over two hundred ratings, 'Requestmen and Defaulters' was a constant weekly event that, with the need to examine papers and other background, meant a full morning devoted to this form of administration alone. Nevertheless, I had had a bad month if I didn't achieve around fifteen hours' flying time.

There were also numerous conferences, visits and other external matters in which I would become involved, discussing progress and the next step forward, arranging co-operation with other agencies, planning the build-up to carrier programmes with manufacturers: it seemed never ending. Most visits could be undertaken by air, and I had for this purpose a most useful two-seat Balliol with which I was able to take Denis to various outstations or to manufacturers. He welcomed these opportunities to consolidate his own flying experience, and during my time at Boscombe he would reach the stage where he could land the aeroplane with little help from myself. He had many years before been put through a limited flying course to 'solo' standard, but had not had the opportunity to maintain proficiency. I always felt it important to keep Denis in touch with the 'sharp end', and ensured that whenever possible he had first-hand experience by participating in the flying.

During the recent Sea Vixen auto-throttle trials in *Hermes*, I had encouraged him to ride in the navigator's seat for one sortie, an experience I would not normally inflict on anyone, since it is rightly called 'the Dark Hole of Calcutta', or other unprintable names, by Sea Vixen navigators who have to suffer a view of the pilot's feet on the rudder pedals, and little else.

About this time at the end of 1964, I had turned my thoughts to a suitable location for tropical trials of the Buccaneer, essential to the final clearance of the aircraft for front-line operations. There were a number of considerations, not least the availability of an aircraft carrier for the embarked phase. This, coupled with the need for very high temperatures, narrowed it down considerably. In discussions with the Naval Staff and the Operations Officer at Fleet HQ, I discovered that HMS *Eagle* would be in the vicinity of the Gulf of Aden about July/August and could be programmed for a short period to conduct the carrier phase.

This seemed promising, and with more research I became aware of a Royal Air Force base at Masira, a small island off the coast of Oman, which might be a second option after the obvious one of the naval and RAF facilities at Aden. But we needed more information, particularly the logistic support we could expect. I discussed the matter generally with the scientists involved, and decided, with the agreement of Superintendent Flying, to fly out to see for myself early in the New Year.

I now leaned on the 'B' Squadron Commander to borrow a Canberra for early February, and also to use one of his navigators for the trip. 'No problem', said Keith Fletcher. We were quite used to exchanging aircraft for *ad hoc* reasons, and he readily agreed to provide a navigator. When it came to near the time there was no shortage of volunteers, but I selected Flt Lt Newbury, whom I knew well, and who had occasionally flown with us in one of our aircraft. From Boscombe, we now signalled the various overseas locations, obtaining diplomatic clearances where these were necessary, and dealt with other in-flight procedures, landing fees, refuelling arrangements and so on.

On 5 February, taking my air engineer officer, Lt Cdr Whitley, with me to assess the aircraft engineering aspects of the forthcoming trials at the two provisionally selected bases, I took off for RAF Luqa in Malta, the first stop on our way south. Our route would take us across the Mediterranean to Cyprus and then on to Tehran before heading south for Masira. This route avoided over-flying a number of Middle Eastern countries generally less than welcoming to foreign military aircraft. The flight to Malta had taken over three hours, and I had planned an overnight stop there in the RAF mess so that we could make Tehran the following day after a short refuelling stop in Cyprus.

Before leaving Boscombe a signal had arrived from the air attaché in Tehran, advising one or two things about servicing and accommodation, and adding that he would welcome us at the airport. Iran at that time was still pro-Western, the Shah still clung to power, and America provided the bulk of the Iranian Air Force aeroplanes, mainly Northrop F105s. On landing, these were much in evidence, scores of them, as I taxied in towards the control tower to park, causing much interest from the ground staff, who I suspect had seldom, if ever, seen a Canberra before.

The atmosphere everywhere was friendly. Wg Cdr 'Whatshisname' was there to meet and transport us to the hotel, and later would collect the three of us for dinner and a show – all on the Embassy! The following day, doing the round of the shops under the guidance of the air attaché, I lost my head to a beautiful Persian carpet, well beyond my means to afford, but I bought it. It would later cost me an arm and a leg with a rather over-zealous customs officer to whom I had unwisely declared it.

After this short break, we took off for the three-hour flight to Masira, flying over the Persian Gulf and skirting the Rub 'al Khali, part of Arabia known as the *Empty Quarter*, a godforsaken area of total desolation visited only occasionally by nomads, until, a short while later, we crossed the coast to land at Masira.

The RAF base was very much a staging-post, a transit camp geared to the reception and onward movement of the few RAF transport aircraft that had occasion to use it. The natives – the RAF personnel – were friendly, over friendly, and had much looked forward to our coming. They were clearly bored with inactivity and hoped we might put some spice in their lives for a few weeks, but it was immediately obvious that this was no base for a trials programme. Apart from one runway and a couple of hangars, other facilities were strictly limited, and the logistical difficulties of supporting a trials programme were all too plain. In a way I was sorry to disappoint them. They had gone out of their way to accommodate us as far as they could, but it was just that, a staging-post, with none of the support of a thriving operational base.

The next day we started early to fly to Aden, a relatively short hop along the coast of Oman and Yemen. I was well aware at this time that the Aden Command was heavily engaged in a phased orderly withdrawal from the area, and at the same time still much preoccupied with fighting elements of the Yemen to the north. I was not surprised, therefore, when I landed and reported to the Station Commander at RAF Khomaksar, to receive a fairly frigid reception and pointed remarks about his inability to cope with the needs of a trials group when he had more important things to think about. I well understood his viewpoint, but equally we had a job to do and I doubted whether the trials flying would affect his operational requirements. So I told him I would make his views known on my return to the Naval Staff at the Ministry of Defence, who I felt would take a different view of the importance of getting the Buccaneer into operational service, and that, meanwhile, I would discuss his objections with some of the naval people in the Joint Command at Aden Headquarters.

The Joint Force Commander at Aden at that time was Adm Michael Le Fanu, soon to be Chief of Naval Staff and First Sea Lord, so from a naval point of view there was no lack of support if it should come to a conflict of interests.

However, it soon became clear from talks with the Naval Staff, that a confrontation would not arise. HMS *Eagle*'s programme had been changed. She was now programmed to be in the Far East during the period of the planned trials, and thus would not be available for us. This was a whole new ball game. Either we would have to conduct the trials in two phases or we would be forced to consider alternative locations. With this, I decided there was little point in prolonging our stay in Aden, declared my intention to return to the UK and left the following day for the long flog to Bahrain, where we would have an overnight stop before flying on to Tehran.

By the time we landed, the temperature was already well into the nineties and I regretted not having planned to go straight on to Tehran. But a late start from Aden and the need for over-flying clearances to be negotiated now made this impossible. Instead we enjoyed some local hospitality for the rest of the day and departed early the next morning for Tehran, Cyprus, Malta and then home.

It was not an entirely wasted journey. It might still be necessary to consider Aden for the land phase of the trials, and Ted Whitley had had an opportunity to assess the maintenance and servicing facilities there. But I was cross that we hadn't been made aware by the Fleet Staff of the change to *Eagle*'s programme before we left. However, it was now water under the bridge, and the more immediate matters concerned the forthcoming heavyweight trials in HMS *Ark Royal* due within a few weeks. These would be the last before the final tropical trials and completion of the full clearance of the Mk 2 Buccaneer, scheduled for squadron service in October.

A feature of the test-flying world was its international exchange between US and UK establishments which had been fostered for some years. In alternate years Boscombe would host or visit the test centre at Edwards Air Force Base or the Naval Test Centre at Patuxent River for discussions on the latest test techniques and an opportunity to fly the others' latest aircraft. This year it was our turn to travel to the States, and in April we had the necessary authority and finance for a small team of two scientists and two test pilots to spend ten days at Patuxent. Nick Bennett, my Senior Test Pilot, would form part of the party, with Mr Sharpe backing up Denis.

The heavyweight trials in *Ark*, involving a variety of stores and armament, went without a hitch. The aircraft was now up to an all-up weight of 62,000 lb, the absolute maximum permissible, and we were pleased to be able to report to the Ministry our recommendations for clearance to this figure after the conclusion of these highly successful carrier trials. The final launches were made with the aircraft carrying four 1,000 lb bombs and four 36RPs (rocket projectiles), not at all bad for a naval aircraft, and a good deal more than most Second World War bomber aircraft.

On 24 April our little party boarded a Boeing 707 at Heathrow for the flight to Washington. I had added one more to the team, Lt Cdr Ed Beadsmoore, the Senior Observer, who I thought would be useful when flying the larger aircraft to add his views on the 'back seat'. Motoring down from Washington, courtesy of a car arranged by the Embassy, we arrived at PAX, as it is generally known, provided with quite luxurious accommodation at the base, and then, later, a typically American warm welcome. A young lieutenant had been detailed off to look after us to make sure we wanted for nothing, and for the next ten days, when we were not being entertained by all and sundry from the Admiral down, or flying, there was golf and water-skiing, both available within the base.

For the next week, with usual American attention to detail, sometimes seemingly petty, we went through briefings and anecdotes about the aircraft we were to fly while we were there. They had made available three: the Douglas Sky Warrior, a large twin-engined strike and reconnaissance aeroplane, heavier than the Buccaneer but without its performance; the F4B Phantom; and the Chance Vought F8U Crusader, a supersonic fighter capable of Mach 1.2 in level flight, with a performance similar to our own English Electric Lightning. Unfortunately, another aircraft on the list to fly, the A6 Intruder, was not available due to unserviceability

In all I was allowed three flights each in the Sky Warrior and Phantom, and two in the Crusader, enough to get a fairly good impression of their individual characteristics and capabilities, and I felt very privileged to have been given the opportunity to do so. The renewed acquaintance with the Phantom only endorsed my impression of several years before at Oceana that this was an exceptional aircraft that far surpassed anything in British service, and I looked forward with anticipation to its adoption by the Royal Navy, scheduled for 1968. In its British form it would have Rolls Royce Spey engines to replace the American General Electric J79s, a decision that had generated considerable reservations in various quarters.

The A3 Douglas Sky Warrior was a large carrier-borne aircraft designed for long-range nuclear strike, but more lately used as a tanker for in-flight refuelling. It compared well with the Canberra in both size and performance, and so was a large aircraft for operations from carriers. It had been in service for some years, so any comparison with the Buccaneer, a much smaller aircraft, would have been unfair. It was, however, equipped with an auto-throttle, a facility that must have given its pilots a great advantage during deck landings, since control response on the approach was not particularly good, especially in the single-engine case.

The Crusader, on the other hand, I found pleasant to fly, with excellent performance and handling. It possessed a number of novel innovations, including a two-position, variable-incidence wing. This provided a high angle of attack for take-off and landing while permitting the fuselage to remain parallel to the flight path for good pilot visibility. Supersonic flight was easily attainable in level flight, and it was streets ahead of anything we possessed in the Royal Navy.

It was a most successful visit in cementing relations as well as the technical experience gained from the many discussions we had with our opposite numbers. A report to the staff of the British Embassy in Washington at the end of any visit to the States was a long-established requirement, as was 'reporting-in' on arrival. So leaving the others to enjoy a touch of Washington sightseeing, Dennis joined me for debriefing.

The head of the Joint Staff was Adm Peter Compston, an aviator whom I knew only slightly, but who at once put you at your ease and made you welcome. I had met him, of course, some ten days or so previously, on arrival, but he was now very anxious to learn how we had got on, whom we had met and whether there was anything of importance that he or his staff should have known about before our visit to Patuxent which, in the normal course of things, he ought to have reported back to the UK. He and the Joint Staff were always alert to new developments in the military world there, and disliked being found wanting! He was reassured on this.

We talked about the visit, and then, 'What about the Buccaneer,' he asked, 'when are we going to see it in service?' So I gave him a run-down of the work we had done so far, and mentioned my recent flight to Aden to find a location for tropical trials.

'Have you thought of coming here?' he asked.

'Well, yes,' I replied, 'it has been considered but I need a carrier, and no British ship is scheduled for this side of the Atlantic in 1965.'

He raised his somewhat bushy eyebrows with a quizzical look on his face, but said no more, and I left him to talk to one or two of his staff. After a while his secretary came on the telephone: 'Would you call on the Admiral before you leave?' So I did. 'I've been thinking,' he started, 'could you not explore the possibility of borrowing an American carrier? I would give you all the support I could.'

This was a fast ball. There were all sorts of considerations. High enough temperatures, preferably around 30 Centigrade, logistics, getting the aircraft over here, back-up support and many others. But he had sown the seed, and I left, assuring him that the possibility would be fully assessed on my return to the UK and that I would keep his staff informed.

The upshot of this was that following a good deal of signal traffic with the Embassy and US Navy people in the Pentagon, I returned to Washington with Denis Higton towards the end of May for discussions in the Pentagon to assess the feasibility of using the US naval base at Pensacola for the shore-based trials. Behind all this was a good chance of sharing time in a training carrier if dates could be mutually agreed. Wg Cdr Bob Cherry from the

Embassy had been allocated to us to provide continuity if the talks came to anything, and he now accompanied us to the Pentagon. He would prove invaluable.

The talks went very well indeed. Charges for fuel, transport, and use of facilities were regarded as side issues and swept under the carpet for later resolution. The most important thing at that moment was to agree in principle to carrying out the trials in the States, and on this point I had no reservations. I had some experience of the US Navy from cross-operating with their carriers during exercises, and more recent experience at Oceana and Patuxent. At the end of these preliminary discussions I reported back to Adm Compston, who was highly delighted that things had gone so well.

Returning home, we went to work to make it happen. Superintendent Flying, David Dick, pledged heavy-lift aircraft support for maintenance requirements, and we started to consider various alternatives for flying the aircraft across, selected the various team members and so on. Meanwhile signals were flashing between the many authorities involved, which raised no insurmountable difficulties and indicated much promise. Then the icing on the cake: subject to finalising and agreeing dates, the US Navy would allow us shared time in the USS *Lexington* for up to one week during the proposed time at Pensacola. Everything seemed to be falling into place.

We planned to leave with three Buccaneers on 3 August, flying to Keflavik in Iceland, Goose Bay, Canada, and then down to Patuxent, where the initial catapult trials would take place to check American gear and crew familiarisation. Support aircraft were allocated, including an Argosy for the whole period and a provisional offer of a Vulcan should we need additional navigational assistance. It was beginning to develop into quite a party.

Looking back, it is extraordinary that for the two months of the deployment, facing a number of unknown challenges, we never once encountered any major difficulty which we couldn't cope with or that was beyond our resources. The flights out proved uneventful, and our arrival at Patuxent provoked considerable interest. But not as much interest or amusement as the sight of Ed Beadsmoore, during a period of relaxation on the golf course, putting three consecutive balls in the water on a short hole which he was destined never to reach! Only a shortage of golf balls stopped him trying more.

With the catapult assessment completed, all three aircraft flew down to Pensacola, where we would stay for the next two months. The support, co-operation and facilities we received were outstanding. From the Captain downwards – whose pleasure it was to entertain us in his large motor launch for picnics and at his splendid house overlooking the Gulf – technically and socially we wanted for nothing. The trials ashore and in Lexington, where we spent three days, went without a hitch.

I recall only one hiccup during the whole period, which, ironically, followed a kindly gesture from one of our sailors. Driving an open-back pickup, lent to us courtesy of the USN, he stopped on his way to lunch to give a young US Navy midshipman, on a short course from the US Naval Academy, a lift to the other side of the airfield. Unfortunately his good intentions caused a minor international incident when he rolled the truck, severely injuring the midshipman, who was thrown out of the back. I visited the midshipman in the naval hospital near Washington later on with Bob Cherry. He was recovering and in good heart, but would be put back a course at the Academy, which obviously upset him. It was not a great disaster but a blot on all the good work we had done, and I was cross; but the responsibility was mine. The Embassy was not too happy, either!

At the end of August I flew home and left the Senior Pilot in charge for the remaining trials. One aircraft was due to return for maintenance, and there was work to be done back at Boscombe, so I made the return flight via Goose and Keflavik, taking just over eight hours from Pensacola.

A few days before I left, I'd had a call from Patuxent, which followed up a conversation during the catapult trials at the beginning of the month when I had been briefed for a flight in the Grumman A6 Intruder, an aircraft on the list for us to fly during our exchange visit in April/May, but at that time unserviceable. Would I be able to get to PAX to fly it now, they asked. This was an opportunity not to be missed, so I made my way to Patuxent three days before departing for the UK.

The A6 is a formidable package with outstanding endurance in its role as a low-level attack bomber, and therefore much to be compared with the Buccaneer. The very large cockpit incorporates side-by-side seating, with the bombardier/navigator slightly behind and below the pilot, in contrast to the tandem seating in the Buccaneer. I spent a little over an hour working it over, and found no rough edges. It is subsonic but not quite the same low-level ride to be experienced in its British counterpart. I had been interested to fly the A6 since Oceana days when it first made its appearance in VA-42

Squadron, but had to be satisfied with the Phantom. Now I realised what a prize we had with the Buccaneer.

On my return to Boscombe I discussed with David Dick the feasibility of flying the last Buccaneer non-stop back to this country at the conclusion of the trials in October. Fuel consumption figures were encouraging, and provided there were no unusual adverse winds it seemed hopeful, although tight. So I got his provisional agreement that the Naval Staff should be informed for whatever publicity they thought advisable to illustrate the long-range capability of the aircraft. With that in mind I returned to the States, where, as a last gesture to our American hosts, I had agreed to let the Air Force test pilots and their engineers (scientists) at Edwards Air Force Base cast an eye over the 'Limeys' latest.'

At the end of September, with all tropical tests completed, we took the Buccaneer to the US Air Force and NASA Space Agency Test Center, near Las Vegas, a vast establishment with two landing areas covering some twenty miles in the desert. In the next two days, while Eric Palmer, the Senior Pilot, gave several of their chaps a ride in the navigator's seat, I was given an opportunity of a lifetime, to fly in the Lockheed F-104 Starfighter to observe the incredible sight of the launch of the X15A research aircraft from a B52 Stratofortress. This was a research programme to investigate flight at very high altitudes, which had already achieved 350,000 ft and speeds exceeding Mach 6, and would be the forerunner to the future Space Program. The aircraft is effectively a highly sophisticated manned rocket with conventional aircraft controls, powered by a liquid-propellant rocket engine.

It was unbelievable. We took off as one of four 'chase' aircraft, maintaining fairly close formation on this very large 'mother' ship, with the X15 strapped to the starboard wing for an air launch. I was sitting in the back of the 104 listening to the radio, waiting for the countdown, but when it came, I was ill prepared for what happened next. 'Zero' was called by the Captain of the Stratofortress, and, with that the X15 dropped away about thirty feet, lit its rocket engine and then achieved a quite astonishing acceleration. Within microseconds it was a dot in the upper atmosphere and out of sight. After burning the engine for about one minute, achieving very high Mach numbers and a height of over 300,000 ft, which qualified the pilot for a US Astronaut's 'wings', he would land at China Lake, largely under automatic control. Meanwhile, we landed at Las Vegas to give me an opportunity to experience landing the F-104, and then returned to Edwards.

That evening there was an invitation to fly to Las Vegas for a gambling run, but I declined. The following day came another invitation, the opportunity to fly the C130 Hercules with Sqn Ldr Carver, a Royal Air Force exchange pilot with the USAF. I spent an hour and a half in this delightful, easy-to-fly, large aircraft, which handled more like a fighter than the four-engined heavy transport that it was. Using reverse thrust immediately, or just before touch-down, the landing could be accomplished with a run of less than one hundred yards. Soon after this flight, I left to return to Patuxent, where Buccaneer 974 awaited me for the flight home.

On 3 October, with Lt Cdr Tony Tayler as my navigator, I flew up to Goose Bay, the departure point for my transatlantic crossing to RNAS Lossiemouth. This was not the shortest crossing by any means, but Goose had all the basic facilities and equipment we required, such as low-pressure air starting, and of course they were by now familiar with the aircraft. Shortly after arrival, the weather closed in, and within a very short time snow had arrived in depth! This, coupled with an adverse wind forecast at altitude, meant that the flight would have to be delayed until the following day when the runway could be cleared. This was a pity, since I had already signalled Lossiemouth of our expected time of arrival before departure from Patuxent.

Next day, the weather had improved. There was still a considerable covering of snow, but the airfield staff had managed to clear a narrow strip on the perimeter track and on the runway, sufficient for take-off. So without wasting any more time we manned the aircraft for an 0900 take-off. Then came the first of our problems: the starboard engine was reluctant to start. All the engine settings, of course, had been geared to hot weather, and now the Spey showed some reluctance to perform under the arctic conditions of Goose. It resulted in a short delay, but eventually, after four attempts, it burst into life and we were in business.

The flight took four hours and twenty minutes to touch down at Lossiemouth, and was full of incidents, too many to record here (a full account was published in the *World Aerospace Systems Magazine*), but for the most part we were without any form of navigation other than DR (dead reckoning) and unreliable and misleading TACAN (tactical navigation). Added to this, we suffered an adverse wind at altitude instead of the westerly component which had been forecast, so our fuel state was not as rosy as we had hoped. Anyway, we made it and were greeted with champagne by the

Captain at Lossiemouth, before flying on to Boscombe later on, arriving in the dark.

Apart from a few bits and pieces, we had cleared the Buccaneer for full and unrestricted service, and my time with 'C' Squadron was coming to a close. Before leaving I was invited, with Dennis, to Blackburn, the aircraft designers, for an official dinner and presentation commemorating the work with the Buccaneer, and in particular the non-stop Atlantic crossing, a very nice gesture for two years' rewarding work.

Ever the scrounger for more aircraft to experience, during my time at A&AEE Boscombe Down I had added a fair number of aircraft to my repertory, including the English Electric Lightning, Folland Gnat, Aero Commander, and a number of others, including the Handley Page Victor, as 2nd Pilot, and helicopters; it all added to the experience. But shortly I would, metaphorically speaking, come down to earth. In January 1966 I was appointed to the Joint Warfare Staff in the dreaded Ministry of Defence.

But prior to, and in anticipation of, this, we had bought a house in Farnborough, which I thought would be suitable for commuting. And so it proved. A short walk to the station and a relatively easy, if crowded, journey to Waterloo meant a few minutes' walk over Hungerford Bridge to my office on the ninth floor of Main Building, as MOD was known. The JWS was an odd fish really, almost a throwback to the old Amphibious Warfare organisation of the Second World War, but which had yet to be fully incorporated within the new Ministry of Defence.

CHAPTER 21

Joint Warfare Staff

The staff was headed by a renowned former paratrooper, Maj Gen 'Tubby' Butler (quite why the nickname I don't know, he was as thin as a rake and fit as a fiddle), a delightful fellow, but he left shortly after my arrival and his place was taken by a rather stuffy air commodore. On the ninth floor we had palatial accommodation and our own private bar! But it wasn't to last. Jealousy from certain Civil Service quarters had discovered our little paradise, and we were moved to the sixth floor in the process of a considerable reorganisation, an event that occurred at least every decade.

The sixth floor housed the VIPs – the Minister of Defence, his Permanent Secretary, Chiefs of the three Service Staffs, and others, such as the Minister responsible for Defence Procurement and Director-General of Defence Intelligence. The Defence Secretary at the time was Dennis Healey, whom I would meet frequently in the lift to the sixth floor. Whether he was early or I was late I don't know, but he was always friendly and chatty.

Our claim to fame was that following Mountbatten's recommendations of some years previously, we were all about to become Joint Defence Staff; it would take some time, but we were the forerunners of that economic reorganisation. My boss was now Rear Adm O.H.M. St J. Steiner, Otto for short, who held the position of Assistant Chief Defence Staff (Joint Warfare), later to become (General), reflecting the broadening of his responsibilities.

There was at the time huge opposition from the three services to being 'Jointed', much reflected later on when I chaired a Joint Service Team to report on the future command and control of helicopters. At every stage of progress, I would encounter opposition from either the Air Force or the Army, leading to acrimonious meetings with very senior officers who were not prepared to make concessions in the interests of the new philosophy.

The primary problem was as to who should own helicopters operating in the battlefield. The Army wished to regard them as another item of long-range artillery and a means of transport to replace the horse! The Air Force, of course, had always taken the view that if it 'flew' it belonged to it. The Navy had had a hard time between the two Great Wars suffering from this entrenched policy before overcoming the Lord Trenchard attitude in 1938.

Anyway, I and my committee could make little headway with these rival positions. At every stage objections would lead to a veto, and my final submission to the Chiefs of Staff was a wishy-washy report, reflecting the irresistible force meeting the immovable object. It would need more authority than I and my committee possessed to resolve such a lofty issue that, once more, questioned the need for an independent Air Force. Much of my time in Whitehall would be spent encouraging more integration between the services, but it was a losing battle, and many years would pass before the concept of a true Joint Service policy was accepted and evolved.

I learnt one other thing there: the parsimonious attitude of those in authority at spending their own money! I had been there about a year when I was asked to arrange a suitable activity for an afternoon's free time during the course of a visit by very senior Americans from the Supreme Allied Commander's staff in Brussels. As they were Americans, my thoughts turned immediately to golf, and we signalled, 'Would this be acceptable?' 'No problem, delighted', was the answer, so play was arranged at a well-known golf club in Berkshire

In accordance with current MOD regulations, our guests could be entertained at government expense but the hosts, headed by the Permanent Secretary, would suffer their own individual costs. I had trouble extracting the appropriate, and not inconsiderable, share from only one, the exalted and very highly paid Permanent Secretary, who flatly refused, despite much effort by his own secretary, claiming he was too busy to deal with such trifles. I just stopped short of requesting the golf club to send him an individual bill when his secretary paid, saying he would get it back somehow!

Unbeknown to me when I left Boscombe, I had been recommended for the award of an Air Force Cross, and this was duly gazetted in the Queen's Birthday Honours List of 1966. It naturally reflected as much on the efforts of 'C' Squadron as a whole as it did on me personally, and I thought we had all done well to get the Buccaneer Mk 2 and Sea Vixen Mk 2 into service as quickly as we had done. However, there it was, it was nice of Gp Capt Dick and Air Cdre Bird to put forward my name; perhaps in the latter case, a little return for the catapult ride in the navigator's seat of the Buccaneer when I flew him from the deck of HMS *Ark Royal* back to Boscombe twelve months before – or was it for the occasions when I allowed him to beat me on the golf course?

In November came an invitation for Pat and myself to Buckingham Palace for the Investiture. These occasions have an air of pomposity, rather than impressiveness, about them, and on entering the Palace through various reception rooms before being seated for the presentation, I was struck by the general run-down appearance of the furnishings and carpets. However, it was a moving experience, performed with great dignity by the ADCs who briefed and seated us, before I was called to receive the award from Her Majesty. She was extremely charming, a large smile put you at ease and, as far as I can recall, she said, 'Now what have you been up to?' She knew broadly, of course, from the briefing notes, but I made a suitable rejoinder, we shook hands and she duly made the presentation. All very typically British, the whole thing carried out with military precision. We left through the main entrance to lunch nearby.

I would spend the minimum time in Whitehall of just under two years, for which I was grateful. The daily commuting and general hustle and bustle to and from work, arriving home late as a result of delays caused by the electrification of the railway line, had begun to pall, and I looked forward to getting out of the 'Madhouse'. I had also been promised an overseas appointment next as compensation for just missing the opportunity of an appointment as Commander Air in HMS *Ark Royal*, which went to my friend Bill Hawley; his time on the Naval Staff coincided with the timescale of the appointment, and mine did not.

CHAPTER 22

Fleet Aviation Officer, Far East Fleet

The appointment, when it came, I received with mixed feelings. I had hoped to get back to sea in some capacity, but in my new job, as Fleet Aviation Officer to the Commander Far East Fleet, my expectations would only be partially fulfilled. However, it was a plum job. I would be back within the true naval orbit again, having been away for far too long. My career had been jeopardised by, perhaps, an unthinking officer's Appointer, whom I knew, although my Machiavellian thoughts turned to other reasons..

Before flying out to Singapore with my family, I spent two weeks at Lossiemouth getting back in flying practice again after two years at the Ministry. I knew that a small naval unit with a naval Hunter aircraft was based at the RAF station at Changi, in Singapore, and would be available to fly when I could spare the time, but this apart, the job demanded current flying experience.

Taking a totally realistic view of my future, I knew now that there was little or no chance of further promotion. On arrival in Singapore, there would only be time for a single report to be made on me, and that would not be enough. I had spent two and more years in America, three at Boscombe and then two at the Joint Staff, none of which carried the weight of a 'Naval' assessment, a prerequisite for promotion. But I had no regrets. Had I been promoted, my destiny would have been a series of appointments sitting behind desks, in contrast to what lay in store for me, although I knew not of it at the time. After all I didn't join the Royal Navy to sit behind desks, which I could equally have done as a civilian.

My arrival overlapped my predecessor, Duncan Lang, which unfortunately prevented the family moving into the assigned married quarter straightaway. As a temporary measure we found accommodation in the Johore Bahru Rest House for a week or so until we moved into an extremely pleasant house in Straits View Gardens. It was spacious, largely open plan on the ground floor to allow maximum ventilation in the hot and humid climate, with enough accommodation for Eye Ing, our living-in Amah, and countless 'Chit-Chats' who would entertain us every evening on the wall, particularly around the pictures. They were harmless little creatures, unlike the voracious cockroaches which invaded the kitchen area but scarcely ventured much further.

Living the other side of the Causeway from Fleet HQ, based in the north of Singapore Island, entailed a journey of some eight miles, but more importantly it meant negotiating the border customs post twice a day. In itself this was not a great problem, except for the queues which formed from the dilatory attitude of the customs officers. I overcame this by buying a Honda motor-cycle to circumvent the long queues of cars, and because I was in uniform I was generally waved straight through. Johore Bahru was a popular choice to live, and generally preferred to the hustle and bustle of downtown Singapore.

It was a generally enjoyable period of eighteen months for me, never a dull moment, with plenty of variation. As FAVO I divided my time between the normal staff work of the Fleet Commander, Adm Bill O'Brien, and his second-in-command, Adm Griffin, whenever he went to sea, which, during my time, amounted to three opportunities. Adm Griffin was an intelligent and clever man but had preconceived ideas on how a supporting operations staff should function during embarked time at sea.

He was known to be in favour of a single Staff Operations Officer who would combine and advise on all the duties of gunnery, torpedo, anti-submarine and aviation. It is doubtful if such an animal existed. He himself was a signals specialist, although he had been exposed to the aviation world in his capacity as a carrier captain. His views on this considerable departure from long-standing practice would eventually find support within the Naval Staff in the form of a new body called an 'Air Warfare Officer'. But that was a long way off, and if it were to work at all it would require careful selection and training of the chosen few. Meantime, he attempted to operate as if this were already a *fait accompli*, rendering pointless the additional specialist officers provided to him from the Fleet Staff.

Life for the family centred around schools, a very nice swimming-pool at the 'Terror' Officers' Club and several holidays 'up country' to cool off at Fraser's Hill in central Malaya. The hill station there was a pleasant place to relax, little to do except play golf on a nine-hole course or follow the paths off the Padang to look for the wonderfully coloured butterflies to be found in the jungle. We acquired quite a collection, but on reflection I am a little saddened by it.

The Hill boasted one tavern-type hostelry run by an English couple which acted as a social centre. Our first visit to this establishment shortly after our arrival caused quite a sensation and not a little embarrassment. A 'One-Armed Bandit' machine in the bar caught the eye of the two children, and we misguidedly gave them a few pennies to keep them out of mischief. From then on there was the steady sound of winnings until, inevitably, the 'Jackpot', with coins all over the place. They could do no wrong, but it hardly enhanced the reputation of the Higgs family.

Dating back from pre-war colonial days, the Admiralty had acquired a number of properties on the Hill, much as the Army had done further up country at the much larger hill station, Cameron Highlands. They were essentially rest centres, an opportunity to get away from the heat and humidity of Singapore and the Straits. We were fortunate to have the opportunity to use the large Navy-owned Admiralty bungalow, Bishop's House, on two occasions. Comfortably furnished and with domestic staff, it was in a prime position and wanted for nothing. It was also provided at minimum costs.

They were pleasant days, marred only on the second occasion by a totally unexpected recall after barely having started my leave and arrived there. There had been an aircraft accident in HMS *Hermes*, a Board of Inquiry had been convened and I had been appointed by the Fleet Commander as President – in my absence on leave! Nothing new in this in the services, and a quick telephone call revealed the details. A car would be provided to take me to Kuala Lumpur for the flight to Singapore and a briefing at Fleet HQ. But then the tricky bit – the ship was many miles away off the Philippines, and the most expedient way of getting there was to fly to Bangkok in Thailand and then take another flight to Manila, where *Hermes* would send a helicopter ashore to transport me on board. A long flog and a schedule that would take all the next day.

I arrived on board to discover a Gannet had been lost overboard in circumstances that had a strong suggestion of pilot negligence. My task, with the support of the three other officers on the board, was to determine the facts and whether they amounted to a case for a court martial. After three days we, as a board, arrived at our conclusions, and as President I submitted my report to Adm Griffin. Meanwhile the ship had headed north towards Hong Kong, and I wasted no time in requesting a helicopter to airlift me to Kai Tak International for onward flight to Singapore and a subsequent flight to Kuala Lumpur to rejoin my family.

If I had known how much they had settled in and been enjoying themselves, I might not have been in so much haste. We had previously become quite friendly with a wealthy and influential Malay, Dato Eddy (Dato is a title equivalent to a knighthood), a man of infinite charm who owned a substantial property at Fraser's Hill, liked to play a few holes of golf and would invariably get half a dozen local boys to accompany him to carry his bag and other things, solely to justify giving them money. Anyway, he had taken the family under his wing when I left to the point where he allowed Pat to drive his Rolls Royce motor car from time to time and generally made sure they came to no harm. Towards the end of the holiday he very kindly housed us when we overran our time at the bungalow, and then insisted that we stop off at one of his clubs on our return journey for refreshments. 'Just say Dato Eddy asked you to call', said he. 'I would be honoured if you would be my guest there.'

A particularly enjoyable short break occurred almost as an accident. These were troubled times in Malaya, with Communist infiltrators causing unrest up and down the country, and a planned holiday on the west coast had to be abandoned when the area was put out of bounds. So we settled for Kuantan on the east coast, which, typically, amounted to a decent hotel but little else – except for one thing. It was renowned as a habitat for very large turtles which would come ashore to lay their eggs on the beach late in the evening. It was a must, of course, and so off to the beach we went, quite dark by this time, and began the long trek to witness this rare phenomenon.

On a typically Malayan deep sandy beach, we were soon struggling with the two children, one on piggy-back. We were not alone; others were walking in the same direction, and before long, and before we realised it, David had been hoisted on the shoulders of a tall Malay and was striding ahead of us, disappearing in the dark, towards our common goal. It all seemed perfectly natural and there was no hint of alarm at the time, but on reflection – we wondered! However, no cause for concern, we all arrived at the appropriate place, and watched these huge turtles waddle up the beach to scratch holes in the sand to lay their eggs. An experience to behold, it made the holiday.

David seemed to have a capacity for attracting help from the local people. Kate at this time was taking ballet lessons, a few miles further along Straits View, and on this occasion David was left by the school bus at the bottom of the road, complete with wicker basket, to be picked up by Pat on return from collecting Kate. He suddenly appeared at the ballet class premises shortly after Pat's arrival there. He had been given a lift by a young Malay on the pillion of his motor-cycle! He was just seven years of age.

But despite the troubles up country, Johore Bahru was generally very safe, with little crime apparent. The opulent properties in the area tended to attract the attention of criminals from time to time, but not often enough to cause any concern. Our own area of Straits View Gardens was not entirely immune from break-ins, and there was at one time a spate of incidents, one of which so alarmed the resident naval officers that two of us appeared in pyjamas, in the area of the break-in, brandishing hastily drawn swords to defend the honour of the teenage daughter of a naval captain who had screamed that someone had prised the steel window-bars apart and got into her bedroom. We saw no one, but the theatrical spectacle of two sword-wielding naval officers was high entertainment value.

By the early part of 1969, from an age point of view, we were conscious of the need to have the children in suitable schools at home, and while my appointment was not due to end until March 1970, we decided the family would return in August, in time for the commencement of the next school year. Thus, with the appropriate notice given to our tenants, they returned to our home in Sycamore Road.

They were, however, given one more memorable occasion to take home with them. We had somehow made the acquaintance of the Area Chief of Police during our travels, an influential man who, apart from other perks, had the use of a large police launch, which was invariably tied up near the Causeway. During the course of a Grand Prix-type motor-race round the roads of Johore Bahru, it naturally held a prime position, and quite out of the blue we were honoured to be his guests. It was a splendid occasion, the racing was first class, perhaps Formula 3, and only exceeded by the generous hospitality of the Police Commissioner. It was a nice send-off.

The following months for me were in many ways unsatisfactory. I had moved into comfortable quarters in the wardroom mess at HMS *Terror*, but time was clearly going to hang heavily, not only because of the loss of the family, but because the government's great run-down of overseas bases had already started to bite, and, with that, the workload. There were now very few ships on the Far East Station, much of the dockyard had already been reduced to care-and-maintenance and the general atmosphere was one of waiting for the inevitable about to happen.

Only a short while after I had moved into the wardroom mess, a court martial was convened of a Roman Catholic priest, and I was appointed to the Board to try him. Unlike their counterparts in both the Army and the Air Force, Padres in the Navy are treated as officers but carry no rank, it always being held that a 'neutral' position aids their work with all ranks, but they are, nevertheless, subject to the Naval Discipline Act.

In this particular case he had unfortunately been discovered 'drunk' on board ship, quite unacceptable behaviour at any time in a ship, but aggravated because he was found on a ratings' mess deck. It was an unpleasant business seeing a man of the 'cloth' in front of the Board, but the embarrassment was minimised by the said Padre offering no defence, and it was dealt with quickly.

Shortly after this unfortunate occurrence, it happened that an AFO (Admiralty Fleet Order) arrived on my desk, promulgating a forthcoming conference to be held at Greenwich, with terms of reference enquiring into the future of the Royal Navy in the latter half of the twentieth century. It was to be held in November and was scheduled for three weeks. Ah, thought I, that would be a very interesting three weeks, and so with no thoughts, of course, of the opportunity to see the family, I started making noises about representing the views of the Far East Fleet Command at said conference.

The bait was taken, COMFEF signalled the Admiralty that I would be his representative, and then it all fell into place. The Staff was being gradually reduced, and it seemed a sensible time to suggest that the general workload had dropped so much over recent months that I could hand over to my Number Two, a competent lieutenant-commander, and cut short my appointment. So it happened. In November I left the Far East Fleet for Greenwich and, in the New Year, my next appointment at DOAE.

DOAE

My acquaintance with the Defence Operations Analysis Establishment was one of personal convenience. I had requested an appointment to suit my domestic circumstances, one that would enable us to stay in the family house for the time being until we decided on the longer-term future. 'How would DOAE, West Byfleet, appeal to you?' I was asked, and while I had no knowledge of its function, it seemed an ideal stop-gap. So I agreed. It was within easy driving distance of home, and as it turned out was an interesting and educational two years.

DOAE enjoyed a reputation for reducing defence matters to numbers, analysing everything that came its way to the point where numerical comparisons would be an essential part of defence planning. From this it was possible to form coherent judgements and make an extremely valuable contribution to future war plans, much of it, therefore, based on past experiences. The ratio of scientists to service personnel was of the order of six or seven to one, just enough service input to keep their feet on the ground. It seemed to work. There was a good deal of interchange with defence planners in the three service staffs in Whitehall, recognised by the fact that all service personnel at DOAE held full MOD passes.

My immediate superior was Capt John Stevens, recently Commodore Hong Kong and a former Commanding Officer of HMS *Leander*, an appointment which carried with it life-long membership of the Leander Yacht Club on the Thames. It was on one such occasion, when he invited half a dozen of the naval officers to lunch at the club, that I persuaded him to divert a few miles to take a little refreshment at a pub run by my old friend Adam MacKinnon from *Illustrious* days. He was long since retired, but clearly enjoyed running this very nice country inn with his wife. I hadn't seen him for nearly twenty years, but he had changed very little and was very much the laid-back Mac of former days.

I would spend two years at Byfleet. I cannot say it was the most exhilarating time of my life but it had served its main purpose as far as the family was concerned, and I had found the Honda motor-cycle, which I had had shipped back from Singapore on the open deck of a frigate, more than useful in avoiding the traffic in the daily commuting run – except for one occasion when the engine failed returning home in the dark late one evening, half-way across the deserted common near Pirbright. No mobile telephones in those days, so, nothing daunted, I pushed the b——y thing the last three miles home.

But then, towards the end of my time there, I had a telephone call from the Admiralty: 'How would you like to go to Bedford as CO?' And I thought my flying days were long since over! It opened up a whole new world. Not only would I now return to Lossiemouth for two weeks' refresher flying, but there was an added bonus, a helicopter course at RNAS Culdrose. My previous experience of helicopters had been cursory, a few flights at

Farnborough during the Test Pilots course and a flight or two at Boscombe. But I was now about to become fully qualified to fly a variety of helicopters in the two to three weeks I would spend at Culdrose in August/September of 1972, at the age of 47.

It was an ideal time for the family to come to Cornwall for a short holiday. After staying in the wardroom mess for a few days, I elected to have the convenience of a caravan nearby, with a naval car to transport me to and fro. This attracted a living-out allowance, and, of course, the caravan proved a bonus during the family's visit.

By the first week of September I had achieved over twenty hours' flying, mainly in the Westland Whirlwind, in which I had accumulated a fair number of 1st Pilot hours. There had also been exposure to the Sea King, Wasp and Hiller, but time would not permit 1st Pilot time in these three. So with twenty hours' flying time in the Hunter at Lossiemouth and now with an equivalent number of helicopter hours under my belt, I was well equipped to tackle Bedford, where I would be reacquainted with a number of old friends from my past time there.

CHAPTER 23

RAE Bedford – Again!

It hadn't changed a great deal. The organisation was much the same, the Aerodynamics Dept/Flight was still quite busy, though less so than when I last knew it, but BLEU, the Blind Landing Experimental Unit, had grown in size and importance. There was now no official Naval Flight, although the Naval Air Department was still active to support the still existing but declining RN Fixed-Wing operations in the fleet. Without a Naval Flight test pilot, continuing catapult and the new (DAX) direct-acting arrester gear requirements would fall to me.

My first intention was to familiarise myself with as many of the test aircraft as I could reasonably expect to do. One of my principal tasks as Commanding Officer was the clearance of all flight tests, particularly the safety aspects, and I felt it necessary to have first-hand knowledge of the aircraft involved. Thus, very early on I qualified to fly as 1st Pilot, the Hawker Siddeley 125, a twin-jet, high-performance executive aircraft; the HS 748, a twin-engined turboprop medium-range airliner capable of carrying up to sixty passengers; and its RAF equivalent, the Andover, a military transport.

I would also fly the Handley Page 115, a research vehicle designed to investigate the low-speed handling characteristics of slender delta-wings for supersonic transport aircraft; the Auster AOP9, a splendid little light, high-wing monoplane which investigated turbulence; and several others. But the bulk of my flying would be in the Whirlwind helicopter and the Sea Vixen. Both aircraft were under my direct control and could be used for support work such as photography or as transports. My aim was to achieve sufficient flying hours to remain proficient without affecting the general administration of the base, which was my *raison d'être*.

Now, with David already away at prep school, the rest of the family took up residence in married quarters at Sharnbrook – 'old hat' to Pat of course, since she had lived in the same village in a delightful cottage with her family those many years ago. So with Sam, our Dalmatian, we settled into our new home, leasing our own house until we determined later where to lay our roots, recognising that I would have one more appointment before final retirement from the Royal Navy after thirty-five years.

Overseeing the various departments and sections at the base entailed numerous weekly and monthly meetings, occupying much of my time. And, as Base Commander I also sat on the main management board of RAE Bedford. Some of these regular meetings, I felt, were pure indulgence. There was, as an example, a monthly meeting with the Bedford local authority to discuss noise and nuisance caused by the aircraft, and other matters. Mostly, there was little problem and little to discuss, but it was guaranteed to take the better part of an afternoon, which, I suspect, served to enhance the expense claims of the Councillor representatives.

At internal board meetings, we frequently co-opted local Trades Union leaders when there were matters to discuss which affected them or their members, and I recall one such after I had introduced measures for bird control on the airfield to prevent aircraft bird strikes.

Shortly after my arrival it was apparent to me that the risk of a bird strike was high enough to warrant protective measures, and I sought the advice of a local chap, recommended to me by the RSPB. He was a peregrine falcon handler with experience in the dispersal of nuisance birds, so I got him along to look at our problem, mainly plovers, but also gulls and other large birds, all capable of catastrophic damage to an aircraft during take-off or landing. Fortunately it hadn't come to that, but there had been a number of bird strikes, and I now employed him to operate his falcons to 'deter', which is what they were trained to do.

I was quite pleased with his efforts, only to find opposition from a union leader at a board meeting. 'You're a bird killer!' he ranted, and went on to other silly accusations about my attitude towards wildlife in general and how he would call his members out, etc., etc. Well, it was all a little unpleasant, but I eventually threatened to hold him responsible for an aircraft accident resulting from a serious bird strike if I stopped the falconry. He went a little quiet and said no more. He really was on a losing wicket; he was talking to one of the world's greatest bird lovers!

I recall another incident involving a union at Bedford, related to me by Ted Whitley, my old air engineer officer from 'C' Squadron, who having left the Navy was now employed in a similar capacity at Bedford. A shop steward running the maintainers' part of the strike was holding a meeting outside one of the hangars when a Hastings aircraft, running-up its engines, carefully lined up the slipstream on the meeting! This deflated the meeting somewhat, but then, as he was pronouncing that a Wessex helicopter, involved in a very important trial, would not fly again until he gave the order for his chaps to sign the various trades, it flew overhead! He had failed to appreciate that Ted was authorised to sign for all trades and had done so.

By the end of the year I had accumulated a fair number of test hours in the HS 748, in the capacity of both Captain and 2nd Pilot. It now bore fruit. Sqn Ldr Terry Downey, CO of BLEU Flight, came to see me in my office with a proposition that had more than a hint of blackmail about it.

'Sir,' he said, 'we are due for a long-range navigation training flight, and I hoped you would approve it.'

'Oh,' said I, 'and where are you thinking of going?'

'Well, it would depend on your approval to go overseas – uh, to Berlin. In which event, I was going to ask if you would come as 2nd Pilot. It's a demanding navigational flight through the corridor, and I would assist with that part of it while you do most of the flying.' Outright coercion, but how could I refuse?

Accordingly, on 1 December we departed from Bedford to land at Wildenrath in West Germany for clearance before the onward flight through the narrow corridor over Russian-controlled East Germany to West Berlin. There were occasional problems in the corridor when the Russians flexed their muscles with buzzing fighters, but we had none, and we duly landed at the RAF base in the British Occupied Zone of Berlin. It was an interesting few days in the divided German city, especially as the Air Force laid on a bus to take us, and a number of others, across the heavily guarded border into East Berlin.

At the border crossing, we remained in the bus to be checked, while the East German guards photographed us with long-range cameras from their position high in the Security Tower. It took a while for the deliberately protracted formalities to be completed, but eventually we were on our way.

On the other side, the contrast was incredible. The Russian sector of Berlin was much as it had been during the war. Grey, unattractive buildings, a lot of rubble, no sign of any rebuilding or shops during our drive to the war cemetery, which was as far as we were permitted to proceed. We witnessed the Changing of the Guard at a military HQ, and returned across the border, carefully counted back in, to the more agreeable and comparatively opulent British Western Sector. Two days later, we flew back, having enjoyed our short stay, but a little sorry to have witnessed that after nearly twenty-five years the situation in Germany was what it was.

By the end of 1972 I had well and truly settled in to my various responsibilities. There was more than enough flying available, but I could not always spare as much time as I might have wished. It had been common practice to hold a meteorological briefing before the start of the day's flying, and when it was over I would discuss what test flights I would like to become involved in during the day, always recognising that the flight commanders, in conjunction with the scientific staff, would make the final decision on the daily programme. The procedure worked quite well; I was able to maintain a working knowledge of what they were doing, and why.

Early in 1973 I received a signal appointing me to the board of a court martial convened to try a Royal Navy lieutenant-commander charged with hazarding his squadron's aircraft. He was the CO of a Gannet AEW aircraft detachment at a Royal Air Force station, and the circumstances revolved around the loss of two aircraft during a night-flying exercise, which a preliminary Board of Inquiry considered to have been recklessly authorised in view of the adverse weather forecast and subsequent conditions.

Well, there wasn't much doubt about it, there were no mitigating circumstances: the CO had made a clanger, and it didn't take the board long to arrive at our findings. The verdict was guilty as charged. Capt David Kirke, the same who had greeted me at Lossiemouth on my flight from Canada, was President, and together we made our submission to 'higher authority' for confirmation.

However, the process required the convening Flag Officer's endorsement before disciplinary action was taken. Despite the indisputable evidence, the findings were quashed by the Admiral, who, it so happened, was the accused's godfather, quoting extenuating circumstances for so doing in his forwarding of the case to the Admiralty. But the officer in question, a very nice intelligent chap, and generally competent, was not further promoted and would retire as a lieutenant-commander.

Towards the end of March 1973, and not to be outdone by BLEU, the CO of Aero Flight proposed a long-range navigation exercise with the HS 125, and since by this time I had flown a good many trial flights in the aircraft, he was kind enough to suggest I crew it with Flt Lt John Rudin, one of the Aero

Flight pilots. These exercises were generally conducted over the weekend, and my other commitments would not suffer, and so, expressing my appreciation, I readily agreed.

It should have been a straightforward down and back to Gibraltar, clearing customs at RAF St Mawgan before stopping at Porto in Portugal for fuel; and indeed, with John in the 2nd Pilot's seat and a couple of passengers in the back, we landed at RAF North Front, Gibraltar, on time.

Then on the Monday morning we suffered a set-back; the maintenance crew had found a major fault with the port engine, requiring its replacement, which would have to be flown out from the UK. So the overnight stop developed into a frustrating week, with signals flashing to and fro, trying to locate a spare and then arranging air transport. Frustrating it was, but no great hardship. We were comfortably accommodated in the RAF officers' mess and had an opportunity to potter around the town, but uncertainty about the arrival of the spare engine curtailed any travels further afield. Eventually, with the spare engine installed, we left for home, flying direct to Bedford after refuelling at Porto again. Inevitably, there was a good deal of banter and mickey-taking! How did we fix it to stay in Gib for a week, and so on, to which John would tease of bribing the engine fitter and the very attractive Women's Royal Air Force officer he met in the mess there.

RAE/Concorde Flight Tests – Da Yu (Heavy Rain [Malay])

Half-way through the year, Peter Parrot, the group captain in charge of flying at Farnborough, rang me; could I pop down to see him in the next day or two to discuss a Structures Department proposal for a flight trial in support of the Concorde aircraft? So a few days later I pottered down in the Auster and he came out to meet me on the tarmac, and we both returned to his office in the control tower.

In brief, Structures was seeking to use a Phantom aircraft to investigate the effects of heavy rain and ice, at high altitude and Mach numbers on the aircraft surfaces in simulation of that to be expected by Concorde. Peter pre-empted my first question by explaining that normally this sort of trial would fall to the Structures and Mechanical Engineering Flight at Farnborough, but they didn't have pilots with that sort of experience, and he felt that we at Bedford were better suited. His thought was that the project should be put to an Aero Flight pilot, and that in the event it involved a detachment away from base, I should take it fully under my wing. I left to give it some thought and to contact the project scientist, a Mr Andrew Fyall.

From my subsequent discussions with him I discovered the background and realised that he had already spent some months, if not years, studying the dangers of rain erosion in flight. With the imminence of Concorde entering service he had been authorised to use a suitably modified supersonic fighter to evaluate the practical problems, and after considering the Lightning, had discarded it in favour of the Phantom with its greater flexibility. After further study of various regions which might be expected to experience severe thunderstorms, he had concluded that the months of January to March in Singapore and the South China Seas offered the most promise.

One pilot in Aero Flight, Flt Lt John Fawcett, had served in a Phantom squadron and was a natural choice. All that remained was for myself to refamiliarise on the aircraft and to take an equal part in the flying. This was arranged through the Ministry of Aviation and MOD Navy, and as I was a naval pilot, Naval Air Station Yeovilton was directed to provide suitable refresher training. In July I flew down to Yeovilton in preparation for a short simulator course and the necessary number of flying hours in the Phantom to prepare for what was obviously going to be a demanding test programme.

But having completed the four-day simulator course, I met with opposition. Objections from station level, that they had insufficient flying-hours available to cope with a strictly non-naval requirement, found support from the local Flag Officer and, eventually, cancellation of an arrangement previously agreed at Naval Staff level. I had no doubt then – and now – that there had been skullduggery behind all this, but the decision had been made.

Peter Parrot was, understandably, hopping mad at this, and straightaway arranged, through the Ministry of Aviation, for the RAF to provide training, which they did in great style at RAF Leuchars, just south of Dundee. While I was there, and towards the end of the short course, I thought I would tweak the tail of the offending person at Yeovilton by arranging a navigation exercise to terminate in a landing at Yeovilton. I have little doubt that my arrival was brought to his notice.

By the end of the year, the nominated Phantom had arrived at Boscombe Down from Holme-on-Spalding-Moor, where Hawker Siddeley Dynamics had prepared the aircraft with various protective coatings to minimise any damage caused during the trial's flights. Two drop-tanks were also fitted with

'Concorde samples' which could be changed between flights. At the beginning of January, after a number of familiarisation flights by Fawcett and myself, which entailed flying to Boscombe from Bedford, usually in the Auster, the aircraft was deployed to RAF Tengah, supported by in-flight refuelling VC10s and Hercules aircraft, and a Britannia transport aircraft which flew out the ground support crew, together with a mass of spare parts and equipment. The enormous cost of this operation was already beginning to show.

In all, during the two months of the trial, over thirty flights were made. My contribution was fifteen, during which I made sure I flew every one of the phases from the lower speeds up to 850 knots TAS (true air speed), well over Mach 1.2 at that height, to experience, and approve of, the developing conditions. I was, after all, first and foremost responsible for the safe conduct of the trial.

It was exhilarating stuff, finding the largest thunderstorms and deliberating penetrating them for as long as possible, wondering how much more the aircraft could take from this savage and brutal battering The noise of the rain on the aircraft surfaces at these very high speeds was quite incredible, and the ride in the cockpit was at times exceedingly uncomfortable, aggravated by the concentration needed to fly solely on instruments in the very dark conditions experienced in the centre of thunderstorms. It was akin, perhaps, to taking a family saloon car at high speed over a tank range. Fortunately, because of the high speed, penetration into the storms would be of relatively short duration before running out of the required heavy rain conditions, and sometimes airspace, but I found it hard to imagine any pilot, in his right senses, deliberately flying through thunderstorms of this magnitude, let alone a Concorde pilot with the safety and comfort of his passengers at the forefront of his mind.

Although all the vital aircraft surfaces had been coated with protective layers of synthetic material, it says much for the sturdiness of the Phantom that we experienced no major damage, the worst being a cracked windscreen, which fortunately held together until after landing, when it was examined and replaced. It proved to be a highly successful trial and a rain-erosion certificate for Concorde was completed in the following year, but I doubt if it would ever have been authorised if the final cost had been known in advance.

To celebrate the end of the trial, I gave Andrew Fyall a familiarisation flight in the navigator's seat shortly before leaving for home. I spared him the conditions under which most of the flying had been conducted in favour of a short flight round some of the Malayan islands off the east coast.

Back at Bedford, I had one very pleasant commitment. Earlier in the year Peter Parrot had phoned one day: 'Would you like to attend the biennial Society of Experimental Test Pilots affair in the States, as the RAE representative?' he asked. 'Unfortunately, I have planned to be on holiday and can't go, so I thought I would give you first refusal.'

I needed little prompting, and just before my birthday I departed for Washington and then on to Los Angeles, where the Society of Experimental Test Pilots Symposium was to be held. In Washington I met up with Duncan Simpson, the deputy chief test pilot of Hawker Aircraft, whom I had known for a very long time, and together we tackled the rest of the journey, booked into the Beverly Hilton Hotel, Beverly Hills, for the next two days and made the acquaintance of many of the large number of other international delegates.

It was a prestigious affair, a typically American 'no expense spared' occasion, laid on to impress the rest of the world with their past achievements in space and their continuing position as number one in the field of aeronautics, which they doubtlessly were. At the symposium, Alan Shepard, one of the original seven NASA astronauts, and the first man in space, was the Master of Ceremonies, with almost all the past and current astronauts in attendance acting as chairman of this or that aspect of the four days' proceedings.

Prior to the four-day symposium at the Beverly Hilton, on 25 September there had been an opportunity to visit the NASA and Air Force Flight Test Center at Edwards Air Force Base, and also SETP International HQ. But I had not long since been to Edwards and so arranged to arrive in Los Angeles that evening from Washington where I had stayed overnight with my ex-Senior Pilot, Nick Bennet, who was now with the British Defence Staff.

For the next three days there was a succession of high-powered international lectures from the industry and military, very professionally presented, all with a message to make. A poolside cocktail party concluded events after the visits on the first day, and the formal opening ceremonies on the second day concluded with a number of talks on current flight test activities, followed by more cocktails. A formal luncheon was arranged for the third day, when that outstanding scientist von Braun was the guest speaker. This left two evenings virtually free before the final day's programme and concluding dinner.

As far as possible, each table at luncheon and the concluding dinner was assigned one of the astronauts to act as host. We were fortunate at my table to have the pleasure of Capt John Young USN, whose claim to fame included a number of 'firsts'. He had been one of the two crew of the first manned Gemini flight in 1965, followed by another a year later before achieving two Apollo missions, including the first to orbit the Moon. And then, subsequently, only a little more than a year before this symposium, he had been one of the two astronauts to land on the Moon itself from the last flight before NASA suspended the Moon Program.

He was a delightful fellow to talk with, very self-effacing and reluctant to talk about his exploits with NASA, preferring instead to talk about his time in the US Navy, which he was passionate about. He was not alone. From the opportunities I, and others, had to talk with the astronauts during the course of the symposium, they shared this common attitude of retreating into their shells about their space experience, as though it had made such an indelible impression on them that they felt it was somehow too personal, like family confidences. (Some time later, reading the book *Apollo to the Moon*, I found this reticence was emphasised, and it became quite clear that their various experiences had had a profound effect on their future behaviour.) But they were all exceptional men and it was a privilege to meet them.

By far the most significant and fascinating feature of the third day was the lengthy talk by the guest speaker, Dr Wernher von Braun, the former German rocket pioneer and scientist who, after becoming a US citizen at the end of the Second World War, had been responsible for the development of the Saturn rocket for the Apollo and Moon landings. After the formal luncheon, he spoke, without notes, for nearly an hour, mostly about his work in America, but he also gave a short account of his early rocket work in Germany. I was surprised to find him much younger than I expected, still only 62 years of age, and yet he had been the leading German rocket scientist in the V2 project which so threatened London and other cities thirty years earlier. He was now vice-president of Fairchild Industries Inc., and his talk, 'Space Program after Apollo', was an example of how far forward he and his colleagues were looking.

The rest of the day was devoted to manned space-flight reports given by a number of astronauts, which included accounts of manoeuvring in space, testing the shuttle, a comparison of the Apollo and Soyuz projects, and a particularly interesting report by Col Bill Pogue of his three months in space.

Several awards were made on the final day at the concluding dinner, but the one that gave me most pleasure was the 'Ivan Kincheloe' award commemorating the name of my former class-mate at ETPS, who had so tragically died in an F-104 aircraft accident when on the verge of taking part in the early space flights. It was awarded to an American test pilot who was considered to have made the most outstanding contribution to aviation in 1974.

There was another notable moment when the society's 'Wings of Man' award to the Smithsonian Institution was accepted on its behalf by Gen James Doolittle, an outstanding US Air Force aviator who, during the Pacific war in 1943, had successfully led a flight of Mitchell heavy bombers to attack the Japanese mainland, having flown off an American aircraft carrier some hundreds of miles south, and then landed in China, since he had neither the fuel nor the facility to land back on board. This had been the first air attack on mainland Japan after Pearl Harbor, and in recognition of this outstanding and enterprising achievement he had been made an honorary KCB. He was now a very young 80-year-old.

Apart from the almost boyish fascination of meeting for the first time these pioneers of space, I took great pleasure in renewing the acquaintance of others in the test-flying world whom I had not met up with for some time either at NAS Patuxent, Edwards Air Force Base or elsewhere. However, there had been a number I had met more recently, only a little more than a year ago, when, on the occasion of the arrival of twenty or so senior representatives of SETP at Bedford in March 1973, I had hosted them for the day with a tour of the establishment and lunch, and then laid on a two-hour air display in the afternoon. From their comments now, they had obviously enjoyed the visit. Bill Bedford, the chief test pilot of Hawker, and an official of SETP, had escorted them on that occasion and had used his influence to persuade Hawker to display the new Harrier 'Jump Jet', superbly flown by John Farley, and in turn the RN Historic Flight had joined in the spirit of things by sending in a Swordfish, Firefly and Sea Fury. To provide a little naval input I flew the Sea Vixen off the catapult and landed into the arrester gear, which, together with demonstrations of several Bedford research aircraft, went down very well.

But it had all been almost surpassed by the sumptuous dinner at the Law Courts later that evening to which Pat and I had been invited. Hosted by Brian Trubshaw, on behalf of the European Section of SETP, it was an exceptional occasion in quite palatial surroundings, rivalling the best, and which I am sure impressed everyone there. But that had been some time ago.

Before leaving UK for this symposium, it had been suggested that, from the budget point of view – justification of costs – it would be sensible to maximise the long flog to the west coast by looking at other appropriate visits I could make while I was there, such as Navy or Air Force establishments. I had therefore made a provisional arrangement to call at the naval air base at Monterey, just south of San Francisco. So with the symposium over, I hired a car to drive the two hundred miles to Monterey, where I was shown round the base, entertained for the evening and accommodated overnight.

The following day I continued to San Francisco, had a brief excursion around this impressive city, looked across the Bay to Alcatraz and the Golden Gate Bridge, and then booked into a hotel for the night. The administrative people at the Embassy in Washington make life very easy for the traveller. Cars, hotel rooms and air flights are all booked with great efficiency, and after a telephone call to them querying a flight from Washington to the UK, I discovered an RAF VC10 was leaving the next day for Brize Norton. It was the personal transport of Adm Ashmore, C in C Fleet, and his staff, but they were sure he would accept another passenger, and so I departed from San Francisco for Washington and the next day boarded the VC10 for home.

To my pleasure I found Dick Fitch a few seats back, travelling with the Admiral as his Chief Staff Officer. I hadn't seen him since Singapore days, when, as Ops Officer to Adm Griffin in HMS *Hermes*, he had kindly vacated his cabin for my occupation, in deference to my seniority, settling instead into a small sea cabin for the whole of the period of the exercises for which I and two other Fleet Staff had been embarked. Meeting him now made the long, tedious flight pass both quickly and enjoyably.

The rest of 1974 was uneventful. In August the family had departed for our new home in Portishead in order that the two children could start their new schools in the new academic year. It was the start of a great many commuting weekends and early Monday-morning starts to make the eight o'clock met. briefings. Eventually the driving palled a little, and I resorted to flying to BAC Filton in Bristol occasionally, where a small RAF detachment would look after the aircraft. Mostly, however, it meant driving through the Cotswolds at some godforsaken time, avoiding the foxes and other wildlife bent on trying to commit suicide in the darkness of the hour.

By the middle of 1975 I expected news of my next, and final, appointment. In October I would have spent three enjoyable and outstanding years at Bedford, and while, from a professional point of view, I was not anxious to depart, the separation from the family assumed an increasing desire to settle into a new job nearer home. I had already made overtures to the Appointers and been given a sympathetic ear. So it was with considerable satisfaction that I received a telephone call asking if an appointment to the staff of the Director-General Naval Weapons at Ensleigh, Bath, would be acceptable. I knew nothing about the organisation, not even where Ensleigh was. But Bath was within striking distance of the new home, and with a little flexibility I felt sure that it would resolve the problems of the 'school run'.

But before leaving Bedford I had one outstanding mission. A fall-out from the Phantom rain erosion tests we had carried out earlier had been an invitation from the Concorde chief test pilot, Brian Trubshaw, for a flight in Concorde, and this had been arranged for a date in the middle of 1974. As luck would have it, just days before a planned family holiday and the Concorde flight, I managed to incapacitate myself by breaking an Achilles tendon playing squash, and I was unable to join the rest of the trials party to Fairford for this justly deserved return of services rendered. Now, better late than never, I rang Brian in early December 1975 to resurrect the invitation and arrange a mutually convenient date to fly with him on one of his supersonic runs down to the Bay of Biscay.

So in early January 1976, I climbed aboard Concorde, fitted out for passenger service, to be mildly astonished at the cramped seating and headroom, and wondered what sort of traveller, notwithstanding the time factor, would prefer this to the more spacious and very comfortable First Class seating in one of the wide-body jets, at far less cost.

We took off about mid-morning, climbing towards the Devon coast to commence a supersonic run south over the English Channel. We never made it. One of the engines failed to respond to reheat, so we reluctantly returned to Fairford to rectify the fault. Two hours later, fault rectified, we were airborne again, and at 35,000 ft, passed through Mach 1, accelerating to the planned profile of M=2.2. There was no sensation of speed, and only the read-out on the bulkhead made us aware that we were now at maximum cruising speed. We spent over three hours in the air, flying down as far as the Bay of Biscay before returning to base. It was all a little boring, and it scarcely took a genius to ponder the cost-effectiveness of this sort of commercial transport. Quick and only just comfortable, versus a little longer and luxurious, was hardly a problem choice for most of us

In January 1976 I left Bedford for the second time. To be able to continue active flying as a commander in two appointments was quite exceptional in the Royal Navy and beyond anything I could have expected. And to have had the benefit of such varied flying over the last three years was really the icing on the cake. I left reluctantly but feeling that I had led a charmed life, pursuing a flying career that I could never have anticipated in 1943 when I first sat before that intimidating, but very understanding, Royal Navy Selection Board. My flying days were finally over; I would now fly a desk until I retired!

In all, over a period of thirty-three years, I had been privileged to fly close to one hundred types of aircraft (including marks where they were significantly different), ranging from basic and advanced trainers, fighters, strike and ground attack, light and heavy bombers, medium- and long-range transport, helicopters and a wide range of fascinating research aircraft, usually one-off prototypes. In operations from a dozen naval aircraft carriers, belonging to both the UK and USA, I had completed around one thousand day and night carrier landings, including several hundred intentional 'rollers', or touch-and-go landings, where these were required to expedite the training of Landing Signal Officers or as part of a test programme for particular aircraft. The latter involved the standard approach and landing on to the deck, with the hook up, before immediately taking off again, down the flight deck and over the ship's bow.

I felt I could look back with a degree of satisfaction. To have been described as an 'exceptional' pilot in my last seagoing carrier appointment was both humbling and pleasing, particularly after such a chequered start all those years before at the start of my flying training in Canada. But there were occasions when I seem to have been extremely fortunate, fallen on my feet in one way or another. I could also be grateful for the opportunity which had befallen me to attend a number of first-class courses, ranging from six to twelve months, which had been inspirational and educational. Notable among these were the Central Flying School (six months), Empire Test Pilots School (twelve months), Air Warfare College (six months), US Armed Forces Staff College (six months) and several other shorter tactical courses of lesser duration. They were all courses of the highest standard, embodying excellent tutors or instructors, which attracted guest speakers of international reputation – politicians, diplomats, scientists, industrialists and occasionally philosophers and others, and, of course, high-ranking military officers.

On balance I could have no regrets: it was all 'purely by chance'.

CHAPTER 24

Director-General Weapons, Ensleigh

I was vaguely aware of the existence of the establishment at Bath. During my time in Whitehall, the Director-General Ships Department at Bath had become well known to me, but DGW(N) was a new animal, one that I would not have encountered had it not been for my request to be appointed somewhere near my home. Nevertheless it would prove to be an interesting and educational couple of years, with an opportunity for travel that broke the daily routine of dropping the children off at school before negotiating the city traffic on my way to my office.

I had within my domain the control of a number of warships and support vessels with which to programme trials of weapons and equipment around the world to meet the needs of Admiralty establishments concerned with underwater and above-the-surface research. It called for tact and patience in dealing with scientists whose concept of meeting timescales suggested complete indifference or lack of understanding to the realities and difficulties of ship planning. But despite these vicissitudes, which occasionally merited the firm stick of the headmaster, we usually met targets and avoided costly overruns.

Off the coast of Andros Island in the Bahamas is a stretch of water known as the Tongue of the Ocean, an area of very deep water entirely suited to submarine equipment and weapons trials. These occupied a good deal of my time and occasioned a number of visits to West Palm Beach in Florida, the HQ of AUTEC (Allied Underwater Test and Evaluation Centre), and then on to Andros, where the Americans were responsible for the test range, although the island itself is British territory. As such it was necessary to make a courtesy call on the Governor of the Bahamas in Nassau during the course of each visit. He never failed to greet us very warmly, and his luncheons were much looked forward to.

One of the two plum jobs for a 'passed-over' lieutenant-commander must have been the appointment to AUTEC at Andros as resident British Naval Officer (the other was surely Officer-in-Charge of the RN Training Centre at Fraser's Hill). The incumbent during my time was an exceptionally pleasant chap who lived with his wife in an Admiralty bungalow with his own pier and powered boat, and whose hospitality knew no bounds. He acted as a naval liaison officer with the Americans, smoothing the way for the arrival of such as I, and generally ensuring that the needs of visiting British submarines were well catered for. It was not an onerous job, and necessarily entailed long periods with little or no activity, but what he had to do he did very well. I spent many a happy hour with him in his boat, snorkelling in the reefs off shore, where the marine life was quite fantastically beautiful.

As always it was necessary to report proceedings to the Defence Staff in Washington before returning home, but none of this was very hard to bear, and these working visits, involving water and air transport, made the two years at DGW(N) both interesting and pleasant.

Not long before completing my time at Ensleigh, I and my wife received an invitation to a Royal Garden Party at Buckingham Palace to be held in July 1978, which we accepted, and of course it was the excuse for a new dress for Pat. So it was in through the large gates again, through the Palace, to the Royal Gardens at the rear. A gloriously sunny day, a very large marquee attended by countless lackeys to serve refreshments to the several hundred guests, made for a relaxed and pleasant late afternoon. The military band played the usual stuff, and in due course the Queen and Duke of Edinburgh made their entrance, accompanied by more lackeys ushering guests this way and that to create a passageway for the Royal couple to proceed and acknowledge whomsoever they felt inclined. This created an almighty undignified surge and scramble for a position to the front, near the Royal procession, to be shaken by the hand or acknowledged. It created an occasion for some guests to show their true colours. But it was really quite pointless since it was perfectly obvious that the pecking order had been previously ordained, and the honoured ones had already established their positions.

As garden parties go, it was a pleasant affair in nice surroundings, but scarcely rose above the level of the local church fête, and fell short of many similar service occasions.

So on 25 September 1978, exactly thirty-five years after I had first been officially accepted for service in the Royal Navy, I was given a fine send-off at Ensleigh and returned to civilian life. It proved to be the beginning of another chapter. Through golf and a cocktail party and a meeting with someone who later became a good friend of the family, I embarked on another career as different as chalk from cheese, but which, in its way, proved to be the perfect antidote. But that is another story.

APPENDIX 1

Provosts to Burma

INTRODUCTION

After the Second World War the United States and the UK, in particular, possessed a huge surplus of war materials, notably ships and aircraft, most of which would become available for export to approved nations. This continued well into the fifties, and Britain had already established ready markets in the Middle East with the sale of excess Spitfires and other aircraft. By the middle of 1950 the market extended to the Far East, and Burma in particular had shown interest in the acquisition of less sophisticated aircraft, such as Hunting Percival Provost trainers.

The Provost, an aircraft of similar performance, but with the advantage of side-by-side seating, had been developed as a replacemeßnt for the ageing Harvard, an aircraft that had done sterling service as an advanced trainer when the training syllabus was split into elementary and advanced stages. The advent of the jet aircraft and modern thinking on all-through training tended towards one aircraft for both stages, and the piston-engined Provost therefore became both obsolescent and available for disposal.

Hunting had established Fieldair Ltd, a subsidiary company, to act as its marketing agents, and following negotiations with the government of Burma, a contract was signed for the delivery of a number of T Mk 53 aircraft to Mingladon, the principal airfield at Rangoon. The delivery of the first three aircraft is the subject of the following narrative, and follows the brief reference to it in the main text. It owes much to the notes and observations compiled during the return journey by the author and Bill Williams.

Delivery flight

With all the formalities over, Admiralty authority to proceed abroad, inoculations and other mundane matters dealt with, I flew to Croydon airport with Johnny Walker on 11 March 1955 for final briefing, collection of passports with numerous valid visas and other documents relating to the aircraft, such as fuel carnets, logbooks, list of spares and various receipt forms; and finally, a return civil air flight ticket to return to UK.

The third pilot was Bill Williams, a wartime RAF pilot, currently serving in an RAF Reserve squadron, flying Meteors, whose day job was a solicitor with a firm in the City. John was nominated as flight leader. He had previous experience with an air delivery flight and was therefore a natural to undertake the various administrative tasks *en route*, but each pilot was responsible for the safety and navigational aspects of his aircraft. During transit, weather or other factors permitting, the three aircraft would fly in loose formation as a formed flight. This all seemed a straightforward and satisfactory arrangement. Route planning, emergency procedures and overnight stops were agreed. John would be the holder of a 'flight float' of several hundred pounds for emergencies. Fuel, aircraft handling and, as far as possible, overnight accommodation would be paid in London.

We now flew back to Farnborough, having arranged to meet up again the following Monday at RAF Biggin Hill, where we would spend the night before departure the following day, 15 March 1955. The arrangement was that we would use RAF or foreign services facilities as far as possible throughout the transit flight in order to minimise the delivery costs to Fieldair, but as it turned out, much was left to our own discretion! If we didn't like the 'cut of its jib' at any stop we would seek an alternative.

During breakfast in the RAF officers' mess at Biggin Hill on the morning of our departure there was a slight hiccup. Enthusiastically shaking the Lea & Perrins, I omitted to ensure the flip cap was firmly on the bottle, with the inevitable result – it flew everywhere – over my white shirt and shorts and, more particularly, over the Mess Steward, dutifully hovering nearby. March it may have been, but we were about to fly to warmer climes, and had dressed in semi-tropical kit accordingly. Nothing daunted, a change of dress was required, and this meant disturbing carefully packed baggage. It cost us a delay of fifteen minutes, and for me, the sort of contemptuous look from the RAF Mess Steward that they usually reserve for the more junior officers.

But with no further mishap we were on our way to Croydon, signed all the necessary documentation accepting the aircraft and spares on personal charge, cleared customs and reported to the control tower to file the flight plan to Dijon, some 300 miles away. The forecast weather over the Channel and into France was not encouraging. Low cloud could be expected, and the likelihood of maintaining close formation was far from assured. This was not a problem: we had the standard agreed procedure in the event of breaking formation through poor visibility or dense cloud, and if necessary we would make our own way to Dijon.

Some weeks before departure, I had approached the School of Aviation Medicine to enquire whether the flight was of any interest to it for any of its research work. At ETPS and subsequently at RAE we enjoyed a close working relationship with the doctors and medical staff there, particularly in the field of ejection seats and aircrew equipment. Well, there wasn't much I could offer them on this occasion, but they turned out a newly developed tropical flying-helmet and several other bits and pieces, such as eye protectors from the sun, copious quantities of concentrated food packs and specially prepared concentrated orange juice in easy-to-manage containers with long tubes for consumption in flight. These I distributed to the other two, and stored my ration in the aircraft, on top of the vast quantity of spares that occupied the whole of the second seat. Shortly after 11 a.m., we departed Croydon for the three-hour flight to Dijon, the first of twenty legs to Rangoon, nearly six thousand miles away. We soon encountered the expected bad weather, entered cloud at less than 1,000 ft, and with very heavy rain the visibility became so poor that I lost the leader's navigation and rendezvous lights, and was barely able to see the outline of his aircraft. 'Hell's teeth,' I thought, 'there's no percentage in this.' With the cloud layer tops previously reported by the meteorology office to be between five and six thousand feet, maintaining close formation was not a sensible option, and over the R/T I advised John that we should proceed independently, as previously briefed, which was to turn starboard 30 degrees for one minute, then resume the original course. Bill heard the transmission and pre-empted the leader by declaring his intention to do the same, except that he would turn to port. Thus we proceeded on our parallel courses, spaced several hundred yards apart, and continued through the murk, flying solely on instruments, maintaining the original airspeed and hoping to be in visual touch when we broke cloud at the top. Five minutes later I was in the clear, and up ahead, on my port side and a little higher, I sighted the leader. A moment or two later, Bill appeared, much where he should have been. We chatted over the R/T and resumed 'normal service', as the BBC is prone to say.

For some time the French regional air traffic control organisation had been notorious for refusing to acknowledge any over-flying aircraft unless they transmitted in the French language, despite the fact that *English* was the internationally accepted language for air traffic throughout the world. We now experienced this insular national trait, and for the whole transit across France there was a deafening silence from the regional controllers. Fortunately this absurd attitude did not extend to the local airfield controllers, and with fifteen minutes to go before our estimated time of arrival (ETA) we made two-way contact with Dijon military ATC, landed and taxied to the designated dispersal area.

After suffering typical French customs fussiness and indifference, we eventually made our way to the Château Rouge hotel, where we were to lodge overnight. Later, embarking on our quest for food, 'I know a restaurant', announced our intrepid leader, 'where the mussels are unmatched.' An hour later, after a prolonged wait and no mussels, we settled for indifferent ham and eggs and retired to the hotel bar! We were not impressed, and he would earn no 'Brownie' points.

The following morning we had a little trouble starting one of the aircraft, which delayed our departure, but shortly after 0800 we were on our way to Nice, the first of the two legs planned for the day. Two-and-a-half hours later, arriving at Nice, the weather had now turned noticeably warmer, and after checking customs, John was dispatched the twenty-minute walk to the meteorological office for the weather forecast to Rome. Shortly after midday we were on our way to Ciampino, Rome's main airport, where we landed just over two hours later.

It had now taken us nearly eight hours' flying, and we felt we had hardly made an impact on the journey. It was going to be a long flog. However, Rome was worth a visit, and our schedule allowed us a clear day to explore as much as we could in the time available. Italian customs were singularly co-operative compared with the French officials, and we were shortly bus-bound for the Hotel Quirinale, passing, *en route*, the magnificent *stationne*, Rome's main railway station, built almost entirely of marble. The following day, Thursday, we devoted to sightseeing, including St Peter's basilica, where the climb to the top of the most beautiful dome in the world was more than worth the effort. In the next six or seven hours we pounded the pavements to visit the Venetian Palace, the monument to Victor Emanuel II, the Flavian Amphitheatre, or Colosseum, and other places of interest, including the not-to-be-missed Trevi Fountain, a rather dirty-looking pool, to throw coins and make a wish, as custom demanded. Our commitment to sightseeing over, we returned to the hotel to prepare for the next stage of our journey.

Next day we caught the early workmen's bus to the airport, took off shortly afterwards for the one-hour flight and brief stop at Brindisi, on the heel of Italy, before continuing to Athens. Here misfortune got in the way again. Hardly had we got airborne from Brindisi than one of the aircraft suffered fuel venting, forcing a return for topping-up. Not a problem in the usual way, except that the Shell gentleman at the airport only appeared when aircraft were due, and by this time he had returned to town after our departure. This was annoying. However, within the hour he was seen bicycling furiously through the airport gates, and, aircraft refuelled, we were off again.

One of the advantages of flying a Provost-type aeroplane is that the cruising altitude of less than eight thousand feet allows a panoramic view of the land below and thus relieves the boredom implicit in much of modern jet flying. The flight to Athens was a fine example, with magnificent views of the islands and the Greek coast before entering the circuit at Athens International airport. The same extravaganza would be experienced the next day after departing Rhodes.

It was becoming a feature of the journey so far that we received a warm welcome, and at Athens it was no exception. Admittedly, these were the days before international air travel became commonplace, and at some of our stops they would not see an aircraft for days on end. But here at Athens, it took much of the pressure from us to be shepherded by the manager through customs and immigration and then to be driven in his own car to the Hotel Minerva for our overnight stop. It was much appreciated. We had now been on the road for five days, still had a long way to go and had visions of a quiet evening – or so we thought! You must visit the Surprise Bar, just down the road, we were urged by the hotel concierge, 'It's just the place for you young people.' It was bad advice. Our doughty leader got completely out of hand and was last seen waving a bottle of Champagne in the air with a bright young thing in tow – or it may have been the other way round!

We rose early the next morning, breakfasted, and were transported to the airport, courtesy of a USAF vehicle that happened to be headed that way. The flight to Rhodes was breathtaking, with the magical panorama of the Dodecanese below us, all the houses built on relatively steep slopes on the sunward sides of the islands, some grouped together, nestling at the foot of the hills, with the early-morning sunlight playing on them.

After little more than an hour at Rhodes for refuelling we were on our way, refreshed by the friendliness of the staff and their coffee. Then, only a quarter of an hour later, we struck violent thunderstorms, which caused a major change of course and a later-than-intended arrival at Nicosia, not popular on a Saturday afternoon. The place was deserted except for the inevitable customs fellow, and it was some time before we were able to persuade reluctant RAF maintenance people, alerted by air traffic control, to turn out to refuel the aircraft. 'You were supposed to be here half an hour ago', they complained, and we in turn had to explain that only God fashioned the weather. Peeved with their unreasonable attitude, we made our way to the Carlton Hotel.

John knew Nicosia well, as he had been stationed there some years before, and after a jug or two of ale at John Odge's Bar, removed ourselves to Antonarki's, a fashionable but inexpensive restaurant, before ending up at the Chanteclair, the best night spot in Nicosia, where we requisitioned a large section of the bar to watch the cabaret. By Mediterranean standards it was about average. Later on we met one of the performers. An American by birth, he had apparently done much globe-trotting and described himself as a 'hobo with talent'. Thinking back to the previous night, we were only half-inclined to agree.

The following day was our day of rest. We had flown seventeen hours in the past five days and spent many hours dealing with flight plans and other matters, such as customs and immigration. We had a long way to go. But at tea that afternoon we were waylaid by a Scottish engineer, 'Mac', who insisted we return home with him to meet his family. His wife, a Greek Cypriot, totally unfazed by the intrusion of three unexpected guests, conjured up an excellent local dish, as if long planned. We left much later than perhaps we would have wished, but the hospitality knew no bounds, and it is always difficult in these circumstances to 'draw stumps'.

We were off relatively early on Monday morning, with a long flying-day ahead of us. This leg would take us to Kleyate (Tripoli) airport in Lebanon, a route deliberately chosen to avoid the experience of another pilot flying a Spitfire on a delivery flight. He had unwisely landed in Israel for refuelling before crossing into Syria, where his aircraft was immediately impounded and he was carted off to the nearest prison. His passport, of course, showed his previous stopping-point, and as he was flying an obviously military aircraft this was a red rag to an Arab country. It took many diplomatic hours of discussion to get him freed two days later.

However, we had no such problem. After the short hop from Cyprus, we were cordially received at Kleyate, and, with every assistance, were on our way again within the hour. Ahead of us was a long flog across the Syrian desert, featureless apart from the odd wadi and occasional nomad or shepherd's track. This was back to basic navigation, course and time, until we managed to discern the features of a sunken pipeline pointing in the direction of our destination. Crossing the Iraq border, we lost it and were back on our own. This was our longest leg, and after three-and-a-half hours we touched down at Habbaniyah, just west of Baghdad. A former RAF air base, but now in some decline, it was Baghdad's principal airport.

The controller looked harassed as we walked in, attempting to answer several telephones at the same time, operate the R/T with a departing light aircraft, and now he was landed with us, wishing to sign for fuel and landing-fees and arrange our departure time. He seemed to cope surprisingly well under the circumstances, if with a little impatience. By late afternoon, refuelled, we pushed on to Basra, at the head of the Persian Gulf, our next stop, arriving just as darkness closed in. By the end of the day we would have been well over six hours in the air. It had been a long day but we were on schedule and had experienced no major problem. The Airport Hotel was adequate, hideously expensive, but at least within walking distance.

It was now Tuesday, a week on from our departure in the UK. At the end of the day we would be pretty well half-way and on the down slope. The temperature had now soared, and the orange juice, so thoughtfully provided by my friends at the Institute of Medicine, was now undrinkable with the heat in the cockpit. Bahrain, our refuelling stop on the way to overnight in Sharjah, cost us no more than half an hour, and we were glad to get back in the air again, flying over a longish stretch of the Persian Gulf. A little short of two hours later we sighted the coast, and shortly afterwards landed at Sharjah.

There is Sharjah, a small coastal town, and some miles inland the airport, a nondescript place boasting a Beau Geste-style fort, built in former times to resist tribal warfare, but now housing the air traffic control building, as well as serving as 'hotel accommodation'; and it was there that we were put up for the night. It seemed unlikely that Sharjah airport saw many overnight travellers, but oddly, early that evening an old Rapide biplane landed, piloted by a German, westbound, on his way through to North Africa. It marked the beginning of a most illuminating evening.

He was an interesting fellow, had fought in the last war in several *Luftflotten* (squadrons) as a fighter pilot, and happily related a number of his experiences, most of which seemed to be against himself. He was, I suppose, a few years older that we three, had obviously had a rough time during his wartime flying and felt lucky to have survived. Like most *Luftwaffe* officers he was no Nazi but would do his duty for Germany. At midnight, when they closed the reception rooms, we retreated to the small roof of the fort to continue our yarns, accompanied by the servant boy who kept us supplied with copious quantities of cold beer to ward off the still high temperature. Eventually, with dawn almost upon us, we turned in. Our planned take-off time of eight o'clock would arrive all too soon.

Rising shortly after seven, we discovered our German friend had long since gone. In fact we were told he had taken off soon after six without sleep and after only a light breakfast. And we thought we were pushing it a bit! In the event, we left on the dot of eight o'clock, climbed to 7,000 ft and prepared for the long flog over the water to Jiwani, to refuel, before continuing to Mauripur, the Pakistani Air Force base at Karachi. Jiwani, a coastal town on the Iran–Pakistan border, was a desolate and sun-scorched place. We understood there were some oil interests there, but it lacked any form of land communication to the point where it was necessary to transport stores of all description – even water – by sea from Karachi. On arrival we felt like honoured guests to be given one glass of water to share between us.

It was unbearably hot, and even in the short stay of a quarter of an hour, the aircraft metal became untouchable, so that it was a relief to get back in the air for the flight to Mauripur. Always with an eye to an export sale, Fieldair had arranged for the Provost to be demonstrated to senior brass of the Pakistan Air Force, which entailed a complete day and overnight stop. However, from our point of view, a short rest would be welcomed, as would the hospitality of the Pakistan Air Force mess. On arrival we were received by the PAF Station Commander and the senior officer of the small RAF staging-post personnel, who relieved us of the worries of servicing. As it happened, this was a mixed blessing, since the aircraft were topped up with the wrong grade of oil, which caused several hours' work for them in the early afternoon.

The following day, in starting up for the first demonstration, a safety disc blew in the Coffman starter. I had most of the spares in my aircraft, and so, consulting the spares sheets, I eventually located a replacement disc in the large sack in the second, or passenger, seat. The RAF mechanic managed to make the repair in under a quarter of an hour, and the subsequent demonstration went without a further hitch. Standing around, with nothing to do for the moment, I watched the mechanic replace the offending disc, a prudent precaution as it turned out, although at the time I had no thoughts that it might happen again.

The Fieldair representative and organiser of the demonstration was a Maj Bates, a plump little man of some 40-odd years and indifferent appearance. His association with the world of aviation, or indeed any other occupation, in that very warm climate was difficult to understand since, for most of the time, he would be seen sitting under the aircraft wing, mopping his brow, murmuring to anyone nearby, 'It must be at least 101 degrees, ol' boy.' But he was a kindly chap, and lent us his car to travel the few miles to a nearby bay for a swim, which was much appreciated.

The senior PAF officers seemed impressed with the aircraft's potential. Their interests were in this, the armed version T Mk 52/53, which had already secured future orders from the Irish Air Force, Iraq and Sudan, as well as Burma. The unit cost was very reasonably priced, it was relatively easy to maintain and hence the operating costs were low. However, no order ensued, possibly for political rather than military reasons.

The following day, Friday 25 March, we crossed into India on our way to stay overnight at the Indian Air Force base at Cawnpore, stopping *en route* for fuel at Jodhpur. Five hours of easily forgettable flying over barren and uninteresting territory, punctuated by a lengthy and exhausting examination of just about everything by customs at Jodhpur, left us at the end of the day in ill humour. We had come from Pakistan, and that raised the hackles of the Indian customs officials, who were clearly bent on making us pay for it. But we should have expected this, given the state of affairs between the two countries. Then, it would seem the Indian Air Force officers' mess at Cawnpore was being renovated, and all they could offer was a large tent, camp-beds and mosquito nets. But they made up for it with a dinner of banquet proportions. With no shortage of cold Indian beer, sleep later was not a problem.

Rising early, our intention was to make Calcutta, but for once the weather was unkind to us. Violent thunderstorms were being reported from Barrackpore (Calcutta), and it was only after a considerable delay that we managed to obtain clearance as far as Gaya, a little over half-way, where the weather was reported fair. This was important to us since we needed to make Rangoon the next day, Sunday. As it was, the forecast proved to be pessimistic, but we abandoned any thoughts of going on to Calcutta since the unexpected flight to Gaya had caused our fuel states to be insufficient for any further diversion from Calcutta, should that have been necessary. As it turned out, it was a wise decision, for the actual weather at Calcutta was foul all day, with heavy thunderstorms and gale-force winds.

Landing at Gaya, the aircraft were picketed and accommodation was arranged for the night in the passengers' rest room, an adequate but unimposing building near the equally inconspicuous edifice that served as the control tower. Within half an hour a severe dust-storm blew up, followed by an even worse thunderstorm. The associated high wind was strong enough to break a picketing line on one of the aircraft, and left to its own devices it slewed round perilously close to making contact with another. It was a nasty moment and the delivery flight could well have ended there and then – at least for two of the aircraft. Airframe damage we had not anticipated, and it is doubtful if any spare parts could be found outside the UK. Fortunately we were spared the horrors of such an unwarranted termination of many hours of flying.

We had just arrived in the control tower when this happened, but a warning shout from Burmah Johnny, who was waiting to refuel the aircraft, stirred us and one or two others into a commendable sprint to restrain the offending aircraft. For the moment, in the high wind and very heavy rain, we could no more than resecure the picket line, but as soon as the storm had abated, we separated the aircraft to avoid any repeat performance.

Under the circumstances – Gaya being at best only a diversionary landing strip – the hospitality was nothing short of astounding. Burmah Johnny mounted his ancient bicycle, rode two miles into the nearest small town in a fierce wind, and returned with a sumptuous meal: beer, soup, roast chicken, fruit salad and coffee, all piping hot in metal containers, all carried in wicker baskets from several miles away! Astonishing, he had been away less than two hours. In the meantime, the French wife of the airport manager, Mr Mullic, had most kindly cooked us a little meal, to 'tide us over', she said.

Mr Mullic was a most interesting man. An Indian, he had served with the RAF during the war as a bomber pilot and attained the rank of wing commander before leaving in 1946. He talked little about the many operations he flew, mainly in Lancasters, but from his conversation, during a long evening, he was obviously well read and had travelled far. He knew London far better than any of us, and waxed lyrical about his time there, and in England, and how he missed the odd bottle of Bass! Gaya would have been an odd place to find him but for the fact that he was born there and had returned to his roots.

The following morning, having avoided a near-calamity the previous day, we came unstuck with a minor irritation in starting engines. Had it not been for the experience at Karachi it might have cost us a delay we could ill afford. Another safety disc blew, this time on Bill's aircraft. But I was well prepared for this one, having watched the mechanic at Mauripur. I also knew now where to look for a replacement. Within twenty minutes, I had a new disc in place, we restarted engines, took off and climbed to our cruising altitude for Barrackpore, where we landed just under two hours later. On arrival there were tea and sandwiches waiting for us in the control tower, courtesy of the Indian Air Force officers. Apparently they had been told by Mr Mullic at Gaya that we had departed without breakfast. These little civilities had been much in evidence throughout our journey. The IAF officers, although disappointed we had not been able to make it the night before, were not surprised. The weather had been dreadful. They had been looking forward to our arrival for some time and had arranged a small reception to celebrate. We expressed our regrets, and, sorry that we were, told them of the hospitality we had received at Gaya, and of Mr Mullic, whom they knew well.

Departing an hour later, the flight to Akyab, on the north-west coast of Burma, took a little over two hours, entirely across water, utterly boring; we would be glad now to see the end of this saga. By the end of the day, we would have been 'on the road' for thirteen days, with only short stops, and flown more than forty-four hours. Added to the normal test flying at Farnborough, my total flying for the month would be a commendable sixty plus hours.

Now, with the last leg from Akyab to Mingladon, Rangoon's main airport, just two hours' flight time away, we were within hailing distance of our final destination. Clearing customs at Akyab was a pleasantly short experience compared with our arrival in India, and by mid- afternoon, having flown the entire leg over forbidding-looking jungle, we were only a few miles away from Mingladon airport. I called John over the R/T: 'Shall we announce our arrival properly, a little bit of a show, perhaps?' and so, with his concurrence and having warned ATC, we formed up in a pretty tight three for some fairly basic manoeuvres, nothing extravagant, all within the airfield boundary, before doing a fairly close-stream landing. It made a nice impression on the waiting VIPs and Brass.

So that was that: we had delivered the first three Provosts and formally handed them over to the Fieldair representative, Mr Kinnear. We had experienced no major problem with the three aircraft over a distance of 6,000 miles, which itself was a great credit to the Provost.

Our task on arrival was greatly simplified by Fieldair's overseas sales manager, Charles Bond, who cleared the way through customs, provided liquid refreshment and then saw us on our way to the Strand Hotel. Later on he called to take us to a most excellent Chinese restaurant in what appeared to be a very doubtful quarter of the city, where we came to no more harm than resisting the importuning of the Chinese girls to feed you during the exceedingly long meal. It was great fun. Later we retreated to Charles Bond's favourite night spot before calling it a day.

The following day we were on our way home, courtesy of 'Air Something or Other', richer by the hundred pounds fee, but also by far more than that. The experience of the last two weeks was priceless.

There was a slight sequel to the end of our journey. During the previous evening, Charles had made us aware of a Fieldair Dakota leaving Delhi for the UK in which he could arrange passage if we wished. All that was required was to get ourselves from Rangoon to Delhi by the Tuesday, easily possible by civil air, he said, and the Dakota was scheduled to arrive in the UK on Wednesday, only two days later than the scheduled flight by civil air. 'You would save over a hundred pounds', he said, but he felt he should warn us that there was always the possibility of delays with the Dakota flight schedule. It was an attractive proposition, but in the end we decided we shouldn't push our luck any further. We had had a good run and would leave it at that.

APPENDIX 2

Aircraft Types Flown as 1st Pilot/Captain

Single Engine/Propeller

Aircraft	Engine
DH Cornell	Ranger
Na Harvard	P&W 134
DH Tiger Moth	Gipsy
CV Corsair IV	P&W 28
G Hellcat I, II	P&W
S Seafire III	Merlin
P Prentice	Gipsy
F Firefly I	Griffon
M Master	Mercury
Sea Fury	Centaurus
Auster	Bombardier
P Provost	Leonides
Sea Balliol	Merlin
DH Chipmunk	Gipsy Major
H Hart	Kestrel
P Proctor	Gipsy Queen
AF Junior	Walter Mikron II
F Storch (German)	Argus
S Spitfire XIV	Griffon
M Whitney Straight	Gipsy Major
Aero Commander	Lycoming
G Avenger	Cyclone
S Seafire XV	Griffon
F Firefly IV	Griffon
P 51D Mustang (US)	Merlin

Multi-Engine/Propeller

Aircraft	Engine
A Oxford	Cheetah
A Anson	Cheetah
M Marathon	Gipsy (4)
HP Hastings CI/II	Hercules (4)
V Varsity	Hercules
DH Dominie	Gipsy 6
DH Mosquito	Merlin
V Valetta C1 T3	Hercules
DH Sea Hornet XX, XXI (NF)	MerlinH
DH Devon	Gypsy
P Pembroke	Leonides
C 119 Packet	Cyclone

Single Engine/Jet

Aircraft	Engine
S Attacker	RR Nene
H Hunter I, II, IV, VI	Avon
DH Vampire III, V	Goblin
Sea Venom	Ghost 104
F Gnat	Orpheus
V F8E Crusader (US)	P&W
F-104 Starfighter (US)	GE 179
D Sky Hawk (US)	P&W J52
Sea Vampire XX	Goblin
G F9F Tiger (US)	Wright J65

H Sea Hawk	Nene
H Hunter V	Sapphire
DH Venom FB1	Ghost 103

Single/Multi-Engine/Turboprop Jet

W Wyvern	Python
F Gannet	D Mamba
S Sea Mew	Mamba
A Breguet 1050 (Fr)	Dart
Hs 748	Dart
C130 Hercules	Allison T56

Multi-Engine Jet

G Javelin	Sapphire
EE Canberra	Avon
G Meteor IV *et al*	Derwent/S
S Scimitar	Avon
DH Sea Vixen	Avon
EE Lightning 2 5	Avon
A3D Sky Warrior (US)	P&W
G A6 Intruder (US)	P&W J52
Fouga Magister (Fr)	CM Zephyr
MD Phantom F4B (US)	GE 79
HS 125	Viper
B Buccaneer 1	Gyron Junior
HP Victor (2nd)	Conway
Comet (2nd)	Avon
BAC 111 (2nd)	Spey
B Buccaneer 2	Spey
M Phantom F4M Mk 1, 2 (US/UK)	Spey

Experimental & Prototype

R&S Bobsleigh	Gypsy Moth	Prone Position
G Meteor F8	Derwent	Prone Position
HP 115	Viper	Extreme wing sweep SST trials
G Meteor F8/10/11/4	Nene	Deflected Jet

DH 110	Avon	Prototype (Sea Vixen)
N113 Type 544	Avon	Prototype (Scimitar)
Short SB5	Derwent	High sweep investigations
BP Delta P111	Nene	Delta wing investigations
Sea Venom	Ghost	Blown flap investigations
H Hunter VI	Mod Avon	Blown flap trials
Avro 707A	Nene	Delta investigations for Vulcan
Sea Meteor Mod 3	Derwent	Deck landing trials
H N7	Nene	Prototype Sea Hawk

Helicopters

W Whirlwind	Gnome
W Wessex	Gnome
Alouette (Fr) (2nd)	Artouste
Saro Skeeter (2nd)	Gipsy Major
Hiller	

Gliders

Slingsby
Olympia
Kranich

Index